101 387 147 2

D1587654

CHRISTINA ROSSETTI
Maude

DINAH MULOCK CRAIK
On Sisterhoods
A Woman's Thoughts about Women

CHRISTINA ROSSETTI

MAUDE

DINAH MULOCK CRAIK

ON SISTERHOODS

A WOMAN'S THOUGHTS
ABOUT WOMEN

Edited by
ELAINE SHOWALTER

Textual Notes by
PENNY MAHON

LONDON
WILLIAM PICKERING

Published by Pickering & Chatto (Publishers) Limited
17 Pall Mall, London SW1Y 5NB

British Library Cataloguing in Publication Data
Rossetti, Christina
   Maude and On Sisterhoods. – (Pickering
   Women's Classics Series)
   I. Title   II. Craik, Mrs.
   III. Showalter, Elaine   IV. Series
   823.8

ISBN 1–85196–027–9

Printed and bound in Great Britain by
Redwood Press Limited
Melksham

CONTENTS

INTRODUCTION

SINGLE WOMEN AND VICTORIAN SISTERHOODS

Christina Rossetti and Dinah Mulock Craik never met, although they belonged to the same generation, and lived close to each other in mid-nineteenth-century literary London. Rossetti, the reclusive sister of the Pre-Raphaelite poet and artist Dante Gabriel Rossetti, was a dedicated poet, the author of *Goblin Market* (1862) and of highly praised books of religious commentary and devotional verse. Craik was the daughter of an eccentric Nonconformist preacher who deserted his teenage children after his wife's death. In 1850, when Rossetti was writing *Maude* within the protective confines of her artistic family, Dinah Mulock was living in lodgings with a woman friend and supporting herself and her two younger brothers with her writing – novels, stories, and essays for the lending libraries and magazines. Best known as the author of the moralizing novel *John Halifax, Gentleman* (1856), she wrote relatively conventional popular fiction. Rossetti was an intellectual, a major artist. Craik, in George Eliot's words, was 'a writer who is read only by novel readers, pure and simple, never by people of high culture.' Eliot did not wish to be compared to her, and we could say that Craik and Christina Rossetti also belonged 'to an entirely different order of writers.'[1]

Yet from their very different perspectives and backgrounds, Rossetti and Craik both wrote about the problems of single women and female vocation, and looked to the Anglican sisterhoods as models of female community that offered women meaningful work. This book reprints three of their texts with common themes: Rossetti's *Maude*, a novella unpublished during

her lifetime; Craik's essay 'On Sisterhoods', which appeared in
Longman's Magazine in 1883; and Craik's anonymously published
and immensely popular *A Woman's Thoughts About Women*.
Together they illustrate the tensions between the solitary and
the collective ideals for women attempting to define an independent life, raising not only questions about the differences in
power between brotherhoods and sisterhoods, but also whether
women's aesthetic, social, and spiritual longings could best be
met with individual effort or community organization.

Portrait of the Poet as a Young Woman

In 1850, when she wrote the autobiographical novella *Maude:
Prose and Verse*, Christina Rossetti was nineteen years old. For the
precocious young poet, the work was only one of several
projects of her teens. Her poems had already been published in
The Athenaeum and in the Pre-Raphaelite journal, *The Germ*; and
a book called *Verses* had been privately printed by her grandfather in 1847.

Growing up in London as the youngest child in a gifted and
unusual family of artists and writers, Rossetti had early developed a poetic vocation. Like her brothers Dante Gabriel and
William Michael, she was steeped in religious imagery, Gothic
fiction, and Italian poetry. As children, the Rossettis competed
in poetic games called *bouts-rimés*, in which they had to write a
sonnet incorporating given rhymes; Christina became so adept
at the game that she could write a sonnet in less than ten
minutes. When she was only eleven, she wrote a set of elegant
birthday quatrains to her mother; indeed, William later claimed
that there was never a time 'when, knowing what a verse was,
we did not also know and feel what a *correct* verse was.'

In a memoir of his sister, William described her as a 'viva-
cious' girl who might have been expected to 'develop into a
woman of expansive heart, fond of society and diversions, and
taking a part in them of more than average brilliancy.' But by
the time she wrote *Maude*, the lively, passionate, and adventurous

little girl who had hated needlework, delighted in fiercely competitive games of chess, and explored the country with her brothers became a painfully constrained, sickly, and over-scrupulous teenager. During the years from fifteen to eighteen, she began to suffer from a variety of ailments: bronchitis, anaemia, breathlessness, palpitations, and chest pain. One of the doctors who treated her during this period thought she was 'then more or less out of her mind (suffering . . . from a form of insanity . . . a kind of religious mania).' While her symptoms were over-determined by many possible causes, including the family's straitened finances, the fear of having to work as a governess, the sexual turbulence of puberty, and a religious crisis, in which she tormented herself over minor lapses in piety, *Maude* makes clear that at least some of Rossetti's 'insanity' came from her anxieties about poetic achievement, her wishes both to be admired for her genius and to renounce it as unfeminine.

'Where Were the Poetesses?'

It would have been even more remarkable if Rossetti had *not* felt such anxieties, for there were few female models of a poetic career, let alone visions of a female poetic tradition. All the Rossetti children admired Elizabeth Barrett Browning, but for Christina especially, her poems were treasure-houses of metrical innovation, rhyme, and form. Along with the sentimentalists Felicia Hemans and Letitia E. Landon ('L.E.L.'), Barrett Browning offered hope that a woman might win fame as a poet. Yet in 1845, Barrett Browning herself had looked at the learned women of the past and asked, 'Where were the poetesses? The divine breath . . . why did it never pass, even in the lyrical form, over the lips of a woman? How strange! And can we deny that it was so? I look everywhere for grandmothers and see none.'

Women poets faced a special set of difficulties and barriers: the high aesthetic and even priestly status of poetry among the literary genres; the traditional links between English verse and the classical education, and the contradictions between feminine self-effacement and the lyric poet's assertive 'I'. Furthermore, even a Barrett Browning was praised only when her writing conformed to Victorian stereotypes of pure femininity; when she tackled political subjects, critics condemned her 'coarseness' or even accused her of madness. And fame, with its publicity and self-assertion, was a troubling antithesis to Victorian notions of proper feminine selflessness and privacy. In a famous Victorian poem on the death of Felicia Hemans, L.E.L. lamented the costs of women's poetic gifts in loneliness and pain:

> Didst thou not tremble at thy fame,
> And loathe its bitter prize,
> While what to others triumph seemed,
> To thee was sacrifice?

During her long career, Rossetti would often make the problems of the woman artist the themes of her verse and the subjects of her correspondence with female contemporaries such as Dora Greenwell and Jean Ingelow. But for the young woman who wrote *Maude*, there were already shadows upon the page.

Brotherhoods and Sisterhoods

The shadows began at home. By 1848, Christina had already experienced the first profound divergence between her life and those of her brothers. As children, their interests and projects had generally been shared. Together they read, wrote, argued about politics, and studied painting. Both Christina and Gabriel – the 'storms' of the family, where Maria and Michael were the 'calms' – were pupils of the artist Ford Madox Brown.

Victorian sisters and Victorian brothers, however, even those with similar interests and close attachments, lived in very different worlds. The Rossetti boys were sent to school, while the girls were taught by their mother at home. The sons became religious sceptics, while the daughters shared their mother's devout High Church faith. But the formation of the Pre-

Raphaelite Brotherhood of artists and writers in 1848–9 elevated the sexual divisions within the family into the sexual difference of Victorian institutions, and divided the brothers who created art from the sister who inspired it. The Rossetti brothers, John Everett Millais, Thomas Woolner, Frederick Stephens, James Collinson, and William Holman Hunt were the founding members. These very young men, ranging in age from nineteen to twenty-three, revelled in the idea of a secret male society. Although William and Gabriel would have liked Christina to sit in on P.R.B. meetings, the others would not permit it. Nonetheless she shared the aesthetic values and beliefs of the group, as expressed in their journal *The Germ*: a commitment to nature, interest in symbolism, self-conscious medievalism, and a preference for melancholy subjects.[2]

From this time on, Rossetti's connection to the brotherhood of the Pre-Raphaelites was defined in conventional feminine terms. Her role was to be the 'High Priestess of Pre-Raphaelitism', the model who sat for D. G. Rossetti's 'Girlhood of Mary Virgin', a picture he intended to be 'a symbol of female excellence'.[3] She posed not only for her own brothers but for others in the fraternity who could not afford to pay professional sitters.[4] Conversely, her frail, serious, pious looks shaped their pictorial style. According to Leslie Parris, a curator at the Tate Gallery, 'it was as much the appearance of Christina Rossetti that determined the emaciated and angular style of the Brothers as any return . . . to the Raphael frescoes in the Campo Santo at Pisa.'[5]

Another sanctioned connection was romantic; a woman might marry into the group. In the fall of 1848 Rossetti became engaged to James Collinson, an apparently dull and dumpy young man whose main attraction for her seemed to be his membership of the P.R.B. Her awkward visit to stay with his family may have contributed to some of the strained gatherings in *Maude*. As she wrote to her brother William, she had stoically joined in lace-making, gardening, and enforced sociability, but wished desperately that they could 'write bouts-rimés and sonnets and be subdued together'.[6]

In addition to being excluded from the Pre-Raphaelite Brotherhood, Rossetti was also shut out of what Jan Marsh calls the Pre-
Raphaelite Sisterhood – the loosely connected group of working-
class models, mistresses, and wives around the circle: 'Not only
was she too unlike them in education, habits of life, and social
and religious values; more important, to be one of them would
have meant not being one of the artists.' As Marsh observes, the
Pre-Raphaelite Sisterhood has a dominant image in art: a brood-
ing face with large, lustrous eyes and surrounded by a mass of
loose hair, looking soulfully out of the canvas. . . . As depicted,
they are silent, enigmatic, passive figures, not individuals engaged
in activity but objects to be gazed upon by painter and
spectator.'[7] Often frozen into this image herself, Rossetti
nonetheless continued to imagine spheres of more activity and
power. Lacking a sisterhood of poets to match the poetic
fraternity of the P.R.B., her imagination often turned to the
newly established Sisterhoods of the Anglican Church, Protestant religious orders in which unmarried English women could
find community and vocation.

By 1850, when Rossetti wrote *Maude*, the Anglican Sisterhoods were very much the topic of the day. Despite centuries of
superstition and calumny against nunneries, religious sisterhoods and Anglican convents had a strong Victorian revival.
Women were demanding more meaningful roles in church
ritual and more serious work than the embroidery of altar
cloths. The controversy over female religious communities began in England in the 1840s, even before the agitation for
women's rights. They originated with the high-church Tractar-
ian or Oxford movement of the 1840s, which founded the first
Anglican order, the Sisters of Mercy at Park Village West,
Regents Park, in 1845. Two other sisterhoods followed in 1848;
and by 1873, there were forty-three in operation.

The sisterhoods were controversial in part because they
challenged the place and duty of women in the family, the plight
of the unmarried woman, and the rights of women to partici-
pate in the ministry of a patriarchal church – in short, because
they raised feminist issues. The religious historian Michael Hill

calls sisterhoods 'the first signs of incipient feminism among women in the middle class', and, in her important study, *Independent Women*, the social historian Martha Vicinus demonstrates that despite their problems and limitations, 'Anglican Sisterhoods were clearly in the vanguard of women's single-sex organizations, in both their organizational autonomy and their insistence upon women's right to a separate religious life.'[8] Membership in a religious community paradoxically gave unmarried women meaningful work and a mobility they otherwise could not possess. While respectable young women could not venture into the slums, let alone speak with prostitutes and vagrants, the Sisters, in their habits and veils, could move freely about the city, and indeed often specialized in 'rescue work', or the reform of prostitution.

Secondly, the sisterhoods allowed women to choose a celibate life without sacrificing social and emotional supports and meaningful work. John Shelton Reed points out that the sisterhoods posed a challenge to the tyrant of Victorian family values, and to the supremacy of female devotion to masculine comfort. The Anglican convent 'took women out of their homes. It gave important work and sometimes great responsibility. It replaced ties to fathers, husbands, and brothers by loyalties to church and sisterhood. It demonstrated that there were callings for women of the upper and middle classes other than those of wife, daughter, and "charitable spinster".'[9] Indeed, Rossetti's older sister Maria joined the Sisterhood of All Saints in 1873, and Rossetti herself did rescue work for the St Mary Magdalene House of Charity of the Sisters of Mercy in Highgate Hill from 1860 to 1870. She was an associate of the order, and wore their habit, described by her friend Letitia Scott as 'very simple, elegant even; black with hanging sleeves, a muslin cap with lace edging, quite becoming to her with the veil.'[10]

Nevertheless, Rossetti, like Maude Foster, was well aware that she had no serious inclination for the monastic life. In a letter to her friend Caroline Gemmer, she explained that she had never seriously 'trembled on "the Convent Threshold"' although she once 'went thro' a sort of romantic impression on the subject like many young people. No, I feel no drawing in that direction: really, of the two, I might perhaps have less unadaptedness in some ways to the hermit life . . . Nor, I think I may truly say, did I ever wish to devote myself at any period of my prolonged life. It was my dear sister who had the pious, devotional, absorbed temperament: not I.'[11]

The Nun's Tale

The convent in *Maude*, represented through Magdalen Ellis, who leaves her mother for the care of 'poor children', is also a Victorian literary convention. Rossetti's fascination with the nun's life in *Maude* was shared by many contemporary artists and writers, and Magdalen's story has many counterparts in mid-Victorian painting and literature. The art historian Susan Casteras describes the 'Victorian pictorial cult of the nun' in the 1840s and 1850s, when 'the beautiful virginity and inaccessibility of the women were key components' of voyeuristic male fantasies about convent life.[12] In paintings such as William Collins's *The World or The Cloister* (1843), Charles Eastlake's *A Visit to the Nun* (1846), Charles Allston Collins's *Convent Thoughts* (1851), or Alfred Elmore's *The Novice* (1852), artists played up the contrast between feminine 'nature' and the 'unnatural' celibacy of the convent world. Eastlake's picture in the Royal Academy exhibition depicted a veiled young nun being visited by her married sister and her children. As *The Art-Journal* noted, the painting was seen as an argument against the monastic life; even the youngest child 'holds up a small nosegay of wild flowers, as if to indicate how much there is a world beyond the dreary walls of the convent from the enjoyment of which, no less than from the sacred lessons all the works of Nature teach us, the Nun has voluntarily excluded herself.'[13]

These themes appear in the literature of the time as well. *Punch* regularly satirised the Anglican Sisterhoods in such pieces as 'Convent of The Belgravians' (18 October 1850) and 'Fashions for 1850; – or A Page for the Puseyites' (30 November

1850).[14] Charles Kingsley's novel *Yeast* (1850) condemns a woman who thinks of becoming a Sister of Charity, 'to fill up the little ideal of a life of romantic asceticism and mystic contemplation.' Lurid accounts like R. MacCrindells' *The Convent; A Narrative, Founded on Fact* (1848), Harriet Martineau's *Sister Anna's Probation* (1861), the anonymous *A Woman's Way; or, the Chelsea Sisterhood* (1865), and Miss E. J. Whately's *Maude; or the Anglican Sister of Mercy* (1869) criticized those 'erring and misguided' women who let 'disappointed feeling, boredom, vain craving for excitement' pass as 'devotedness to God's service'.[15]

Maude

Of course, Maude is harder on her own faults and flaws than anyone else. Most critics have observed that in *Maude*, Rossetti gives a fairly close picture of her own appearance and habits as a fifteen-year-old, and 'a fussily critical assessment of her own character.'[16] Maude is secretive and guilt-ridden over her desire to write, and self-tormenting about minor deviations in piety. In the view of William Michael Rossetti, Christina's

> main object in delineating Maude was to exhibit what she regarded as defects in her own character, and in her attitude towards her social circle and her religious obligations . . . Maude is made the subject of many unfavourable comments, from herself and from her strict-minded authoress. The worst harm she appears to have done is, that when she had written a good poem, she felt it to be good. She was also guilty of the grave sin of preferring to forego the receiving of the eucharist when she supposed herself to be unworthy of it. . . . If some readers opine that all this shows Christina Rossetti's mind to have been at that date overburdened with conscientious scruples of an extreme and even a wire-drawn kind, I share their opinion.' (Prefatory Note, London, 1896)

Yet we should not be too quick to read *Maude* as autobiography, for there are many signs, even in this brief text, that Rossetti drew on literary conventions to ironize and complicate her heroine's motives. Angela Leighton reminds us that while *Maude* 'is one of the most searchingly autobiographical of Rossetti's writings, it is also one which playfully confounds the biographer's questions. . . . [and] is as emotionally secretive as any of the poet's best verse. . . . This most girlish and personal of Rossetti's works turns out to be as arch and unconfessional as any of them.'[17]

To begin with, *Maude* is an embryonic *Kunstlerromane*, or novel of the woman artist. This genre, which Elizabeth Barrett Browning would extend fully in her verse-novel *Aurora Leigh* (1856), had special meanings for a Victorian woman writer, since it accentuated the tensions between creativity and femininity. As Rachel DuPlessis points out, 'Using the female artist as a literary motif dramatizes and heightens the already-present contradiction in bourgeois ideology between the ideal of striving, improvement, and visible public works, and the feminine version of that formula: passivity, "accomplishments", and invisible private acts.'[18]

In most nineteenth-century instances, the story of the woman artist has an unhappy or at least a compromised ending; the heroine must give up the primacy of art in order to win love, and if she is unable to renounce art, she cannot survive. Sandra Gilbert and Susan Gubar see Maude's story as predetermined by these myths; Maude Foster, 'the ambitious, competitive, self-absorbed and self-assertive poet – must die, and be replaced by either the wife, the nun, or most likely, the kindly, useful spinster.'[19] Even in the scenes where she is shown as successful and acclaimed, there is a subtext of struggle. Gilbert and Gubar note that the scene of writing – or indeed reading poetry – is always a source of anxiety to Maude. 'Plainly, the very act of poetic assertion, and its challenge to attempt self-definition or at least self-confrontation, elicits evasions, anxieties, hostilities, in brief "painful preoccupation," from all competitors, so that the jolly poetry game paradoxically contains the germ of just the gloom it seems designed to dispel.'[20]

Moreover, in stories about women artists, relationships between mothers and daughters take on symbolic importance.

Often, 'the daughter becomes an artist to extend, reveal, elaborate her mother's often thwarted talents.'[21] Christina Rossetti's loyalty and dedication to her own mother were strong, and it is striking that in this early work, she imagines a world in which fathers and brothers are nameless and marginal, while mothers, sisters, aunts, and female cousins and friends are at the centre. Maude writes her poems for, and about, other women.

These women are both rivals and doubles. As critics have frequently noted, Rossetti often uses pairs or trios of sisters in her writing to explore aspects of her own personality, 'the warring factions within [her] own divided self.'[22] The split between poetic and sexual creativity, between the introspective and the extroverted life, is represented in the rivalry between Maude and her cousin Mary Clifton. Rossetti draws explicit distinctions between them at several points: 'The two made a strong contrast: one was occupied by a thousand shifting thoughts of herself, her friends, her plans, what she must do, and what she would do; the other, whatever might employ her tongue . . . had always an under-current of thought intent upon herself.'

Maude is the introspective intellectual; Mary the impetuous hoyden who will be the first to marry and have children. Whereas Maude seems prematurely adult, Mary is childlike and direct. When she meets Maude at the train she is bubbling with enthusiasm over the 'unlimited strawberries and cream' ordered for her party, and offers to introduce Maude to all the farm animals, including the pig who is her 'special protégé.' Maude, on the other hand, is beyond juvenile interests, and coolly unimpressed even by meeting the 'new and very fat baby', who reciprocates with 'a howl of intense dismay'. Intellectually, however, Maude gets the upper hand; Mary is unable to rhyme even a couplet, while she easily dashes off a clever poem. Nonetheless, Maude seems sufficiently jealous of her cousin to preach away about feminine beauty and to make a catty remark about 'wax-dollish' girls with 'fair complexions'.

A year later the differences between the two girls are even more obvious. Mary comes bouncing into Maude's house in

London with an 'imperious' appetite; Maude can barely get through the tea-party at Mrs Strawdy's; and indeed the very arrival of her cousins seems to plunge her into further unsociability. To Mary, the life of the nuns is pitiable – 'All day long they are at prayers, or teaching children, or attending the sick, or making poor things, or something.' Maude, however, thinks the life of the convent is happy for those who choose it.

Finally, Mary marries Mr Herbert, and goes off for a wedding-tour to Scarborough and the Lakes, while Maude is 'overturned' on her way to be a bridesmaid, and dies of her injuries. Here too Maude's destiny seems linked to Mary's in ways she does not wish to admit. Her 'Epithalamium for the fair fiancée' turns out to be the gloomy 'Three Nuns', in which Mary's part is the rejected woman. She also designs a pillow for Mary, 'worked in glowing shades of wool and silk.' This gift is carefully wrapped and packed for the cab-ride which ends in Maude's overturning. Writing to Agnes from her sickbed, Maude apologizes for missing the wedding, and asks for 'a detailed account of the lovely bride, her appearance, deportment, and toilet,' as well as an opinion on the groom's handsomeness; 'how I should love a baby of hers,' she notes unconvincingly. Partly for the sake of exposition, but also in what seems like competition with Mary, Maude dwells on her injuries and pain.

Despite some happy moments, Maude is a moody and finally a morbid girl. From the very first page of the story, she is pale, evasive, and secretive, hiding her poems from her mother. But the reader is let in on something more: Maude's cultivated depression. The concealed answer to her mother's conventional question – 'A penny for your thoughts' – is shocking in a girl of fifteen; for Maude is thinking, Hamlet-like, about death:

> 'Yes, I too could face death and never shrink:
> But it is harder to bear hated life.'

The depth of her depression seems inexplicable. As Rossetti's narrator observes, 'it was the amazement of everyone what could make her poetry so broken-hearted as was mostly the case. Some pronounced that she wrote very foolishly about things she could not possibly understand; some wondered if she really had any secret source of uneasiness; while some simply set her down as affected.' In some respects, Maude reminds us of Freud's Dora, another unhappy nineteenth-century adolescent girl who left suicide notes in her writing-desk. Yet we see no obvious sources of Maude's pain. She is attractive, admired, and loved. Her languor seems innate; Rossetti particularly stresses Maude's pallor, an image which also connects her to the marble statue and to art, as in Rossetti's poem 'A Soul': 'She stands as pale as Parian statues stand.' Magdalen Ellis imagines her as 'pale Sister Maude'.

Maude's perplexing unhappiness, her frenzy of self-abnegation, and her paradoxical self-assertion, suggest the personality modern psychiatry would relate to anorexia. As Hilde Bruch explains in her book *The Golden Cage* (1978), the onset of anorexia and puberty often coincide. Some anorexic girls dread the physical changes of adolescence; others wish to remain children under their parents' nurturant care; for yet others, 'reaching puberty may be the end of a secret dream of growing up to be a boy.' These are surely resonant themes for Christina Rossetti, and reflected in her identification with the fifteen-year-old Maude.

Rossetti/Maude's condition as a poet also generates images of disease, renunciation, and anorexia. Rossetti, Sandra Gilbert observes, is a 'poet of anorexia': 'Denied all other means of self-creation, both the starved woman poet and the starving anorexic transform self-denial into self-assertion, a hunger/pain into a hunger/strike.' The problem of anorexia is also a problem of sisterhood and worship, for men commune at an altar serviced by women, but women's communion 'can occur only parodically, at an altar of emptiness, in a service of refusal disguised as self-denial.'[23]

The phrase 'service of refusal' seems an apt description for the section in which Maude emotionally declares that she will no longer take Communion. Her decision follows the tea-party at which she has experienced not only social frustration and embarrassment at being asked to recite her poems, but also subtle competition in the art of renunciation. The Mowbray girls do not go to the theatre or dance; they sing only simple religious airs. Maude reacts with her own bad manners, coldly refusing to read; and later melodramatically tells Agnes of her intent not to go to Church, since she is a hypocrite and sinner.

The final ceremony of refusal is Maude's death after an accident; and Agnes's subsequent burial and burning of her journal and poems. Yet here too Rossetti has it both ways. In one sense, as Angela Leighton points out, 'death here seems to offer a moral solution to the temptations of vanity to which Maude has fallen prey. To be saved from her own ambition, the girl must die.'[24]

Yet the story itself belies this message. Rossetti's editor Rebecca Crump reminds us that within the story, Agnes acts as Maude's literary executor; she is 'astonished at the variety of Maude's compositions' and, although she destroys some of the poems, she saves the best for posterity. Moreover, Christina Rossetti did not stop writing at the age of nineteen, but continued to develop her poetic gifts for another forty-four years. In her own life and career, Rossetti 'was able to integrate and harmonize the divisive elements within her own personality'; perhaps envisioning a different ending for her heroine helped her to resolve her own conflicts about poetic ambition.[25] Paradoxically, conceding that men were divinely ordained as superior to women in art as in other areas of life (as she writes to brother Gabriel, for example, 'you must not expect me to possess a tithe of your capacities'[26]) may have served to relieve some of Rossetti's guilt about her work, while choosing devotional subjects served to legitimize her poetry as suitably feminine and Christian. While neither Maude nor Rossetti can imagine themselves joining a real Anglican sisterhood, the female religious community offers an alternative outside the expectations of romantic love and marriage, a world elsewhere that Rossetti was able to find in poetry.

In 1897, three years after Rossetti's death, *Maude* was resurrected by William Michael Rossetti and published by James Bowman in London and by the Chicago firm of Herbert S.

Stone, whose list of authors included Shaw, Mallarmé, and the American feminist Kate Chopin. While Maude's fragments, pencil scrawls, and drafts were consigned to the fire, Rossetti's manuscript has survived to be read by a new generation.

Dinah Mulock Craik: On Unmarried Women and Sisterhoods

Posterity has been less kind to Dinah Mulock Craik, and yet her essays on women's issues make an important contribution to our understanding of Victorian feminist thought. Craik's 'On Sisterhoods' offers a useful counterpoint to *Maude*. It describes Craik's attendance at the ceremony where a young novice took her vows to the Sisterhood of the Orphanage of Mercy. While noting all the circumstances which might make conventual life alien and unacceptable to the English Protestant mind – the monastic setting, the smell of lilies and incense, the processions, the nun's habit – and while setting out limits that enforce the priority of family ties and home duties, Craik nonetheless attempts a defence of the sisterhood as a meaningful and useful life for unmarried women. Most of the essay draws distinctions between the Catholic and the Protestant nunneries. In particular, Craik stressed the absence of ecstatic religious mysticism, the comfort and homeliness of daily life, and the freedom to visit family or return to secular life. For her, the strongest argument for the sisterhood is the alternative life it offers to single women with no outlet for their maternal emotions. Her vignette of a nun with three orphaned children sums up this vision:

> Three orphans and a solitary woman,
> husbandless, childless, laughing and toying
> together, kissing and kissed – They made a
> group so pretty, so happy – so full of God's
> great mercy, compensation – that it brought
> the tears to one's eyes.

She saw the Sisterhood as a surrogate family, and a work

collective which would lift women out of depression and apathy, and channel their energy into useful reform. Indeed, she notes, 'It is a strange thing to say – yet I dare to say it, for I believe it to be true – that entering a Sisterhood, almost any sort of Sisterhood where there was work to do, authority to compel the doing of it, and companionship to sweeten the same, would have saved many a woman from a lunatic asylum.' At the same time, Craik softened these radical views with more conventional words about the 'stray sheep' of 'gentlewomanhood', the needy souls 'sure to wander if left alone, but safe enough in a flock with a steady shepherd to guide them.' This was the sort of rhetoric likely to appeal to conservative readers.

As Martha Vicinus points out, however, the feeble sheep Craik describes 'would have wilted under the rigorous regimen of prayer and work undertaken by most sisters.'[27] Margaret Goodman, the author of *Experiences of an English Sister of Mercy* (1862) protested against the theory that sisterhoods were sanctuaries for the hopeless: 'It would appear from the writings of some persons, who urge the multiplication of sisterhoods, that they think them desirable because calculated to prove a blessing to women who have nothing to do: a mode of existence for ladies who, after every effort on their part, from the supply not equalling the demand, are unable to find husbands; or a refuge for the woe-worn, weary and disappointed. For neither of these three classes will a sisterhood prove a home. The work is far too real to be performed by lagging hands.'[28]

Craik herself was no laggard. Left destitute by an eccentric father when she was nineteen, throughout her career, she masked her private feminist views with public disdain for the organized feminist movement and women's public activism. In a letter to Oscar Wilde written just before her death, Craik explained that although she cared 'little for Female Suffrage' and had 'given the widest berth to that set of women who are called, not unfairly, the shrieking sisterhood,' she nonetheless held firmly to her feminist principles, and wanted women 'to be strong and brave – both for themselves and as the helpers, not the slaves or foes, of men.' In her fiction and essays, Craik always advocated the bonds of a traditional sisterhood of womanly friendship, service and sacrifice, and repudiated the 'Shrieking Sisterhood' demanding women's rights.

This conservative approach to the woman question is well represented by *A Woman's Thoughts About Women* (1858), which she published anonymously in *Chambers's Edinburgh Journal* from 2 May to 19 December 1857. Along with Charlotte Yonge's *Womankind* (1876), this book is the Holy Living and Holy Dying of Victorian Anglican Spinsterhood, an avatar of the modern self-help paperback. On the first page, Craik makes clear that she is not concerned with married women who 'have realized in greater or less degree the natural destiny of our sex,' but rather with 'the single women, belonging to those supernumerary ranks, which, political economists tell us, are yearly increasing.' The book is a curious mixture of bitter personal experience, homely piety, hard-headed advice, and democratic concern for women. When she wrote it, Craik was thirty-two years old; it seemed to her that she had been a 'working woman all her life', and the book gave her a chance to test her own theories on survival.

Above all things, she advocated self-dependence, a trait which she knew would come hard to middle-class women, who 'from babyhood are given to understand that helplessness is feminine and beautiful; helpfulness . . . unwomanly and ugly.' Women's energies were not directed to useful work, but rather to 'the massacre of old Time'. Her advice is brisk and bolstering: avoid false pride, get yourself educated and trained, don't worry what men will say. She cites case histories of women who took over businesses, or started them; she talks about handicrafts, trades, and the plight of domestic servants. Craik's belief that 'persistent, consecutive work' was the duty and the fulfilment of men and women alike led her to espouse equal education for boys and girls, and to advocate women's entrance into all the professions. She also believed in the moral imperative of a sisterhood that cut across class boundaries, and thus in her chapter on 'Female Servants', she stressed the responsibility of employers towards their maids: 'To say to these "ladies" that the "women" they employ are of the same feminine flesh and blood, would of course meet nominal assent. But to attempt to get them to carry that truth out practically – to own that they and their servants are of like passions and feelings, capable of similar elevation or deterioration of character, and amenable to the same moral laws – in fact, all "sisters" together, accountable both to themselves and to the other sex for the influence they mutually exercise over one another, would, I fear, be held simply ridiculous.'[29]

Craik's views are neither radical nor rosy. Her advice rests on an ideal of Christian resignation, often grim in its denial of the importance of happiness and personal fulfilment. She has many genteel prejudices, warning women, for example, against the immodesty of acting or singing as a career. She makes frequent heavy jokes about the nonsense of women's rights. For these reasons, American feminists reading the book classed it with the prosings of such writers as Sarah Ellis on the duties of women in all the roles and obligations of their lives. But Craik had enough imagination and daring to see that while women could not depend on men to support them and give them homes, they could, if they wished, depend on each other. When she thought of the single woman, she thought not only of the orphaned young lady, the governess, the poet, or the nun, but also of the cook, the seamstress and the prostitute. With her customary practicality, she suggests that women should help their sisters get off the streets by finding them decent jobs.

Moreover, *A Woman's Thoughts About Women* does not cater to the self-pity of the unmarried woman, nor avoid confronting the emotional issues of her life. Depression, anxiety, hypochondria, the realization of ageing – Craik writes about them all. 'It is a condition to which a single woman must make up her mind,' she firmly notes, 'that the close of her days will be more or less solitary.' Yet the final chapter of the book, 'Growing Old', is also the most optimistic and progressive. In middle age, Craik writes, a woman is more independent and less vulnerable. At peace with her regrets, she can begin to make full use of her abilities. Craik reveals something of her own hard-won independence in her conclusions: 'Would that, instead of educating our young girls with the notion that they are to be wives, or nothing – we could instil into them the principle that, above and before all, they are to be *women*, – women, whose character is of their own making, and whose lot lies in their own hands.'

NOTES

[1] George Eliot, *The George Eliot Letters*, ed. Gordon S. Haight, 9 vols. New Haven: Yale University Press, 1954–78, Vol. 3, p. 302.

[2] For a discussion of these connections, see Jerome Bump, 'Christina Rossetti and Pre-Raphaelite Brotherhood', in *The Achievement of Christina Rossetti*, ed. David A. Kent, Ithaca: Cornell University Press, 1987, pp. 250–273.

[3] Kathleen Jones, *Learning Not to be First: The Life of Christina Rossetti*, New York: St Martin's Press, 1992, p. 28.

[4] Jones, p. 32.

[5] Quoted in Jones, p. 32.

[6] Jones, p. 40.

[7] Jan Marsh, *The Pre-Raphaelite Sisterhood*, New York: St Martin's Press, 1985, xiii, p. 1.

[8] See Martha Vicinus, *Independent Women: Work and Community for Single Women, 1850–1920*, Chicago: University of Chicago Press, p. 48, and Michael Hill, *The Religious Order*, London: Heinemann Educational Books Ltd., 1973, p. 10. See also Elaine Showalter, 'Florence Nightingale's Feminist Complaint: Women, Religion, and *Suggestions for Thought*', *Signs* 6 (1981), pp. 395–412.

[9] John Shelton Reed, '"A Female Movement": The Feminization of Nineteenth-Century Anglo-Catholicism', *Anglican and Episcopal History* 57 (1988), pp. 230–31.

[10] See Georgina Battiscombe, *Christina Rossetti: A Divided Life*, London: Constable, 1981, pp. 94, 153–4.

[11] Undated, unpublished letter in the Koch Collection, Pierpont Morgan Library, New York; quoted by Antony H. Harrison in 'Christina Rossetti and the Sage Discourse of Feminist High Anglicanism', in *Victorian Sages and Cultural Discourse: Renegotiating Gender and Power*, ed. Thais E. Morgan, New Brunswick: Rutgers University Press, 1990, p. 284, no. 29.

[12] Susan P. Casteras, 'Virgin Vows: The Early Victorian Artists' Portrayal of Nuns and Novices', in *Religion in the Lives of English Women, 1760–1930*, Bloomington: Indiana University Press, 1986, pp. 129–60.

[13] 'The Royal Pictures', *The Art-Journal* XVIII (1856), p. 174; quoted in Casteras, 'Virgin Vows', p. 145.

[14] See Casteras, 'Virgin Vows', pp. 132–3.

[15] Casteras, 'Virgin Vows', pp. 138–9.

[16] Angela Leighton, '"When I am dead, my dearest": The Secret of Christina Rossetti', *Modern Philology* 87 (May 1990), p. 373.

[17] Leighton, pp. 373–4.

[18] Rachel Blau DuPlessis, *Writing Beyond the Ending*, Bloomington: Indiana University Press, 1985, p. 84.

[19] Sandra M. Gilbert and Susan Gubar, *The Madwoman in the Attic*, New Haven: Yale University Press, 1979, p. 552.

[20] Gilbert and Gubar, p. 550.

[21] DuPlessis, p. 93.

[22] Rebecca Crump, 'Introduction,' *Maude*, Hamden, Conn.: Archon Books, 1976, p. 22.

[23] Sandra M. Gilbert, 'Hunger Pains', *University Publishing* 8 (1979), p. 11.

[24] Leighton, p. 375.

[25] Crump, Introduction, p. 22.

[26] *The Family Letters of Christina Georgina Rossetti*, ed. William Michael Rossetti, London: Macmillan, 1904, p. 31.

[27] Vicinus, pp. 50–51.

[28] Margaret Goodman, *Sisterhoods in the Church of England*, London: Smith, Elder, 1863, p. 268.

[29] Quotations are from Dinah Mulock, *A Woman's Thoughts About Women*, London: Hurst & Blackwell, 1858. See also Elaine Showalter, 'Dinah Mulock Craik and the Tactics of Sentiment', *Feminist Studies* 2 (1975), pp. 5–23.

CHRISTINA ROSSETTI
CHRONOLOGY

1830   Christina Georgina Rossetti born in London on December 5.

1847   *Verses.*

1848   Formation of Pre-Raphaelite Brotherhood.

1850   Breaks engagement with James Collinson. Writes *Maude.*

1862   *Goblin Market and Other Poems.*

1866   *The Prince's Progress and Other Poems.* Declines proposal from Charles Bagot Cayley.

1870   *Commonplace and Other Short Stories.*

1872   *Sing-Song: A Nursery Rhyme Book.*

1874   *Annus Domini: A Prayer for Each Day of the Year.*

1879   *Seek and Find: A Double Series of Short Stories of the Benedicte.*

1881   *A Pageant and Other Poems.*

1882   Death of Dante Gabriel Rossetti.

1894   Death of Christina Rossetti from cancer on December 29.

1897   First publication of *Maude.*

CHRONOLOGY

1826   Dinah Maria Mulock born April 20 in Stoke-on-Trent, eldest of three children of Dinah Mellard Mulock and Nonconformist preacher Thomas Mulock.

1841   First poems published in *Staffordshire Advertiser*, signed 'D.M.M.'

1845   Mother dies. Father refuses to support Dinah and her two younger brothers, Tom and Benjamin.

1849   First novel, *The Ogilvies*

1850   *Olive*. Moves to lodgings in London with friend, Frances Martin.

1852   *The Head of the Family*

1853   *Agatha's Husband*

1856   *John Halifax, Gentleman*

1857   *A Woman's Thoughts About Women*

1859   *A Life for a Life*

1864   Awarded Civil List Pension of £60 a year.

1865   Married George Lillie Craik.

1866   *A Noble Life*

1869   Adopted daughter Dorothy from parish workhouse. Father dies.

1872   *Adventures of a Brownie*

1875   *The Little Lame Prince*

1879   *Young Mrs Jardine*

1882   *Plain Speaking*, a collection of essays

1886   *King Arthur*, propaganda novel about adoption.

1887   Died 12 October of heart failure.

CHRISTINA ROSSETTI

SELECTED BIBLIOGRAPHY

PRIMARY:

Verses, privately printed, London: G. Polidori, 1847

Goblin Market and Other Poems, London: Macmillan, 1862

The Prince's Progress and Other Poems, London: Macmillan, 1866

Commonplace and Other Short Stories, London: F. S. Ellis, 1870

Sing-Song: A Nursery Rhyme Book, London: Routledge and Sons, 1872

Annus Domini: A Prayer for Each Day of the Year, London: James Porter and Co., 1874

Speaking Likenesses, London: Macmillan, 1874

Goblin Market, The Prince's Progress and Other Poems, London: Macmillan, 1875

Seek and Find, London: S.P.C.K., 1879

A Pageant and Other Poems, London: Macmillan, 1881

Letter and Spirit: Notes on the Commandments, London: S.P.C.K., 1883

Time Flies: A Reading Diary, London: S.P.C.K., 1885

Poems: New and Enlarged Edition, London: Macmillan, 1890

The Face of the Deep, London: S.P.C.K., 1893

Verses, London: S.P.C.K., 1893

New Poems: Hitherto Unpublished of Uncollected, ed. William Michael Rossetti, London: Macmillan, 1896

Maude, London: James Bowden, 1897

The Poetical Works of Christina Georgina Rossetti, with Memoir and Notes, ed. William Michael Rossetti, London: Macmillan, 1904

The Family Letters of Christina Georgina Rossetti, ed. William Michael Rossetti, New York: Scribners, 1908

The Complete Poems of Christina Rossetti, ed. Rebecca W. Crump, 2 vols. to date, Baton Rouge: Louisiana State University Press, 1979–85

SECONDARY:

Bellas, Ralph, *Christina Rossetti*, Boston: Twayne, 1977

Crump, Rebecca W., *Christina Rossetti: A Reference Guide*, Boston: G. K. Hall, 1976

Crump, Rebecca W., ed. *Maude: Prose and Verse*, Hamder, Conn: Archon Books, 1976

Battiscombe, Georgina, *Christina Rossetti: A Divided Life*, London: Constable, 1981

Gilbert, Sandra M. and Susan Gubar, *The Madwoman in The Attic: The Woman Writer and The Nineteenth-Century Literary Imagination*, New Haven: Yale University Press, 1979

Harrison, Antony H., *Christina Rossetti in Context*, Chapel Hill: University of North Carolina Press, 1988

Jones, Kathleen, *Learning Not to be First: The Life of Christina Rossetti*, New York: St Martin's Press, 1992

Kent, David, ed. *The Achievement of Christina Rossetti*, Ithaca: Cornell University Press, 1987

Packer, Lona Mosk, *Christina Rossetti*, Berkeley: University of California Press, 1963

Rosenblum, Dolores, *Christina Rossetti: The Poetry of Endurance*, Carbondale: Southern Illinois University Press, 1986

DINAH MULOCK CRAIK
SELECTED BIBLIOGRAPHY

PRIMARY:

The Ogilvies, London: Chapman & Hall, 1849
Olive, London: Chapman & Hall, 1850
Agatha's Husband, London: Chapman & Hall, 1853
John Halifax, Gentleman, London: Hurst & Blackett, 1856
A Woman's Thoughts About Women, London: Hurst & Blackett, 1858
A Life for a Life, London: Hurst & Blackett, 1859
Christian's Mistake, London: Hurst & Blackett, 1865
A Noble Life, London: Hurst & Blackett, 1866
The Woman's Kingdom, London: Hurst & Blackett, 1869
The Little Lone Prince and His Travelling Cloak, London: Macmillan, 1875
About Money and Other Things, London: Macmillan, 1886
Concerning Men and Other Papers, London: Macmillan, 1888

SECONDARY SOURCES:

R. H. Hutton, 'Novels by the Authoress of "John Halifax"', *North British Review* 29 (1858), pp. 466–81.
Sally Mitchell, *Dinah Mulock Craik*, Boston: Twayne Publishers, 1983.
Louisa Parr, 'Dinah Mulock', in *Women Novelists of Queen Victoria's Reign*, London: Hurst & Blackett, 1897.
Elaine Showalter, 'Dinah Mulock Craik and the Tactics of Sentiment: A Case Study in Victorian Female Authorship', *Feminist Studies* 2 (1975), pp. 5–23.

Maude

MAUDE

Part 1st

I

'A penny for your thoughts,' said Mrs Foster one bright July
morning as she entered the sitting room with a bunch of roses
in her hand, and an open letter: 'A penny for your thoughts,'
said she addressing her daughter, who, surrounded by a chaos of
stationery, was slipping out of sight some scrawled paper. This
observation remaining unanswered, the Mother, only too much
accustomed to inattention, continued: 'Here is a note from your
Aunt Letty; she wants us to go and pass a few days with them.
You know Tuesday is Mary's birthday, so they mean to have
some young people and cannot dispense with your company.'

'Do you think of going?' said Maude at last, having locked her
writing-book.

'Yes dear: even a short stay in the country may do you good,
you have looked so pale lately. Don't you feel quite well? tell
me.'

'Oh yes; there is not much the matter, only I am tired and
have a headache. Indeed there is nothing at all the matter;
besides, the country may work wonders.'

Half satisfied, half uneasy, Mrs Foster asked a few more
questions, to have them all answered in the same style: vain
questions, put to one who without telling lies was determined
not to tell the truth.

When once more alone Maude resumed the occupations
which her Mother's entrance had interrupted. Her writing-book

was neither Common-Place Book, Album, Scrap-Book nor
Diary; it was a compound of all these; and contained original
compositions not intended for the public eye, pet extracts,
extraordinary little sketches and occasional tracts of journal.
This choice collection she now proceeded to enrich with the
following sonnet:

> Yes, I too could face death and never shrink:
> But it is harder to bear hated life;
> To strive with hands and knees weary of strife;
>   To drag the heavy chain whose every link
>   Galls to the bone; to stand upon the brink
> Of the deep grave, nor drowse, though it be rife
> With sleep; to hold with steady hand the knife
>   Nor strike home: this is courage as I think.
> Surely to suffer is more than to do:
>   To do is quickly done; to suffer is
>   Longer and fuller of heart-sicknesses:
> Each day's experience testifies of this:
> Good deeds are many, but good lives are few;
>   Thousands taste the full cup; who drains the lees?[1] –

having done which she yawned, leaned back in her chair, and
wondered how she should fill up the time till dinner.

Maude Foster was just fifteen. Small though not positively
short, she might easily be overlooked but would not easily be
forgotten. Her figure was slight and well-made, but appeared
almost high-shouldered through a habitual shrugging stoop. Her
features were regular and pleasing: as a child she had been very
pretty; and might have continued so but for a fixed paleness,
and an expression, not exactly of pain, but languid and pre-
occupied to a painful degree. Yet even now if at any time she
became thoroughly aroused and interested, her sleepy eyes
would light up with wonderful brilliancy, her cheeks glow with
warm colour, her manner become animated, and drawing herself up to her full height she would look more beautiful than
ever she did as a child. So Mrs Foster said, and so unhappily
Maude knew. She also knew that people thought her clever, and
that her little copies of verses were handed about and admired.

Touching these same verses, it was the amazement of every one what could make her poetry so broken-hearted as was mostly the case. Some pronounced that she wrote very foolishly about things she could not possibly understand; some wondered if she really had any secret source of uneasiness; while some simply set her down as affected. Perhaps there was a degree of truth in all these opinions. But I have said enough: the following pages will enable my readers to form their own estimate of Maude's character. Meanwhile let me transport them to another sitting room; but this time it will be in the country with a delightful garden look-out.

Mary Clifton was arranging her Mother's special nosegay when that lady entered.

'Here my dear, I will finish doing the flowers. It is time for you to go to meet your Aunt and Cousin; indeed, if you do not make haste, you will be too late.'

'Thank you, Mamma; the flowers are nearly done;' and Mary ran out of the room.

Before long she and her sister were hurrying beneath a burning sun towards the Railway Station. Through having de-layed their start to the very last moment, neither had found time to lay hands on a parasol; but this was little heeded by two healthy girls, full of life and spirits, and longing moreover to spy out their friends. Mary wanted one day of fifteen; Agnes was almost a year older: both were well-grown and well-made, with fair hair, blue eyes and fresh complexions. So far they were alike: what differences existed in other respects remains to be seen.

'How do you do, Aunt? How do you do, Maude?' cried Mary making a sudden dart forward as she discovered her friends, who having left the Station had already made some progress along the dusty road. Then relinquishing her Aunt to Agnes, she seized upon her cousin, and was soon deep in the description of all the pleasures planned for the auspicious morrow.

'We are to do what we like in the morning: I mean, nothing particular is arranged; so I shall initiate you into all the mysteries of the place; all the cats, dogs, rabbits, pigeons, etc.; above all I must introduce you to a pig, a special protégé of mine: – that is, if you are inclined, for you look wretchedly pale; aren't you well, dear?'

'Oh yes, quite well, and you must show me everything. But what are we to do afterwards?'

'Oh! afterwards we are to be intensely grand. All our young friends are coming and we are to play at round games,[2] (you were always clever at round games,) and I expect to have great fun. Besides, I have stipulated for unlimited strawberries and cream; also sundry tarts are in course of preparation. By the way, I count on your introducing some new game among us benighted rustics; you who come from dissipated London.'

'I fear I know nothing new, but will do my best. At any rate I can preside at your toilet and assist in making you irresistible.'

Mary coloured and laughed; then thought no more of the pretty speech, which sounded as if carefully prepared by her polite cousin. The two made a strong contrast: one was occupied by a thousand shifting thoughts of herself, her friends, her plans, what she must do, and what she would do; the other, whatever might employ her tongue, and to a certain extent her mind, had always an under-current of thought intent upon herself.

Arrived at the house, greetings were duly and cordially performed; also an introduction to a new and very fat baby, who received Maude's advances with a howl of intense dismay. The first day of a visit is often no very lively affair: so perhaps all parties heard the clock announce bed-time without much regret.

II

The young people were assembled in Mary's room, deep in the mysteries of the toilet.

'Here is your wreath, Maude; you must wear it for my sake, and forgive a surreptitious sprig of bay which I have introduced;' said Agnes, adjusting the last white rose, and looking affectionately at her sister and cousin.

Maude was arranging Mary's long fair hair with goodnatured anxiety to display it to the utmost advantage.

'One more spray of fuchsia; I was always sure fuchsia would make a beautiful head-dress. There; now you are perfection: only look; look Agnes. – Oh, I beg your pardon; thank you; my wreath is very nice, only I have not earned the bay.' Still she did not remove it; and when placed on her dark hair it well became the really intellectual character of her face. Her dress was entirely white; simple, fresh and elegant. Neither she nor Agnes would wear ornaments; but left them to Mary, in whose honour the entertainment was given, and who in all other respects was arrayed like her sister.

In the drawingroom Mary proceeded to set in order the presents received that morning: – a handsomely bound Bible from her Father, and a small Prayer-book with Cross and clasp from her Mother; a bracelet of Maude's hair from her Aunt; a cornelian heart from Agnes, and a pocket bonbonnière from her Cousin, besides pretty trifles from her little Brothers. In the midst of arrangements and re-arrangements the servant entered with a large bunch of lilies from the village school-children and the announcement that Mr and Mrs Savage were just arrived with their six daughters.

Gradually the guests assembled, young and old, pretty and

plain; all alike seemingly bent on enjoying themselves: some
with gifts, and all with cordial greetings for Mary; for she was a
general favourite. There was slim Rosanna Hunt, her scarf
arranged with artful negligence to hide a slight protrusion of
one shoulder; and sweet Magdalen Ellis, habited as usual in quiet
colours. Then came Jane and Alice Deverell, twins so much alike
that few besides their parents knew them apart with any
certainty; and their fair brother Alexis who, had he been a girl,
would have increased the confusion. There was little Ellen
Potter with a round rosy face like an apple, looking as natural
and goodhumoured as if, instead of a grand French Governess,
she had had her own parents with her like most of the other
children; and then came three rather haughty-looking Miss
Stantons; and pale Hannah Lindley the orphan; and Harriet
Eyre, a thought too showy in her dress.

Mary, all life and spirits, hastened to introduce the new-
comers to Maude; who, perfectly unembarrassed, bowed and
uttered little speeches with the manner of a practised woman of
the world; while the genuine, unobtrusive courtesy of Agnes did
more towards making their guests comfortable than the eager
goodnature of her sister, or the correct breeding of her cousin.

At length the preliminaries were all accomplished, every one
having found a seat, or being otherwise satisfactorily disposed
of. The elders of the party were grouped here and there, talking
and looking on: the very small children were accommodated in
an adjoining apartment with a gigantic Noah's Ark: and the rest
of the young people being at liberty to amuse themselves as
fancy might prompt, a general appeal was made to Miss Foster
for some game, novel, entertaining and ingenious; or, as some of
the more diffident hinted, easy.

'I really know nothing new,' said Maude: 'you must have
played at Proverbs, What's my thought like, How do you like it,
and Magic music: – or stay, there is one thing we can try: Bouts
rimés.'[3]

'What?' asked Mary.

'Bouts rimés: it is very easy. Some one gives rhymes, Mamma
can do that, and then every one fills them up as they think fit. A

sonnet is the best form to select; but, if you wish, we could try eight, or even four lines.'

'But I am certain I could not make a couplet;' said Mary laughing. 'Of course you would get on capitally, and Agnes might manage very well, and Magdalen can do anything; but it is quite beyond me: do pray think of something more suited to my capacity.'

'Indeed I have nothing else to propose. This is very much better than mere common games; but if you will not try it, that ends the matter:' and Maude leaned back in her chair.

'I hope' – began Mary: but Agnes interposed:

'Suppose some of us attempt Bouts rimés; and you meanwhile can settle what we shall do afterwards. Who is ready to test her poetic powers? – What, no one? – Oh, Magdalen, pray join Maude and me.'

This proposal met with universal approbation, and the three girls retreated to a side table; Mary, who supplied the rhymes, exacting a promise that only one sonnet should be composed. Before the next game was fixed upon, the three following productions were submitted for judgement to the discerning public. The first was by Agnes:

> Would that I were a turnip white,
> Or raven black,
> Or miserable hack
> Dragging a cab from left to right;
> Or would I were the showman of a sight,
> Or weary donkey with a laden back,
> Or racer in a sack,
> Or freezing traveller on an Alpine height;
> Or would I were straw catching as I drown,
> (A wretched landsman I who cannot swim,)
> Or watching a lone vessel sink,
> Rather than writing: I would change my pink
> Gauze for a hideous yellow satin gown
> With deep-cut scolloped edges and a rim.[4]

'Indeed I had no idea of the sacrifice you were making;' observed Maude: 'you did it with such heroic equanimity. Might

I however venture to hint that my sympathy with your sorrows would have been greater, had they been expressed in metre?'

'There's gratitude for you,' cried Agnes gaily: 'What have you to expect, Magdalen?' and she went on to read her friend's sonnet:

> 'I fancy the good fairies dressed in white,
>   Glancing like moon-beams through the shadows black;
>   Without much work to do for king or hack.
>   Training perhaps some twisted branch aright;
>   Or sweeping faded Autumn leaves from sight
>   To foster embryo life; or binding back
>   Stray tendrils; or in ample bean-pod sack
>   Bringing wild honey from the rocky height;
>   Or fishing for a fly lest it should drown;
>   Or teaching water-lily heads to swim,
>   Fearful that sudden rain might make them sink;
>   Or dyeing the pale rose a warmer pink;
>   Or wrapping lilies in their leafy gown,
>   Yet letting the white peep beyond the rim. –

'Well, Maude?'

'Well, Agnes; Miss Ellis is too kind to feel gratified at hearing that her verses make me tremble for my own: but such as they are, listen:

> Some ladies dress in muslin full and white,
> Some gentlemen in cloth succinct and black;
> Some patronise a dog-cart, some a hack,
>   Some think a painted clarence only right.
>   Youth is not always such a pleasing sight,
> Witness a man with tassels on his back;
> Or woman in a great-coat like a sack
>   Towering above her sex with horrid height.
> If all the world were water fit to drown
>   There are some whom you would not teach to swim,
>   Rather enjoying if you saw them sink;
>   Certain old ladies dressed in girlish pink,
> With roses and geraniums on their gown: –
>   Go to the Bason, poke them o'er the rim.' –

'What a very odd sonnet,' said Mary after a slight pause: 'but surely men don't wear tassels.'

Her cousin smiled: 'You must allow for poetical licence; and I have literally seen a man in Regent Street wearing a sort of hooded cloak with one tassel. Of course every one will understand the Bason to mean the one in St James' Park.'

'With these explanations your sonnet is comprehensible,' said Mary: and Magdalen added with unaffected pleasure: 'And without them it was by far the best of the three.'

Maude now exerted herself to amuse the party; and soon proved that ability was not lacking. Game after game was proposed and played at; and her fund seemed inexhaustible, for nothing was thought too nonsensical or too noisy for the occasion. Her goodhumour and animation were infectious: Miss Stanton incurred forfeits with the blandest smile; Hannah Lindley blushed and dimpled as she had not done for many months; Rosanna never perceived the derangement of her scarf; little Ellen exulted in freedom from school-room trammels; the twins guessed each other's thoughts with marvellous facility; Magdalen laughed aloud; and even Harriet Eyre's dress looked scarcely too gay for such an entertainment. Well was it for Mrs Clifton that the strawberries, cream and tarts had been supplied with no niggard hand: and very meagre was the remnant left when the party broke up at a late hour.

III

Agnes and Mary were discussing the pleasures of the preceding evening as they sat over the unusually late breakfast, when Maude joined them. Salutations being exchanged and refreshments supplied to the last comer, the conversation was renewed.

'Who did you think was the prettiest girl in the room last night? our charming selves of course excepted,' asked Mary; 'Agnes and I cannot agree on this point.'

'Yes,' said her sister, 'we quite agree as to mere prettiness; only I maintain that Magdalen is infinitely more attractive than half the handsome people one sees. There is so much sense in her face, and such sweetness. Besides, her eyes are really beautiful.'

'Miss Ellis has a characteristic countenance, but she appeared to me very far from the belle of the evening. Rosanna Hunt has much more regular features.'

'Surely you don't think Rosanna prettier than Jane and Alice,' interrupted Mary: 'I suppose I never look at those two without fresh pleasure.'

'They have good fair complexions, eyes and hair certainly,' and Maude glanced rather pointedly at her unconscious cousin: 'but to me they have a wax-dollish air which is quite unpleasant. I think one of the handsomest faces in the room was Miss Stanton's.'

'But she has such a disagreeable expression,' rejoined Mary hastily: then colouring she half turned towards her sister, who looked grave, but did not speak.

A pause ensued; and then Agnes said, 'I remember how prejudiced I felt against Miss Stanton when first she came to live here, for her appearance and manners are certainly unattractive: and how ashamed of myself I was when we heard that last year, through all the bitterly cold weather, she rose at six, though she never had a fire in her room, that she might have time before breakfast to make clothes for some of the poorest people in the village. And in the Spring, when the scarlet fever was about, her mother would not let her go near the sick children for fear of contagion; so she saved up all her pocket money to buy wine and soup and such things for them as they recovered.'

'I dare say she is very good,' said Maude: 'but that does not make her pleasing. Besides, the whole family have that disagreeable expression, and I suppose they are not all paragons. But you have both finished breakfast, and make me ashamed of your diligence. What is that beautiful piece of work?'

The sisters look delighted: 'I am so glad you like it, dear

Maude. Mary and I are embroidering a cover for the lectern in our Church; but we feared you might think the ground dull.'

'Not at all; I prefer those quiet shades. Why, how well you do it: is it not very difficult? – Let me see if I understand the devices. There is the Cross and the Crown of Thorns; and those must be the keys of S. Peter, with, of course, the sword of S. Paul. Do the flowers mean anything?'

'I am the Rose of Sharon and the Lily of the Valleys,'[5] answered Agnes pointing: 'That is the balm of Gilead, at least it is what we call so; there are myrrh and hyssop, and that is a palm-branch. The border is to be vine-leaves and grapes; with fig-leaves at the corners, thanks to Mary's suggestions. Would you like to help us? there is plenty of room at the frame.'

'No, I should not do it well enough, and have no time to learn, as we go home tomorrow. How I envy you,' she continued in a low voice as if speaking rather to herself than to her hearers: 'you who live in the country, and are exactly what you appear, and never wish for what you do not possess. I am sick of display and poetry and acting.'

'You do not act,' replied Agnes warmly: 'I never knew a more sincere person. One difference between us is that you are less healthy and far more clever than I am. And this reminds me: Miss Savage begged me to ask you for some verses to put in her Album. Would you be so very obliging? any that you have by you would do.'

'She can have the sonnet I wrote last night.'

Agnes hesitated: 'I could not well offer her that, because –'

'Why? she does not "tower".[6] Oh! I suppose she has some reprehensible old lady in her family, and so might feel hurt at my Lynch-law. I will find you something then before I go.'

And that evening, when Agnes went to her cousin's room to help her in packing, Maude consigned to her a neat copy of the following lines:–

> She sat and sang alway
> By the green margin of a stream,
> Watching the fishes leap and play
> Beneath the glad sun-beam.

I sat and wept alway
Beneath the moon's most shadowy beam,
Watching the blossoms of the may
Weep leaves into the stream.

I wept for memory;
She sang for hope that is so fair; –
My tears were swallowed by the sea;
Her songs died on the air.[7]

MAUDE

Part 2nd

I

Rather more than a year had elapsed since Maude parted from
her cousins; and now she was expecting their arrival in London
every minute: for Mrs Clifton, unable to leave her young family,
had gratefully availed herself of Mrs Foster's offer to receive
Agnes and Mary during the early Winter months, that they
might take music and dancing lessons with their cousin.

At length the rumbling of an approaching cab was heard;
then a loud knock and ring. Maude started up: but instead of
running out to meet her guests, began poking vigorously at the
fire, which soon sent a warm, cheerful light through the apartment, enabling her, when they entered, to discern that Agnes
had a more womanly air than at their last meeting, that Mary
had outgrown her sister, and that both were remarkably good-
looking.

'First let me show you your room, and then we can settle
comfortably to tea; we are not to wait for Mamma. She thought
you would not mind sleeping together, as our house is so small;
and I have done my best to arrange things to your taste, for I
know of old you have only one taste between you. Look, my
room is next yours, so we can help each other very cosily: only
pray don't think of unpacking now; there will be plenty of time
this evening, and you must be famished: come.'

But Agnes lingered still, eager to thank her cousin for the
goodnatured forethought which had robbed her own apartment

of flower-vases and inkstand for the accommodation of her guests. The calls of Mary's appetite were however imperious; and very soon the sisters were snugly settled on a sofa by the fire, while Maude in a neighbouring armchair made tea.

'How long it seems since my birthday party;' said Mary, as soon as the eatables had in some measure restored her social powers: 'Why, Maude, you are grown quite a woman; but you look more delicate than ever, and very thin: do you still write verses?' Then without waiting for a reply: 'Those which you gave Miss Savage for her Album were very much admired; and Magdalen Ellis wished at the time for an autograph copy, only she had not courage to trouble you. But perhaps you are not aware that poor Magdalen has done with Albums and such like, at least for the present: she has entered on her noviciate in the Sisterhood of Mercy established near our house.'

'Why poor?' said Maude: 'I think she is very happy.'

'Surely you would not like such a life,' rejoined her cousin: 'They have not proper clothes on their beds, and never go out without a thick veil, which must half blind them. All day long they are at prayers, or teaching children, or attending the sick, or making poor things, or something. Is that to your taste?'

Maude half sighed; and then answered: 'You cannot imagine me either fit or inclined for such a life; still I can perceive that those are very happy who are. When I was preparing for Confirmation Mr Paulson offered me a district; but I did not like the trouble, and Mamma thought me too unwell for regularity. I have regretted it since though: yet I don't fancy I ever could have talked to the poor people or done the slightest good. – Yes, I continue to write now and then as the humour seizes me; and if Miss Ellis' –

'Sister Magdalen,' whispered Agnes.

'– If Sister Magdalen will accept it, I will try and find her something admissible even within Convent walls. But let us change the subject. On Thursday we are engaged to tea at Mrs Strawdy's. There will be no sort of party, so we need not dress or take any trouble.'

'Will my Aunt go with us?' asked Agnes.

'No. Poor Mamma has been ailing for some time and is by no means strong; so as Mrs Strawdy is an old school-fellow of hers and a most estimable person, she thinks herself justified in consigning you to my guardianship. On Saturday we must go shopping, as Aunt Letty says you are to get your Winter things in London; and I can get mine at the same time. On Sunday – or does either of you dislike Cathedral services?'

Agnes declared they were her delight; and Mary, who had never attended any, expressed great pleasure at the prospect of hearing what her sister preferred to all secular music.

'Very well,' continued Maude: 'we will go to S. Andrew's then, and you shall be introduced to a perfect service; or at any rate to perhaps the nearest English approach to vocal perfection. But you know you are to be quite at home here; so we have not arranged any particular plans of amusement, but mean to treat you like ourselves. And now it is high time for you to retire. Here Agnes,' handing to her cousin a folded paper, the result of a rummage in her desk: 'Will you enclose this to Sister Magdalen, and assure her that my verses are honoured even in my own eyes by her acceptance. You can read them if you like, and Mary too, of course; only please not in my presence.'

They were as follows:

> Sweet sweet sound of distant waters falling
>   On a parched and thirsty plain;
> Sweet sweet song of soaring skylark, calling
>   On the sun to shine again;
> Perfume of the rose, only the fresher
>   For past fertilizing rain;
> Pearls amid the sea, a hidden treasure
>   For some daring hand to gain; –
>   Better, dearer than all these
>   Is the earth beneath the trees:
>   Of a much more priceless worth
>   Is the old, brown, common earth.
>
> Little snow-white lamb piteously bleating
>   For thy mother far away;

Saddest, sweetest nightingale retreating
     With thy sorrow from the day;
Weary fawn whom night has overtaken,
     From the herd gone quite astray;
Dove whose nest was rifled and forsaken
     In the budding month of May; –
          Roost upon the leafy trees;
          Lie on earth and take your ease:
          Death is better far than birth,
          You shall turn again to earth.

Listen to the never pausing murmur
     Of the waves that fret the shore:
See the ancient pine that stands the firmer
     For the storm-shock that it bore;
And the moon her silver chalice filling
     With light from the great sun's store;
And the stars which deck our temple's ceiling
     As the flowers deck its floor;
          Look and hearken while you may,
          For these things shall pass away:
          All these things shall fail and cease;
          Let us wait the end in peace.

Let us wait the end in peace; for truly
     That shall cease which was before:
Let us see our lamps are lighted, duly
     Fed with oil, nor wanting more:
Let us pray while yet the Lord will hear us,
     For the time is almost o'er;
Yea, the end of all is very near us;
     Yea, the Judge is at the door.
          Let us pray now while we may;
          It will be too late to pray
          When the quick and dead shall all
          Rise at the last trumpet call.[8]

II

When Thursday arrived Agnes and Mary were indisposed with
colds; so Mrs Foster insisted on her daughter's making their
excuses to Mrs Strawdy. In a dismal frame of mind Maude,
assisted by her sympathizing cousins, performed her slight preliminary toilet.

'You have no notion of the utter dreariness of this kind of
invitation: I counted on your helping me through the evening,
and now you fail me. Thank you, Mary; I shall not waste eau de
Cologne on my handkerchief. Goodnight both: mind you go to
bed early and get up quite well tomorrow. Goodnight.'

The weather was foggy and raw as Maude stepped into the
street; and proved anything but soothing to a temper already
fretted; so by the time that she had arrived at her destination,
removed her walking things, saluted her hostess and apologized
for her cousins, her countenance had assumed an expression
neither pleased nor pleasing.

'Let me present my nieces to you, my dear,' said Mrs Strawdy
taking her young friend by the hand and leading her towards the
fire: 'This is Miss Mowbray, or, as you must call her, Annie; that
is Caroline, and that Sophy. They have heard so much of you
that any farther introduction is needless;' here Maude bowed
rather stiffly: 'But as we are early people you will excuse our
commencing with tea, after which we shall have leisure for
amusement.'

There was something so genuinely kind and simple in Mrs
Strawdy's manner, that even Maude felt mollified, and resolved
on doing her best not only towards suppressing all appearance
of yawns, but also towards bearing her part in the conversation.

'My cousins will regret their indisposition more than ever,

when they learn of how much pleasure it has deprived them;' said she, civilly addressing Miss Mowbray.

A polite bend, smile and murmur formed the sole response: and once more a subject had to be started.

'Have you been very gay lately? I begin to acquire the reputation of an invalid, and so my privacy is respected.'

Annie coloured and looked excessively embarrassed; at last she answered in a low hesitating voice: 'We go out extremely little, partly because we never dance.'

'Nor I either; it really is too fatiguing: yet a ball-room is no bad place for a mere spectator. Perhaps, though, you prefer the Theatre?'

'We never go to the play,' rejoined Miss Mowbray looking more and more uncomfortable.

Maude ran on: 'Oh, I beg your pardon, you do not approve of such entertainments. I never go, but only for want of some one to take me.' Then addressing Mrs Strawdy: 'I think you know my Aunt Mrs Clifton?'

'I visited her years ago with your Mamma,' was the answer: 'when you were quite a little child. I hope she continues in good health. Pray remember me to her and to Mr Clifton when you write.'

'With pleasure. She has a large family now, eight children.'

'That is indeed a large family,' rejoined Mrs Strawdy, intent meanwhile on dissecting a cake with mathematical precision: 'You must try a piece, it is Sophy's own manufacture.'

Despairing of success in this quarter, Maude now directed her attention to Caroline, whose voice she had not heard once in the course of the evening.

'I hope you will favour us with some music after tea; in fact, I can take no denial. You look too blooming to plead a cold, and I feel certain you will not refuse to indulge my love for sweet sounds: of your ability to do so I have heard elsewhere.'

'I shall be most happy; only you must favour us in return.'

'I will do my best,' answered Maude somewhat encouraged: 'but my own performances are very poor. Are you fond of German songs? they form my chief resource.'

'Yes, I like them much.'

Baffled in this quarter also, Miss Foster wanted courage to attack Sophy, whose countenance promised more cake than conversation. The meal seemed endless: she fidgeted under the table with her fingers; pushed about a stool on the noiselessly soft carpet until it came in contact with some one's foot; and at last fairly deprived Caroline of her third cup of coffee, by opening the piano and claiming the fulfilment of her promise.

The young lady complied with obliging readiness. She sang some simple airs, mostly religious, not indeed with much expression, but in a voice clear and warbling as a bird's. Maude felt consoled for all the contrarieties of the day; and was bargaining for one more song before taking Caroline's place at the instrument, when the door opened to admit Mrs and Miss Savage; who having only just reached town, and hearing from Mrs Foster that her daughter was at the house of a mutual friend, resolved on begging the hospitality of Mrs Strawdy, and renewing their acquaintance.

Poor Maude's misfortunes now came thick and fast. Seated between Miss Savage and Sophia Mowbray, she was attacked on either hand with questions concerning her verses. In the first place, did she continue to write? Yes. A flood of exstatic compliments followed this admission: she was so young, so much admired, and, poor thing, looked so delicate. It was quite affecting to think of her lying awake at night, meditating those sweet verses – ('I sleep like a top,' Maude put in drily,) – which so delighted her friends, and would so charm the public, if only Miss Foster could be induced to publish. At last the bystanders were called upon to intercede for a recitation.

Maude coloured with displeasure; a hasty answer was rising to her lips, when the absurdity of her position flashed across her mind so forcibly that, almost unable to check a laugh in the midst of her annoyance, she put her handkerchief to her mouth. Miss Savage, impressed with a notion that her request was about to be complied with, raised her hand, imploring silence; and settled herself in a listening attitude.

'You will excuse me,' Maude at last said very coldly: 'I could not think of monopolizing every one's attention. Indeed you are extremely good, but you must excuse me.' And here Mrs Savage interposed, desiring her daughter not to tease Miss Foster; and Mrs Strawdy seconded her friend's arguments, by a hint that supper would make its appearance in a few minutes.

Finally the maid announced that Miss Foster was 'fetched'; and Maude, shortening her adieus and turning a deaf ear to Annie's suggestion that their acquaintance should not terminate with the first meeting, returned home dissatisfied with her circumstances, her friends and herself.

III

It was Christmas Eve. All day long Maude and her cousins were hard at work putting up holly and mistletoe in wreaths, festoons, or bunches, wherever the arrangement of the rooms admitted of such embellishment. The picture-frames were hidden behind foliage and bright berries; the bird-cages were stuck as full of green as though it had been Summer. A fine sprig of holly was set apart as a centre-bit for the pudding of next day: scratched hands and injured gowns were disregarded: hour after hour the noisy bustle raged until Mrs Foster, hunted from place to place by her young relatives, heard, with inward satisfaction, that the decorations were completed.

After tea Mary set the backgammon board in array and challenged her Aunt to their customary evening game: Maude, complaining of a headache, and promising either to wrap herself in a warm shawl or to go to bed, went to her room: and Agnes, listening to the rattle of the dice, at last came to the conclusion that her presence was not needed down stairs, and resolved to visit the upper regions. Thinking that her cousin was lying down tired and might have fallen asleep, she forbore knocking; but opened the door softly and peeped in.

Maude was seated at a table, surrounded by the old chaos of stationery; before her lay the locking manuscript-book, into which she had just copied something. That day she had appeared more than usually animated: and now supporting her forehead upon her hand, her eyes cast down till the long lashes nearly rested upon her cheeks, she looked pale, languid, almost in pain. She did not move, but let her visitor come close to her without speaking: Agnes thought she was crying.

'Dear Maude, you have overtired yourself. Indeed, for all our sakes, you should be more careful:' here Agnes passed her arm affectionately round her friend's neck: 'I hoped to find you fast asleep, and instead of this you have been writing in the cold. Still, I did not come to lecture; and am even ready to show my forgiving disposition by reading your new poem: may I?'

Maude glanced quickly up at her cousin's kind face; then answered: 'Yes, if you like;' and Agnes read as follows:

> Vanity of vanities, the Preacher saith,
> All things are vanity. The eye and ear
> Cannot be filled with what they see and hear:
> Like early dew, or like the sudden breath
> Of wind, or like the grass that withereth
> Is man, tossed to and fro by hope and fear:
> So little joy hath he, so little cheer,
> Till all things end in the long dust of death.
> Today is still the same as yesterday,
> Tomorrow also even as one of them;
> And there is nothing new under the sun.
> Until the ancient race of time be run,
> The old thorns shall grow out of the old stem,
> And morning shall be cold and twilight grey. –[9]

This sonnet was followed by another, written like a post-script:

> I listen to the holy antheming
> That riseth in thy walls continually,
> What while the organ pealeth solemnly

And white-robed men and boys stand up to sing.
I ask my heart with a sad questioning:
'What lov'st thou here?' and my heart answers me:
'Within the shadows of this sanctuary
    To watch and pray is a most blessed thing.'
To watch and pray, false heart? it is not so:
    Vanity enters with thee, and thy love
Soars not to Heaven, but grovelleth below.
    Vanity keepeth guard, lest good should reach
    Thy hardness; not the echoes from above
Can rule thy stubborn feelings or can teach. $-$[10]

'Was this composed after going to S. Andrew's?'

'No; I wrote it just now, but I was thinking of S. Andrew's. It is horrible to feel such a hypocrite as I do.'

'Oh! Maude, I only wish I were as sensible of my faults as you are of yours. But a hypocrite you are not: don't you see that every line of these sonnets attests your sincerity?'

'You will stay to Communion tomorrow?' asked Maude after a short silence, and without replying to her cousin's speech; even these few words seemed to cost her an effort.

'Of course I shall; why, it is Christmas Day: – at least I trust to do so. Mary and I have been thinking how nice it will be for us all to receive together:[11] so I want you to promise that you will pray for us at the Altar, as I shall for you. Will you?'

'I shall not receive tomorrow,' answered Maude; then hurrying on as if to prevent the other from remonstrating: 'No: at least I will not profane Holy Things; I will not add this to all the rest. I have gone over and over again, thinking I should come right in time, and I do not come right: I will go no more.'

Agnes turned quite pale: 'Stop,' she said interrupting her cousin: 'Stop; you cannot mean, – you do not know what you are saying. You will go no more? Only think, if the struggle is so hard now, what it will be when you reject all help.'

'I do not struggle.'

'You are ill tonight,' rejoined Agnes very gently: 'you are tired and over-excited. Take my advice, dear; say your prayers and get to bed. But do not be very long; if there is anything you miss and will tell me of, I will say it in your stead. Don't think me unfeeling: I was once on the very point of acting as you propose. I was perfectly wretched: harassed and discouraged on all sides. But then it struck me – you won't be angry? – that it was so ungrateful to follow my own fancies, instead of at least endeavouring to do God's Will: and so foolish too; for if our safety is not in obedience, where is it?'

Maude shook her head: 'Your case is different. Whatever your faults may be, (not that I perceive any,) you are trying to correct them; your own conscience tells you that. But I am not trying. No one will say that I cannot avoid putting myself forward and displaying my verses. Agnes, you must admit so much.'

Deep-rooted indeed was that vanity which made Maude take pleasure, on such an occasion, in proving the force of arguments directed against herself. Still Agnes would not yield; but resolutely did battle for the truth.

'If hitherto it has been so, let it be so no more. It is not too late: besides, think for one moment what will be the end of this. We must all die: what if you keep to your resolution, and do as you have said, and receive the Blessed Sacrament no more?' – Her eyes filled with tears.

Maude's answer came in a subdued tone: 'I do not mean never to Communicate again. You remember Mr Paulson told us last Sunday that sickness and suffering are sent for our correction. I suffer very much. Perhaps a time will come when these will have done their work on me also; when I shall be purified indeed and weaned from the world. Who knows? the lost have been found, the dead quickened.' She paused as if in thought; then continued: 'You partake of the Blessed Sacrament in peace, Agnes, for you are good; and Mary, for she is harmless: but your conduct cannot serve to direct mine because I am neither the one nor the other. Some day I may be fit again to approach the Holy Altar, but till then I will at least refrain from dishonouring it.'

Agnes felt almost indignant: 'Maude, how can you talk so? this is not reverence. You cannot mean that for the present you will indulge vanity and display; that you will court admiration and applause; that you will take your fill of pleasure until sickness, or it may be death, strips you of temptation and sin together. Forgive me; I am sure you never meant this: yet what else does a deliberate resolution to put off doing right come to? – and if you are determined at once to do your best, why deprive yourself of the appointed means of grace? Dear Maude, think better of it;' and Agnes knelt beside her cousin, and laid her head against her bosom.

But still Maude, with a sort of desperate wilfulness, kept saying: 'It is of no use; I cannot go tomorrow; it is of no use.' She hid her face, leaning upon the table and weeping bitterly; while Agnes, almost discouraged, quitted the room.

Maude, once more alone, sat for some time just as her cousin left her. Gradually the thick, low sobs became more rare; she was beginning to feel sleepy. At last she roused herself with an effort and commenced undressing; then it struck her that her prayers had still to be said. The idea of beginning them frightened her, yet she could not settle to sleep without saying something. Strange prayers they must have been, offered with a divided heart and a reproachful conscience. Still they were said at length; and Maude lay down harassed, wretched, remorseful, everything but penitent. She was nearly asleep, nearly unconscious of her troubles, when the first stroke of midnight sounded. Immediately a party of Christmas waits[12] and carollers burst forth with their glad music. The first part was sung in full chorus:

'Thank God, thank God, we do believe;
Thank God that this is Christmas Eve.
Even as we kneel upon this day,
Even so the ancient legends say,
Nearly two thousand years ago
The stalled ox knelt, and even so
The ass knelt full of praise, which they
Could not express, while we can pray.
Thank God, thank God, for Christ was born
Ages ago, as on this morn.

In the snow-season undefiled
God came to earth a Little Child:
He put His ancient Glory by
To love for us and then to die.' –

– Then half the voices sang the following stanza:

'How shall we thank God? how shall we
Thank Him and praise Him worthily?
What will He have Who loved us thus?
What presents will He take from us? –
Will He take gold? or precious heap
Of gems? or shall we rather steep
The air with incense? or bring myrrh? –
What man will be our messenger
To go to Him and ask His Will?
Which having learned, we will fulfil
Though He choose all we most prefer:
What man will be our messenger?' –

– This was answered by the other half:

'Thank God, thank God, the Man is found,
Sure-footed, knowing well the ground.
He knows the road, for this the way
He travelled once, as on this day.
He is our Messenger; beside,
He is our Door and Path and Guide;
He also is our Offering;
He is the Gift That we must bring.' –

– Finally all the singers joined in the conclusion:

'Let us kneel down with one accord
And render thanks unto the Lord:
For unto us a Child is born
Upon this happy Christmas morn;
For unto us a Son is given,
Firstborn of God, and Heir of Heaven.' –[13]

As the echoes died away, Maude fell asleep.

MAUDE

Part 3rd

I

Agnes Clifton to Maude Foster.

12th June 18—

My dear Maude,

Mamma has written to my Aunt that Mary's marriage is fixed for the 4th of next month: but as I fear we cannot expect you both so many days before the time, I also write, hoping that you at least will come without delay. At any rate I shall be at the Station tomorrow afternoon with a chaise for your luggage; so pray take pity on my desolate condition, and avail yourself of the three o'clock train. As we are both bridesmaids elect, I thought it would be very nice for us to be dressed alike, so have procured double quantity of everything; thus you will perceive no pretence remains for your lingering in smoky London.

You will be amused when you see Mary: I have already lost my companion. Mr Herbert calls at least once a day, but sometimes oftener; so all day long Mary is on the alert. She takes much more interest in the roses over the porch than was formerly the case; the creepers outside the windows require continual training, not to say hourly care: I tell her the constitution of the garden must have become seriously weakened lately. One morning I caught her before the glass, trying the effect of seringa (the English orange-blossom, you know,) in her hair. She looked such a darling. I hinted how flattered Mr Herbert would feel when I told him; which provoked her to offer a few remarks on old maids. Was it not a shame?

Last Thursday Magdalen Ellis was finally received into the Sisterhood of Mercy. I wished much to be present, but could not, as the whole affair was conducted quite privately; only her parents were admitted of the world. However, I made interest for a lock of her beautiful hair, which I prize highly. It makes me sad to look at it: yet I know she has chosen well; and will, if she perseveres, receive hereafter an abundant recompense for all she has foregone here. Sometimes I think whether such a life can be suited to me; but then I could not bear to leave Mamma: indeed that is just what Magdalen felt so much. I met her yesterday walking with some poor children. Her veil was down, nearly hiding her face; still I fancy she looked thoughtful, but very calm and happy. She says she always prays for me, and asked my prayers; so I begged her to remember you and Mary. Then she enquired how you are; desiring her kindest love to you, and assuring me she makes no doubt your name will be known at some future period: but checking herself almost immediately, she added that she could fancy you very different, as pale Sister Maude. This surprised me; I can fancy nothing of the sort. At last she mentioned the verses you gave her months ago, which she knows by heart and values extremely: – then, having nearly reached my home, we parted.

What a document I have composed; I who have not one minute to spare from Mary's trousseau. Will you give my love to my Aunt; and request her from me to permit your immediately coming to

Your affectionate cousin,
Agnes M. Clifton.————

P.S. Mary would doubtless send a message were she in the room; I conjecture her to be lurking about somewhere on the watch. Goodbye: or rather, Come. –

Maude handed the letter to her Mother: 'Can you spare me, Mamma? I should like to go, but not if it is to inconvenience you.'

'Certainly you shall go, my dear. It is a real pleasure to hear you express interest on some point, and you cannot be with any one I approve of more than Agnes. But you must make haste with the packing now: I will come and help you in a few minutes.'

Still Maude lingered: 'Did you see about Magdalen? I wonder what made her think of me as a Sister. It is very nice of her; but then she is so good she never can conceive what I am like. Mamma, should you mind my being a Nun?'

'Yes my dear; it would make me miserable. But for the present take my advice and hurry a little, or the train will leave without you.'

Thus urged, Maude proceeded to bundle various miscellanous goods into a trunk; the only article on the safety of which she bestowed much thought, being the present destined for Mary: a sofa-pillow worked in glowing shades of wool and silk. This she wrapped carefully in a cloth, and laid at the bottom: then over it all else was heaped without much ceremony. Many were the delays occasioned by things mislaid, which must be looked for; ill-secured, which must be re-arranged; or remembered too late, which yet could not be dispensed with, and so must be crammed in somewhere. At length, however, the tardy preparations were completed; and Maude, enveloped in two shawls, though it was the height of Summer, stepped into a cab; promising strict conformity to her Mother's injunction that both windows should be kept closed.

Half an hour had not elapsed when another cab drove up to the door; and out of it Maude was lifted perfectly insensible. She had been overturned; and, though no limb was broken, had neither stirred nor spoken since the accident.

II

Maude Foster to Agnes Clifton.

2nd July 18—

My dear Agnes,

You have heard of my mishap? it keeps me not bedridden, but sofa-ridden. My side is dreadfully hurt; I looked at it this morning for the first time, but hope never again to see so shocking a sight. The pain now and then is extreme, though not always so; sometimes, in fact, I am unconscious of any injury.

Will you convey my best love and wishes to Mary, and tell her how much I regret being away from her at such a time; especially as Mamma will not hear of leaving me. A day or two ago I tried to compose an Epithalamium[14] for our fair fiancée; which effort resulted in my present enclosure: not much to the purpose, we must admit. You may read it when no better employment offers. The first Nun no one can suspect of being myself, partly because my hair is far from yellow and I do not wear curls; partly because I never did anything half so good as profess. The second might be Mary, had she mistaken her vocation. The third is Magdalen, of course. But whatever you miss, pray read the mottoes. Put together they form a most exquisite little song which the Nuns sing in Italy. One can fancy Sister Magdalen repeating it with her whole heart.

The Surgeon comes twice a day to dress my wounds; still, all the burden of nursing falls on poor Mamma. How I wish you were here to help us both: we should find plenty to say.

But perhaps ere many months are passed I shall be up and about, when we may go together on a visit to Mary; a most delightful possibility. By the way, how I should love a baby of hers, and what a pretty little creature it ought to be. Do you think Mr Herbert handsome? hitherto I have only heard a partial opinion.

Ugh, my side! it gives an awful twinge now and then. You need not read my letter; but I must write it, for I am unable to do anything else. Did the pillow reach safely? It gave me so much pleasure to work it for Mary, who, I hope, likes it. At all events, if not to her taste, she may console herself with the reflection that it is unique; for the pattern was my own designing.

Here comes dinner; goodbye. When will anything so welcome as your kind face gladden the eyes of

Your affectionate
Maude Foster?———

P.S. I have turned tippler lately on port wine three times a day. 'To keep you up,' says my Doctor: while I obstinately refuse to be kept up, but insist on becoming weaker and weaker. Mind you write me a full history of your grand doings on a certain occasion: not omitting a detailed account of the lovely bride, her appearance, deportment and toilet. Goodbye once more: when shall I see you all again? –

Three Nuns.

1.

'Sospira questo core
E non so dir perchè.'[15]

———

Shadow, shadow on the wall
   Spread thy shelter over me;
Wrap me with a heavy pall,
   With the dark that none may see.
Fold thyself around me; come:
Shut out all the troublesome
Noise of life; I would be dumb.

Shadow thou hast reached my feet,
   Rise and cover up my head;

Be my stainless winding sheet,
    Buried before I am dead.
Lay thy cool upon my breast:
Once I thought that joy was best,
Now I only care for rest.

By the grating of my cell
    Sings a solitary bird;
Sweeter than the vesper bell,
    Sweetest song was ever heard.*
Sing upon thy living tree:
Happy echoes answer thee,
Happy songster, sing to me.

When my yellow hair was curled
    Though men saw and called me fair,
I was weary in the world
    Full of vanity and care.
Gold was left behind, curls shorn
When I came here; that same morn
Made a bride no gems adorn.

Here wrapped in my spotless veil,
    Curtained from intruding eyes,
I whom prayers and fasts turn pale
    Wait the flush of Paradise.
But the vigil is so long
My heart sickens: – sing thy song,
Blithe bird that canst do no wrong.

Sing on, making me forget
    Present sorrow and past sin.
Sing a little longer yet:
    Soon the matins will begin;
And I must turn back again
To that aching worse than pain
I must bear and not complain.

* 'Sweetest eyes were ever seen.' E. B. Browning.

Sing, that in thy song I may
    Dream myself once more a child
In the green woods far away
    Plucking clematis and wild
Hyacinths, till pleasure grew
Tired, yet so was pleasure too,
Resting with no work to do.

In the thickest of the wood,
    I remember, long ago
How a stately oak tree stood,
    With a sluggish pool below
Almost shadowed out of sight.
On the waters dark as night,
Water-lilies lay like light.

There, while yet a child, I thought
    I could live as in a dream,
Secret, neither found nor sought:
    Till the lilies on the stream,
Pure as virgin purity,
Would seem scarce too pure for me:–
Ah, but that can never be.

2.
'Sospirerà d'amore,
    Ma non lo dice a me.'

———

I loved him, yes, where was the sin?
    I loved him with my heart and soul.
    But I pressed forward to no goal,
There was no prize I strove to win.
Show me my sin that I may see:–
Throw the first stone, thou Pharisee.

I loved him, but I never sought
    That he should know that I was fair.

I prayed for him; was my sin prayer?
I sacrificed, he never bought.
He nothing gave, he nothing took;
We never bartered look for look.

My voice rose in the sacred choir,
        The choir of Nuns; do you condemn
        Even if, when kneeling among them,
Faith, zeal and love kindled a fire
And I prayed for his happiness
Who knew not? was my error this?

I only prayed that in the end
        His trust and hope may not be vain.
        I prayed not we may meet again:
I would not let our names ascend,
No, not to Heaven, in the same breath;
Nor will I join the two in death.

Oh sweet is death; for I am weak
        And weary, and it giveth rest.
        The Crucifix lies on my breast,
And all night long it seems to speak
Of rest; I hear it through my sleep,
And the great comfort makes me weep.

Oh sweet is death that bindeth up
        The broken and the bleeding heart.
        The draught chilled, but a cordial part
Lurked at the bottom of the cup;
And for my patience will my Lord
Give an exceeding great reward.

Yea, the reward is almost won,
        A crown of glory and a palm.
        Soon I shall sing the unknown psalm;
Soon gaze on light, not on the sun;
And soon, with surer faith, shall pray
For him, and cease not night nor day.

My life is breaking like a cloud;
    God judgeth not as man doth judge –
    Nay, bear with me; you need not grudge
This peace; the vows that I have vowed
Have all been kept: Eternal Strength
Holds me, though mine own fails at length.

Bury me in the Convent ground
    Among the flowers that are so sweet;
    And lay a green turf at my feet,
Where thick trees cast a gloom around.
At my head let a Cross be, white
Through the long blackness of the night.

Now kneel and pray beside my bed
    That I may sleep being free from pain:
    And pray that I may wake again
After His Likeness, Who hath said
(Faithful is He Who promiseth,)
We shall be satisfied Therewith.

                          3.
            'Rispondimi, cor mio,
              Perchè sospiri tu?
           Risponde: Voglio Iddio,
              Sospiro per Gesù.'

                    ————

My heart is as a freeborn bird
    Caged in my cruel breast,
That flutters, flutters evermore,
    Nor sings, nor is at rest.
But beats against the prison bars,
    As knowing its own nest
Far off beyond the clouded West.

My soul is as a hidden fount
    Shut in by clammy clay,

That struggles with an upward moan;
    Striving to force its way
Up through the turf, over the grass,
    Up, up into the day,
Where twilight no more turneth grey.

Oh for the grapes of the True Vine
    Growing in Paradise.
Whose tendrils join the Tree of Life
    To that which maketh wise.
Growing beside the Living Well
    Whose sweetest waters rise
Where tears are wiped from tearful eyes.

Oh for the waters of that Well
    Round which the Angels stand.
Oh for the Shadow of the Rock
    On my heart's weary land.
Oh for the Voice to guide me when
    I turn to either hand,
Guiding me till I reach Heaven's strand.

Thou World from which I am come out,
    Keep all thy gems and gold;
Keep thy delights and precious things,
    Thou that art waxing old.
My heart shall beat with a new life,
    When thine is dead and cold:
When thou dost fear I shall be bold.

When Earth shall pass away with all
    Her pride and pomp of sin,
The City builded without hands
    Shall safely shut me in.
All the rest is but vanity
    Which others strive to win:
Where their hopes end my joys begin.

I will not look upon a rose
    Though it is fair to see:

The flowers planted in Paradise
        Are budding now for me.
Red roses like love visible
        Are blowing on their tree,
Or white like virgin purity.

I will not look unto the sun
        Which setteth night by night:
In the untrodden courts of Heaven
        My crown shall be more bright.
Lo, in the New Jerusalem
        Founded and built aright
My very feet shall tread on light.

With foolish riches of this World
        I have bought treasure, where
Nought perisheth: for this white veil
        I gave my golden hair;
I gave the beauty of my face
        For vigils, fasts and prayer;
I gave all for this Cross I bear.

My heart trembled when first I took
        The vows which must be kept;
At first it was a weariness
        To watch when once I slept.
The path was rough and sharp with thorns;
        My feet bled as I stepped;
The Cross was heavy and I wept.

While still the names rang in mine ears
        Of daughter, sister, wife;
The outside world still looked so fair
        To my weak eyes, and rife
With beauty; my heart almost failed;
        Then in the desperate strife
I prayed, as one who prays for life.

Until I grew to love what once
        Had been so burdensome.

So now when I am faint, because
Hoped deferred seems to numb
My heart, I yet can plead; and say
Although my lips are dumb:
'The Spirit and the Bride say, Come.' —[16]

———

III

Three weeks had passed away. A burning sun seemed baking
the very dust in the streets, and sucking the last remnant of
moisture from the straw spread in front of Mrs Foster's house,
when the sound of a low muffled ring was heard in the sick-
room; and Maude, now entirely confined to her bed, raising
herself on one arm, looked eagerly towards the door; which
opened to admit a servant with the welcome announcement
that Agnes had arrived.

After tea Mrs Foster, almost worn out with fatigue, went to
bed; leaving her daughter under the care of their guest. The first
greetings between the cousins had passed sadly enough. Agnes
perceived at a glance that Maude was, as her last letter hinted,
in a most alarming state: while the sick girl, well aware of her
condition, received her friend with an emotion which showed
she felt it might be for the last time. But soon her spirits rallied.

'I shall enjoy our evening together so much, Agnes,' said she,
speaking now quite cheerfully: 'You must tell me all the news.
Have you heard from Mary since your last despatch to me?'

'Mamma received a letter this morning before I set off; and
she sent it hoping to amuse you. Shall I read it aloud?'

'No, let me have it myself.' Her eye travelled rapidly down
the well-filled pages, comprehending at a glance all the tale of
happiness. Mr and Mrs Herbert were at Scarborough; they

would thence proceed to the Lakes; and thence, most probably, homewards, though a prolonged tour was mentioned as just possible. But both plans seemed alike pleasing to Mary; for she was full of her husband, and both were equally connected with him.

Maude smiled as paragraph after paragraph enlarged on the same topic. At last she said: 'Agnes, if you could not be yourself, but must become one of us three: I don't mean as to goodness, of course, but merely as regards circumstances, – would you change with Sister Magdalen, with Mary, or with me?'

'Not with Mary, certainly. Neither should I have courage to change with you; I never should bear pain so well: nor yet with Sister Magdalen, for I want her fervour of devotion. So at present I fear you must even put up with me as I am. Will that do?'

There was a pause. A fresh wind had sprung up and the sun was setting.

At length Maude resumed: 'Do you recollect last Christmas Eve when I was so wretched, what shocking things I said? How I rejoice that my next Communion was not indeed delayed till sickness had stripped me of temptation and sin together.'

'Did I say that? It was very harsh.'

'Not harsh: it was just and right as far as it went, only something more was required. But I never told you what altered me. The truth is, for a time I avoided as much as possible frequenting our parish Church, for fear of remarks. Mamma, knowing how I love S. Andrew's, let me go there very often by myself, because the walk is too long for her. I wanted resolution to do right; yet believe me I was very miserable: how I could say my prayers at that period is a mystery. So matters went on; till one day as I was returning from a shop, I met Mr Paulson. He enquired immediately whether I had been staying in the country? Of course I answered, No. Had I been ill? again, No. Then gradually the whole story came out. I never shall forget the shame of my admissions; each word seemed forced from me, yet at last all was told. I will not repeat all we said then, and on a subsequent occasion when he saw me at Church: the end was that I partook of the Holy Communion on Easter Sunday. That was indeed a Feast. I felt as if I never could do wrong again, and yet –. Well, after my next impatient fit, I wrote this;' here she took a paper from the table: 'Do you care to see it? I will rest a little, for talking is almost too much for me.'

I watched a rosebud very long
　　Brought on by dew and sun and shower,
　　Waiting to see the perfect flower:
Then, when I thought it should be strong,
　　It opened at the matin hour
　　　　And fell at evensong.

I watched a nest from day to day,
　　A green nest, full of pleasant shade,
　　Wherein three little eggs were laid:
But when they should have hatched in May,
　　The two old birds had grown afraid,
　　　　Or tired, and flew away.

Then in my wrath I broke the bough
　　That I had tended with such care,
　　Hoping its scent should fill the air:
I crushed the eggs, not heeding how
　　Their ancient promise had been fair:–
　　　　I would have vengeance now.

But the dead branch spoke from the sod,
　　And the eggs answered me again:
　　Because we failed dost thou complain?
Is thy wrath just? And what if God,
　　Who waiteth for thy fruits in vain,
　　　　Should also take the rod? –[17]

'You can keep it if you like;' continued Maude, when her cousin had finished reading: 'Only don't let any one else know why it was written. And, Agnes, it would only pain Mamma to look over everything if I die; will you examine the verses, and destroy what I evidently never intended to be seen. They might all be thrown away together, only Mamma is so fond of them. –

What will she do?' – and the poor girl hid her face in the pillows.

'But is there no hope, then?'

'Not the slightest, if you mean of recovery; and she does not know it. Don't go away when all's over, but do what you can to comfort her. I have been her misery from my birth till now; there is no time to do better. But you must leave me, please; for I feel completely exhausted. Or stay one moment: I saw Mr Paulson again this morning, and he promised to come tomorrow to administer the Blessed Sacrament to me; so I count on you and Mamma receiving with me, for the last time perhaps: will you?'

'Yes, dear Maude. But you are so young, don't give up hope. And now would you like me to remain here during the night? I can establish myself quite comfortably on your sofa.'

'Thank you, but it could only make me restless. Goodnight, my own dear Agnes.'

'Goodnight, dear Maude. I trust to rise early tomorrow, that I may be with you all the sooner.' So they parted.

That morrow never dawned for Maude Foster.

———

Agnes proceeded to perform the task imposed upon her, with scrupulous anxiety to carry out her friend's wishes. The locked book she never opened: but had it placed in Maude's coffin, with all its records of folly, sin, vanity; and, she humbly trusted, of true penitence also. She next collected the scraps of paper found in her cousin's desk and portfolio, or lying loose upon the table; and proceeded to examine them. Many of these were mere fragments, many half-effaced pencil scrawls, some written on torn backs of letters, and some full of incomprehensible abbreviations. Agnes was astonished at the variety of Maude's compositions. Piece after piece she committed to the flames, fearful lest any should be preserved which were not intended for general perusal: but it cost her a pang to do so; and to see how small a number remained for Mrs Foster. Of three only she took copies for herself. The first was dated ten days after Maude's accident:

> Sleep, let me sleep, for I am sick of care;
> Sleep, let me sleep, for my pain wearies me.
> Shut out the light; thicken the heavy air
> With drowsy incense; let a distant stream
> Of music lull me, languid as a dream,
> Soft as the whisper of a Summer sea.

> Pluck me no rose that groweth on a thorn,
> Nor myrtle white and cold as snow in June,
> Fit for a virgin on her marriage morn:
> But bring me poppies brimmed with sleepy death, '
> And ivy choking what is garlandeth,
> And primroses that open to the moon.

> Listen, the music swells into a song,
> A simple song I loved in days of yore;
> The echoes take it up and up along
> The hills, and the wind blows it back again. –
> Peace, peace, there is a memory in that strain
> Of happy days that shall return no more.

> Oh peace, your music wakeneth old thought,
> But not old hope that made my life so sweet,
> Only the longing that must end in nought.
> Have patience with me, friends, a little while:
> For soon where you shall dance and sing and smile,
> My quickened dust may blossom at your feet.

> Sweet thought that I may yet live and grow green,
> That leaves may yet spring from the withered root,
> And buds and flowers and berries half unseen;
> Then if you haply muse upon the past,
> Say this: Poor child, she hath her wish at last;
> Barren through life, but in death bearing fruit. –[18]

The second, though written on the same paper, was evidently composed at a subsequent period:

Fade, tender lily,
   Fade, O crimson rose,
Fade every flower,
   Sweetest flower that blows.

Go, chilly Autumn,
   Come O Winter cold;
Let the green stalks die away
   Into common mould.

Birth follows hard on death,
   Life on withering.
Hasten, we shall come the sooner
   Back to pleasant Spring. —[19]

The last was a sonnet, dated the morning before her death:

What is it Jesus saith unto the soul? —
'Take up the Cross, and come, and follow Me.'
This word He saith to all; no man may be
   Without the Cross, wishing to win the goal.
Then take it bravely up, setting thy whole

Body to bear; it will not weigh on thee
Beyond thy utmost strength: take it, for He
   Knoweth when thou art weak, and will control
The powers of darkness that thou needs't not fear.
   He will be with thee, helping, strengthening,
   Until it is enough: for lo, the day
Cometh when He shall call thee: thou shalt hear
   His Voice That says: 'Winter is past, and Spring
Is come; arise, My Love, and come away.' —[20]

Agnes cut one long tress from Maude's head; and on her return home laid it in the same paper with the lock of Magdalen's hair. These she treasured greatly: and, gazing on them, would long and pray for the hastening of that eternal morning, which shall reunite in God those who in Him, or for His Sake, have parted here.

Amen for us all.

On Sisterhoods

Dinah Mulock Craik

ON SISTERHOODS

'I slept, and dreamed that life was Beauty;
I woke, and found that life was Duty.'

This couplet was the favourite axiom of a dear old friend of
mine, and the keynote of her noble and sorely-tried life of over
eighty years. As I sit writing, watching the same hills and the
same beautiful river that she watched until she died, it seems a
fitting motto for a few words I have long wished to say, and
which a chance incident has lately revived in my mind.

A young lady, who had been for some time a probationer (or
whatever the term may be) in one of those Anglican Sisterhoods
which their friends so much admire, their foes so sharply
condemn, wrote to me that she was about to make her 'profession' there, and wished me to be present at the 'service'. These
two words were my only clue as to what kind of ceremony it
would be, and what sort of 'profession' the girl was about to
make. A 'girl' she still was to me, for I had held her in my arms
when only a day old; but in truth she was a woman of thirty,
quite capable of judging, deciding and acting for herself. She had
had a hard life, was claimed by no very near ties or duties, and I
felt a satisfaction in thinking she had the courage to choose a
decided vocation; which would be to her at once a refuge and

an occupation, for the Sisterhood bore the name of the Orphanage of Mercy. Whatever her life there might be, it could not be
an idle life. I had a certain sympathy with it, which prompted
me at once to say I would go; and I went.

It was one of those grey, wet, summer days which always strike
one with a melancholy unnaturalness, like a human existence lost
or wasted. As I stood in the soaking rain before a large monastic
building, the door of which was opened by a nunlike portress, I
was conscious of a slight sensation of pain at the difference
between this home and a bright, happy English home. But not all
homes are bright and happy, and not all – nay, very few – wives
and mothers have the placid, contented smile of the Sister who
came to welcome me in the parlour – a regular convent-parlour
or 'parloir', which is what the word originally came from.

She explained that Sister —— (*my* girl) was 'in retreat', and
could see no one till after the service; and then we stood talking
for several minutes about her and about the Orphanage. The
Sister's dress, manner, and indeed the whole atmosphere of the
place, were so essentially monastical, that I involuntarily put the
question, 'Are you a Catholic?'

'Not Roman Catholic,' she answered, after a slight hesitation.
'We belong to the Catholic Church – the Church of England.'

Verily – and I will add happily – our mother Church of
England shelters under her broad wings so many diverse broods!
– would that they could keep from pecking one another![1]

When I found myself in the Chapel, it seemed at first exactly
like one of those chapels that we see in Norman cathedrals. The
high altar was brilliantly lighted, and adorned with white lilies,
the faint sweet smell of which penetrated everywhere and
mingled with that of incense. But there were none of those
paltry or puerile images that abound in Roman Catholic churches; nothing except the large crucifix, the sign of all Christians,
to which no good Christian ought to object. Protestant – in the
sense of Luther and Calvin, and of modern Low Church and
Presbyterianism – the place certainly was not; but no unbiassed
eyewitness could have seen any tokens of Mariolatry or saint-
worship in it, or in the service held there.

Gradually the whole Chapel became filled with Sisters, who I saw were divided into three classes – the black-veiled, the white-veiled, and the novices, or probationers. These latter wore the dress of ordinary young ladies, while the Sisters were undeniably nuns; in their plain black gowns and white or black veils of some soft-falling, close-fitting material – a costume as becoming and comfortable as any woman can wear. It seemed to suit all the faces, young and old, and some were quite elderly and not over beautiful; but every one had that peculiar expression of mingled sweetness and peace, which – let the contemptuous world say what it will – I have found oftener on the faces of nuns – Catholic Petites Sœurs des Pauvres or Protestant Sisters of Charity – than among any other body of women that I know; a fact which I neither attempt to account for nor argue from, but merely state it as such.

After a somewhat long pause of waiting, and reading of the printed service which was given us, there was a slight stir and turning of heads. A distant chanting of female voices (some, I own, a trifle out of tune) announced the procession – very like the processions with which we are familiar in foreign churches, save that there were only two priests and no acolytes. The rest were Sisters; except two young ladies dressed in full bridal costume, who, with a motherly nun behind them, came and knelt before the altar. Neither looked excited nor agitated; and when the service began, there followed a series of solemn questions, asked and answered, just like a marriage ceremony, in which I recognised the voice of *my* girl, perfectly natural, collected, and firm.

The chaplain, or priest – his vestments were very like a Roman Catholic priest's, but every word he uttered might have come from an evangelical pulpit – calling each by her Christian name – I, as her godmother, had given my girl hers, and would have been loth she should change it – asked 'if she were joining this community of her own free will, if she would endow it with her worldly goods, and take the vow of obedience to its rules?' I heard no other vow except that something was said about chastity as 'the spouse of Christ'. To all these was answered

distinctly, 'I will, God being my helper.' Afterwards the dress of
each – gown, veil, and cross – was brought to the altar and
blessed in a few simple words, and the two girls went out,
during the singing of a hymn, to reappear presently in another
procession; with their secular dress for ever laid aside. There
was no cutting off of hair, or prostration under a black pall – as
in Catholic countries; merely the change of dress.

But that was very great. In the young nun who walked up to
the altar, taper in hand, I hardly recognised my girl, so spiritual-
ised was her honest face by the picturesqueness of the close
white veil, and by her expression of entire content – as sweet as
that I have seen on some young brides' features as they went
down the aisle to the church-door.

'Are you content?' I said, as, when service was ended, she
came to me, in a large room, where Sisters, clergy, and friends
were standing about, taking tea or coffee, and chatting in a most
mundane and secular fashion. 'Are you really satisfied?'

'Perfectly,' she answered; and kissed me and her other friends
and kindred, not without emotion, but with no excitement or
exaltation; indeed, she was the last person in the world to be
what the French call *exaltée*, or to give way to romantic impulses
of any kind. 'But you must come to speak to the Mother. I do so
want you to see our Mother. It is she who has done it all.'

By which was meant the Orphanage – established almost
entirely by this lady, as I afterwards learnt. And when I saw the
Mother I was not surprised.

Some people strike you at once with their personality, physical and mental, which carries with it an influence that, you feel,
must affect every one within their reach. I have never seen any
one in whom this individuality was more strong, except perhaps
Cardinal Newman,[2] of whom the Mother vividly reminded me.
Tall, stately, and beautiful – the beauty of middle-age just
becoming old age – of few words, but with a clasp of the hand
and a smile beyond all speaking, I could understand how the
Mother was just the woman to be head of a community like this,
ruling it as much by her influence as her authority.

I had some talk with her, and also with the officiating priest

– chaplain, 'spiritual director', the anti-Ritualists would call him:[3] but, if a wolf in sheep's clothing, he looked the most harmless of vulpine foes, as he stood sipping his coffee and chatting to his cheerful flock, who fluttered around as women always will round a clergyman, even in 'the world'. This, though inside a quasi-nunnery, seemed a very merry world, and all the nuns went about conversing much as people do at afternoon teas and garden-parties, except that there was not one who had that jaded, bored, or cross look so often seen on the faces of the rich and prosperous who have nothing to do.

'And now you must come and see our orphans. We have over two hundred. We take them in from anywhere or anybody; no recommendation needed except that they are orphans, and destitute. We feed, clothe, and educate them until they are old enough to work, and then we find them work, chiefly as domestic servants. Come and look at them.'

Orphanages are at best a sad sight: the poor little souls seem such automatons, brought up by line and rule, just No. 1, No. 2, No. 3 – of no importance to anybody. But this class – a sewing-class, I think it was, chiefly of big girls, who rose with bright faces and showed their work with intelligent pride – was something quite different. More different still was the long procession of 'little ones' which we met as it was going out of the Chapel to supper and bed.

'Children, don't you know me?' said the new-made Sister, stopping the three smallest – such tiny dots! – and calling them by their Christian names. They hesitated a minute, then with a cry of delight sprang right into her arms. She held them there: one over her shoulder, the other two clinging to her gown. Three orphans and a solitary woman, husbandless, childless, laughing and toying together, kissing and kissed, – they made a group so pretty, so happy – so full of God's great mercy, compensation, – that it brought the tears to one's eyes.

I went away after having gone over the whole establishment; went away feeling that there was a great deal to be said – much more than we Protestants till lately had any idea of – on behalf of Sisterhoods.

'I slept, and dreamed that life was Beauty;
I woke, and found that life was Duty.'

Alas! this is the experience of almost every woman who has any womanly qualities in her at all, long before she reaches old age! How to combine the two – how to arrange her life so that duty shall not draw all the beauty out of it, while mere beauty shall always be held subservient to duty – this is the crucial test, the great secret which must be learned during those years – most painful years they often are! – between the first passing away of youth and the quiet acceptance of inevitable old age. Should age come and find the lesson unlearned, it is too late.

Marriage is supposed to be the great end of a woman's being, and so it is. Few will deny that the perfect life is the married life – the happy married life – though I have heard people say that 'any husband is better than none'. Perhaps so; in the sense of his being a sort of domestic Attila, a 'scourge of God' to 'whip the offending Adam' out of a woman and turn her into an angel, as the wives of some bad husbands seem to become. But, in truth, any wife whose husband is not altogether vicious has a better chance of being educated into perfection, through that necessary altruism which it is the mystery of marriage to teach, than a woman sunk in luxurious single-blessedness, who has no work to do, and nobody to do it for, and so seems almost compelled into that fatal selfism which is at the root of half the evils and miseries of existence.

Thus we come back to the great question, becoming more difficult as we advance in – shall we call it civilisation? Those women who do not marry, what are they to do with their lives?

For some of them Fate decides, often severely enough, laying on them the sacred burthen of aged parents, or helpless brothers and sisters, or orphan nephews and nieces. Others, left without natural duties or ties, have the strength to make such for themselves. I know no position more happy, more useful (and therefore happy) than that of a single woman, who, having inherited or earned sufficient money and position, has courage to assume the status and responsibilities of a married woman.

She has, except the husband, all the advantages of the matronly position, and almost none of its drawbacks. So much lies in her power to do unhindered, especially the power of doing good. She can be a friend to the friendless and a mother to the orphan; she can fill her house with happy guests, after the true Christian type – the guests that cannot repay her for her kindness. Being free to dispose of her time and her labour, she can be a good neighbour, a good citizen – whether or not she ever attains the doubtful privilege of female suffrage.[4] Her worldly goods, her time, and her affections are exclusively her own to bestow wisely and well. Solitary, to a certain extent, her life must always be; but it need never be a morbid, selfish, or dreary life. I think it might be all the better for our girls of this generation, which understands the duties and destinies of women a little better than the last one, if we were to hold up to them – since they cannot all be wives and mothers – this ideal of a happy single life, which lies before any girl who either inherits an independence, or has the courage and ability to earn one.

But such cases are, and must always be, exceptional. The great bulk of unmarried women are a very helpless race, either hampered with duties, or seeking feebly for duties that do not come; miserably overworked, or disgracefully idle; piteously dependent on male relations, or else angrily vituperating the opposite sex for their denied rights or perhaps not undeserved wrongs. Between these two lies a medium class, silent and suffering, who have just enough money to save them from the necessity of earning it, just enough brains and heart to make them feel the blankness of their life without strength to obviate it – to strike out a career for themselves, and cheat Fate by making it neither a sad nor useless one. It is for these stray sheep, sure to wander if left alone, but safe enough in a flock with a steady shepherd to guide them, that I open up for consideration the question of Sisterhoods.

Not that I defend the mediæval system of nunneries, where, from a combination of motives, good and bad, religious and worldly, girls were separated from all family ties and dedicated to the service of God. It cannot be too strongly insisted that the family life is the first and most blessed life, and that family duties, in whatever shape they come, ought never to be set aside. Also that the service of God is also best fulfilled through the service of man – the utilising of an aimless existence for the good of others. It is this which constitutes the strength and the charm of a community, for such work can best be done in communities. The mass of women are not clever enough, or brave enough, to carry out anything single-handed. Like sheep, they follow the leader; they will do excellent work if any one will find it for them, but they cannot find it for themselves. How continually do we hear the cry, 'I want something to do'; 'Tell me what to do, and I'll do it!' as she very likely would if shown how.

Of course, a really strong woman would never need this; she would under no circumstances be idle – if she could not find work, she would make it. But for one like this, capable of organising, guiding, ruling, there are hundreds and thousands of women fitted only to obey; to whom the mere act of obedience is a relief, because it saves them from responsibility. To them a corporate institution, headed by such an one as the Mother of that Orphanage of Mercy I visited, is an actual boon. It protects them from themselves – their weak, vacillating, uncertain selves – puts them under line and rule, gives them the shelter of numbers and the strength of a common interest. It is astonishing what good can be done by a combined body, who, as indi-viduals, would have done no good at all.

An institution which would absorb the waifs and strays of – let us coin a word, and say – gentlewomanhood – ladies of limited income and equally limited capacity, yet very good women so far as they go; which could take possession of them, income and all, saving and utilising both it and themselves – would be a real boon to society. For what does not society suffer from these helpless excrescences upon it – women with no ties, no duties, no ambition – who drone away a hopeless, selfish existence, generally ending in confirmed invalidism, or hypo-chondria, or actual insanity! – for diseased self-absorption is the very root of madness. It is a strange thing to say – yet I dare to say it, for I believe it to be true – that entering a Sisterhood, almost any sort of Sisterhood where there was work to do, authority to compel the doing of it, and companionship to sweeten the same, would have saved many a woman from a lunatic asylum.

But it must be the ideal Sisterhood, not that corruption of it as seen in foreign countries which rouses the British ire at the very name of 'nun'. It must be exactly opposite in many things to the Roman Catholic idea of a girl giving up 'the world' and becoming 'the spouse of Christ'. Many a wife and mother belonging to and living in the world, is just as much the spouse of Christ – if that means devoting herself to good works for the love of Him – as any vowed nun.

Besides, the Sisterhood ought not to be composed at all of girls, but of women old enough to choose their own lot, or submit to Fate's choosing it for them; who either cannot or will not marry; who have no near ties, but need the support and sweetness of adopted affections and extraneous duties. It may be very pleasant to escape from the irksomeness of tending a crabbed parent's declining years, or enduring the ill-humours of an invalid brother or sister, in order to dedicate oneself to general philanthropy, to put on a picturesque dress and devote one's days to good deeds and choral services; but this ought not to be allowed. Family ties should always come first, and any Sisterhood which attempts to break them merits severe reprobation.

In the heroic life of Sister Dora one is painfully conscious of this, both in herself and in the fact, if it be a fact, that she was prohibited from going to the deathbed of her own father, and sent off to nurse some other person, by order of her Superior.[5] I was glad to hear my girl say that immediately after her 'profession' she was to go away for a month to be with a young married sister in her hour of trial. And in answer to another question of mine she said, 'Oh yes, even though you do not agree with us, our Mother will let me come and see you whenever you please.'

This, the liberty of visiting friends, ought – subject to fit regulations – to be an essential element in all Sisterhoods. So also should be the right of returning entirely to 'the world', if they so choose. Some sort of vow, or promise, must be made – else the community would dwindle into a mere religious boarding-house. But the vow ought to be, like that of marriage, absolutely binding while it lasts, and intended to last in permanence, yet with the possibility of dissolution did inevitable circumstances require this: a possibility which is practically a certainty, since by our English laws no conventual establishment can detain its inmates for life, or against their own will.

And besides being women of an age to exercise their own discretion, they ought to be allowed full time to do so. Two or three years, at least, my girl had been resident with the Sisterhood before she made her 'professional' – that is, assumed the white veil; and three or four years more, she told me, must pass before she was allowed to take the black one. 'And then?' I said. 'Even then we could break our vows; but,' with a quiet smile, 'I think none of us ever do so,' – Which is common sense also. After seven years' trial of their vocation, and being already past middle age, most women would feel that their lot was finally settled, and have no mind to change it.

Another absolute law of the ideal Sisterhood must be work. In this nineteenth century we cannot go back to the mediæval notions of ecstatic mysticism or corporeal penitences. I am sure that the respectable Sisters of the Orphanage of Mercy neither flagellate themselves, nor wear hair shirts, nor sleep on cold stones, nor rise at one in the morning to chant litanies. So far as I could see, these ladies live a simple, comfortable, wholesome life; such as will best maintain their own health, that they may use it for the good of others.

And truly this ought to be the primary object of Sisterhoods. They should never be merely religious bodies – and yet I doubt if a purely secular Sisterhood would long exist. A hospital nurse once said to me, 'To do our work well, we must do it for the love of God.' The same may be said of all work. But it must be done, also, for the love of man; that 'enthusiasm of humanity' which prompts women to devote themselves to charitable labours, such as teaching the young, or nursing the old and sick. Every religious community ought to have distinct and continuous secular work; and a community of women contains so many difficult elements, that nothing but work and plenty of it, guided by a head which is competent to keep the machine perpetually going, will save it from collapse.

Therefore it should combine, if possible, Beauty with Duty. I was glad to see that this particular Sisterhood had made their own dress, and that of their orphans, as picturesque as possible; that their building within and without was not only convenient but elegant, and their chapel and its service as beautiful as God's house should be. And why not? Lives devoted to duty cannot afford to have any beauty taken out of them. And no one can look round on this lovely outside world without feeling that its Creator meant us to love beauty, to crave after it, and to attain it whenever possible.

The Low Church Bible-woman who goes about in her rusty black, with a bundle of tracts in one hand and a basket in the other, is a most useful and honourable person; but the lady in a nun's dress, or with the white cross of the hospital nurse, carries with her a certain atmosphere of grace which cannot be without its influence even upon the roughest natures. In our ardent pursuit of the Good, we are apt to forget, especially as we grow older, that its power is doubled when it is allied to the Beautiful.

Of course, if every woman were strong enough to live and work alone, to carry out her own individual life and make the best of it, without leaning on any one else, there would be no need for Sisterhoods. But it is not so. Very few women can take care of themselves, to say nothing of other people. Some say this is the fault of Nature, some of education – a centuries-long education into helpless subservience. Whichever theory is right, or perhaps half-right and half-wrong, the result is the same.

For such women, the life in community is eminently desirable. It provides shelter, under the guardianship of a capable head; companionship, for only the strong and self-dependent can endure, permanently, their own company – and perhaps even for them this is not always good; sympathy, something on which to expend their barren and shut-up affections; and lastly, it supplies work, that definite and regular work which is the best solace of sorrow, the best safeguard against temptation, the only efficient help to that ideal condition of a 'sound mind in a sound body' which all women, however feeble their minds and ugly their bodies, should strive for to the very end of life.

These advantages – not small, even though weighed against many disadvantages – were no doubt the reason why, for so many centuries, conventual establishments existed, and still do exist, in Catholic countries. When our Protestant horror of them has a little subsided, we may learn – indeed, in many instances we are already learning – to eliminate the good from the evil, and make use of, without abusing it, Hamlet's not altogether unwise advice to Ophelia, 'Go get thee to a nunnery – go – go – go!'[6]

And some of us, who set sail so gaily for the natural port but never found it, and now drift hither and thither, helmless and hopeless, upon the world's desolate sea, – some of us would, perhaps, be not sorry to go, and none the worse for going into some quiet shelter, where they might take up their daily burthen, and grow stronger in the carrying of it, knowing they did not carry it alone. It is the old fable of the bundle of sticks; in which the feeble stick, the crooked stick, the broken stick can bind itself up with the stronger ones, and by association with others be able to cure its own deficiencies and do good service to the end of its days.

For which purpose I say these few words about Sisterhoods.

A Woman's Thoughts

About Women

'He that good thinketh, good may do,
And God will help him thereunto:
For was never good work wrought
Without beginning of good thought.'

PREFACE

These 'Thoughts,' a portion of which originally appeared in 'Chambers' Journal,' are, I wish distinctly to state, *only* Thoughts. They do not pretend to solve any problems, to lay down any laws, to decide out of one life's experience and within the limits of one volume, any of those great questions which have puzzled generations, and will probably puzzle generations more. They lift the banner of no party; and assert the opinions of no *clique*. They do not even attempt an originality, which, in treating of a subject like the present, would be either dangerous or impossible.

In this book, therefore, many women will find simply the expression of what they have themselves, consciously or unconsciously, oftentimes thought; and the more deeply, perhaps, because it has never come to the surface in words or writing. Those who do the most, often talk – sometimes think – the least: yet thinkers, talkers, and doers, being in earnest, achieve their appointed end. The thinkers put wisdom into the mouth of the speakers, and both strive together to animate and counsel the doers. Thus all work harmoniously together; and verily

> 'Was never good work wrought,
> Without beginning of good thought.'

In the motto which I have chosen for its title-page, lies at once the purpose and preface of this my book. Had it not been planned and completed, honestly, carefully, solemnly, even fearfully, with a keen sense of all it might do, or leave undone; and did not I believe it to be in some degree a good book, likely to effect some good, I would never have written or published it.

How much good it may do, or how little, is not mine either to know, to speculate, or to decide.

I have written it, I hope, as humbly as conscientiously; and thus I leave it.

A WOMAN'S THOUGHTS
ABOUT WOMEN

CHAPTER I

SOMETHING TO DO

I premise that these thoughts do not concern married women, for whom there are always plenty to think, and who have generally quite enough to think of for themselves and those belonging to them. They have cast their lot for good or ill, have realised in greater or less degree the natural destiny of our sex. They must find out its comforts, cares, and responsibilities, and make the best of all. It is the single women, belonging to those supernumerary ranks, which, political economists tell us, are yearly increasing, who most need thinking about.

First, in their early estate, when they have so much in their possession – youth, bloom, and health giving them that temporary influence over the other sex which may result, and is meant to result, in a permanent one. Secondly, when this sovereignty is passing away, the chance of marriage lessening, or wholly ended, or voluntarily set aside, and the individual making up her mind to that which, respect for Grandfather Adam and Grandmother Eve must compel us to admit, is an unnatural condition of being.

Why this undue proportion of single women should almost always result from over-civilisation, and whether, since society's

advance is usually indicated by the advance, morally and intellectually, of its women – this progress, by raising women's ideal
standard of the 'holy estate,' will not necessarily cause a decline
in the very *un*holy estate which it is most frequently made – are
questions too wide to be entered upon here. We have only to
deal with facts – with a certain acknowledged state of things,
perhaps incapable of remedy, but by no means incapable of
amelioration.

But, granted these facts, and leaving to wiser heads the
explanation of them – if indeed there be any – it seems
advisable, or at least allowable, that any woman who has
thought a good deal about the matter, should not fear to express
in word – or deed, which is better, – any conclusions, which out
of her own observation and experience she may have arrived at.
And looking around upon the middle classes, which form the
staple stock of the community, it appears to me that the chief
canker at the root of women's lives is the want of something to
do.[1]

Herein I refer, as this chapter must be understood especially
to refer, not to those whom ill or good fortune – *query*, is it not
often the latter? – has forced to earn their bread; but 'to young
ladies,' who have never been brought up to do anything. Tom,
Dick, and Harry, their brothers, has each had it knocked into
him from school-days that he is to do something, to be somebody. Counting-house, shop, or college, afford him a clear
future on which to concentrate all his energies and aims. He has
got the grand *pabulum*[2] of the human soul – occupation. If any
inherent want in his character, any unlucky combination of
circumstances, nullifies this, what a poor creature the man
becomes! – what a dawdling, moping, sitting-over-the-fire,
thumb-twiddling, lazy, ill-tempered animal! And why? 'Oh,
poor fellow! 'tis because he has got nothing to do!'

Yet this is precisely the condition of women for a third, a
half, often the whole of their existence.

That Providence ordained it so – made men to work, and
women to be idle – is a doctrine that few will be bold enough to
assert openly. Tacitly they do, when they preach up lovely

uselessness, fascinating frivolity, delicious helplessness – all those polite impertinences and poetical degradations to which the foolish, lazy, or selfish of our sex are prone to incline an ear, but which any woman of common-sense must repudiate as insulting not only her womanhood but her Creator.

Equally blasphemous, and perhaps even more harmful, is the outcry about 'the equality of the sexes;' the frantic attempt to force women, many of whom are either ignorant of or unequal for their own duties – into the position and duties of men. A pretty state of matters would ensue! Who that ever listened for two hours to the verbose confused inanities of a ladies' commit-tee, would immediately go and give his vote for a female House of Commons?[3] or who, on the receipt of a lady's letter of business – I speak of the average – would henceforth desire to have our courts of justice stocked with matronly lawyers, and our colleges thronged by

'Sweet girl-graduates with their golden hair?'[4]

As for finance, in its various branches – if you pause to consider the extreme difficulty there always is in balancing Mrs Smith's housekeeping-book, or Miss Smith's quarterly allowance, I think, my dear Paternal Smith, you need not be much afraid lest this loud acclaim for 'women's rights' should ever end in pushing you from your stools, in counting-house, college, or elsewhere.

No; equality of the sexes is not in the nature of things. Man and woman were made for, and not like one another. One only 'right' we have to assert in common with mankind – and that is as much in our own hands as theirs – the right of having something to do.

That both sexes were meant to labour, one 'by the sweat of his brow,' the other 'in sorrow to bring forth' – and bring up – 'children'[5] – cannot, I fancy, be questioned. Nor, when the gradual changes of the civilised world, or some special destiny, chosen or compelled, have prevented that first, highest, and in earlier times almost universal lot, does this accidental fate in any way abrogate the necessity, moral, physical, and mental, for a woman to have occupation in other forms.

But how few parents ever consider this? Tom, Dick, and
Harry, aforesaid, leave school and plunge into life; 'the girls'
likewise finish their education, come home, and stay at home.
That is enough. Nobody thinks it needful to waste a care upon
them. Bless them, pretty dears, how sweet they are! papa's
nosegay of beauty to adorn his drawing-room. He delights to
give them all they can desire – clothes, amusements, society; he
and mamma together take every domestic care off their hands;
they have abundance of time and nothing to occupy it; plenty of
money, and little use for it; pleasure without end, but not one
definite object of interest or employment; flattery and flummery
enough, but no solid food whatever to satisfy mind or heart – if
they happen to possess either – at the very emptiest and most
craving season of both. They have literally nothing whatever to
do, except to fall in love; which they accordingly do, the most
of them, as fast as ever they can.

'Many think they are in love, when in fact they are only idle'[6]
– is one of the truest sayings of that great wise bore, Imlac, in
Rasselas, and it has been proved by many a shipwrecked life, of
girls especially. This 'falling in love' being usually a mere delusion of the fancy, and not the real thing at all, the object is
generally unattainable or unworthy. Papa is displeased, mamma
somewhat shocked and scandalised; it is a 'foolish affair,' and no
matrimonial results ensue. There only ensues – what?

A long, dreary season, of pain, real or imaginary, yet not the
less real because it is imaginary; of anger and mortification, of
important struggle – against unjust parents, the girl believes, or,
if romantically inclined, against cruel destiny. Gradually this
mood wears out; she learns to regard 'love' as folly, and turns
her whole hope and aim to – matrimony! Matrimony in the
abstract; not *the* man, but any man – any person who will snatch
her out of the dulness of her life, and give her something really
to live for, something to fill up the hopeless blank of idleness
into which her days are gradually sinking.

Well, the man may come, or he may not. If the latter
melancholy result occurs, the poor girl passes into her third
stage of young-ladyhood, fritters or mopes away her existence,

sullenly bears it, or dashes herself blindfold against its restrictions; is unhappy, and makes her family unhappy; perhaps herself cruelly conscious of all this, yet unable to find the true root of bitterness in her heart: not knowing exactly what she wants, yet aware of a morbid, perpetual want of something. What is it?

Alas! the boys only have had the benefit of that well-known juvenile apophthegm, that

> 'Satan finds some mischief still
> For idle hands to do:'

it has never crossed the parents' minds that the rhyme could apply to the delicate digital extremities of the daughters.

And so their whole energies are devoted to the massacre of old Time. They prick him to death with crochet and embroidery needles; strum him deaf with piano and harp playing – *not* music; cut him up with morning-visitors, or leave his carcass in ten-minute parcels at every 'friend's' house they can think of. Finally, they dance him defunct at all sort of unnatural hours; and then, rejoicing in the excellent excuse, smother him in sleep for a third of the following day. Thus he dies, a slow, inoffensive, perfectly natural death; and they will never recognise his murder till, on the confines of this world, or from the unknown shores of the next, the question meets them: 'What have you done with Time?' – Time, the only mortal gift bestowed equally on every living soul, and excepting the soul, the only mortal loss which is totally irretrievable.[7]

Yet this great sin, this irredeemable loss, in many women arises from pure ignorance. Men are taught as a matter of business to recognise the value of time, to apportion and employ it: women rarely or never. The most of them have no definite appreciation of the article as a tangible divisible commodity at all. They would laugh at a mantua-maker who cut up a dress-length into trimmings, and then expected to make out of two yards of silk a full skirt. Yet that the same laws of proportion should apply to time and its measurements – that you cannot dawdle away a whole forenoon, and then attempt to cram into the afternoon the entire business of the day – that every minute's unpunctuality constitutes a debt or a theft (lucky, indeed, if you yourself are the only party robbed or made creditor thereof!): these slight facts rarely seem to cross the feminine imagination.

It is not their fault; they have never been 'accustomed to business.' They hear that with men 'time is money;' but it never strikes them that the same commodity, equally theirs, is to them not money, perhaps, but *life* – life in its highest form and noblest uses – life bestowed upon every human being, distinctly and individually, without reference to any other being, and for which every one of us, married or unmarried, woman as well as man, will assuredly be held accountable before God.

My young-lady friends, of from seventeen upwards, your time, and the use of it, is as essential to you as to any father or brother of you all. You are accountable for it just as much as he is. If you waste it, you waste not only your substance, but your very souls – not that which is your own, but your Maker's.

Ay, there the core of the matter lies. From the hour that honest Adam and Eve were put into the garden, not – as I once heard some sensible preacher observe – 'not to be idle in it, but to dress it and to keep it,' the Father of all has never put one man or one woman into this world without giving each something to do there, in it and for it: some visible, tangible work, to be left behind them when they die.

Young ladies, 'tis worth a grave thought – what, if called away at eighteen, twenty, or thirty, the most of you would leave behind you when you die? Much embroidery, doubtless; various pleasant, kindly, illegible letters; a moderate store of good deeds; and a cart-load of good intentions. Nothing else – save your name on a tombstone, or lingering for a few more years in family or friendly memory. 'Poor dear – ! what a nice lively girl she was!' For any benefit accruing through you to your generation, you might as well never have lived at all.

But 'what am I to do with my life?' as once asked me one girl out of the numbers who begin to feel aware that, whether marrying or not, each possesses an individual life, to spend, to use, or to lose. And herein lies the momentous question.

The difference between man's vocation and woman's seems naturally to be this – one is abroad, the other at home: one external, the other internal: one active, the other passive. He has to go and seek out his path; hers usually lies close under her feet. Yet each is as distinct, as honourable, as difficult; and whatever custom may urge to the contrary – if the life is meant to be a worthy or a happy one – each must resolutely and unshrinkingly be trod. But – *how*?

A definite answer to this question is simply impossible. So diverse are characters, tastes, capabilities, and circumstances, that to lay down a distinct line of occupation for any six women of one's own acquaintance, would be the merest absurdity.

'Herein the patient must minister to herself.'[8]

To few is the choice so easy, the field of duty so wide, that she need puzzle very long over what she ought to do. Generally – and this is the best and safest guide – she will find her work lying very near at hand: some desultory tastes to condense into regular studies, some faulty household quietly to remodel, some child to teach, or parent to watch over. All these being needless or unattainable, she may extend her service out of the home into the world, which perhaps never at any time so much needed the help of us women. And hardly one of its charities and duties can be done so thoroughly as by a wise and tender woman's hand.

Here occurs another of those plain rules which are the only guidance possible in the matter – a Bible rule, too – '*Whatsoever thy hand findeth to do, do it with thy might.*'[9] Question it not, philosophise not over it – do it! – only *do it*! Thoroughly and completely, never satisfied with less than perfectness. Be it ever so great or so small, from the founding of a village-school to the making of a collar – do it 'with thy might;' and never lay it aside till it is done.

Each day's account ought to leave this balance – of something done. Something beyond mere pleasure, one's own or another's

– though both are good and sweet in their way. Let the superstructure of life be enjoyment, but let its foundation be in solid work – daily, regular, conscientious work: in its essence and results as distinct as any 'business' of men. What they expend for wealth and ambition, shall not we offer for duty and love – the love of our fellow-creatures, or, far higher, the love of God?

'Labour is worship,' says the proverb: also – nay, necessarily so – labour is happiness. Only let us turn from the dreary, colourless lives of the women, old and young, who have nothing to do, to those of their sisters who are always busy doing something; who, believing and accepting the universal law, that pleasure is the mere accident of our being, and work its natural and most holy necessity, have set themselves steadily to seek out and fulfil theirs.

These are they who are little spoken of in the world at large. I do not include among them those whose labour should spring from an irresistible impulse, and become an absolute vocation, or it is not worth following at all – namely, the professional women, writers, painters, musicians, and the like. I mean those women who lead active, intelligent, industrious lives: lives complete in themselves, and therefore not giving half the trouble to their friends that the idle and foolish virgins do[10] – no, not even in love-affairs. If love comes to them accidentally, (or rather providentially), and happily, so much the better! – they will not make the worse wives for having been busy maidens. But the 'tender passion' is not to them the one grand necessity that it is to aimless lives; they are in no haste to wed: their time is duly filled up; and if never married, still the habitual faculty of usefulness gives them in themselves and with others that obvious value, that fixed standing in society, which will for ever prevent their being drifted away, like most old maids, down the current of the new generation, even as dead May-flies down a stream.

They have made for themselves a place in the world: the harsh, practical, yet not ill-meaning world, where all find their level soon or late, and where a frivolous young maid sunk into a helpless old one, can no more expect to keep her pristine position than a last year's leaf to flutter upon a spring bough.

But an old maid who deserves well of this same world, by her ceaseless work therein, having won her position, keeps it to the end.

Not an ill position either, or unkindly; often higher and more honourable than that of many a mother of ten sons. In households, where 'Auntie' is the universal referee, nurse, play-mate, comforter, and counsellor: in society, where 'that nice Miss So-and-so,' though neither clever, handsome, nor young, is yet such a person as can neither be omitted nor overlooked: in charitable works, where she is 'such a practical body – always knows exactly what to do, and how to do it:' or perhaps, in her own house, solitary indeed, as every single woman's home must be, yet neither dull nor unhappy in itself, and the nucleus of cheerfulness and happiness to many another home besides.

She has not married. Under Heaven, her home, her life, her lot, are all of her own making. Bitter or sweet they may have been – it is not ours to meddle with them, but we can any day see their results. Wide or narrow as her circle of influence appears, she has exercised her power to the uttermost, and for good. Whether great or small her talents, she has not let one of them rust for want of use.[11] Whatever the current of her existence may have been, and in whatever circumstances it has placed her, she has voluntarily wasted no portion of it – not a year, not a month, not a day.

Published or unpublished, this woman's life is a goodly chronicle, the title-page of which you may read in her quiet countenance; her manner, settled, cheerful, and at ease; her unfailing interest in all things and all people. You will rarely find she thinks much about herself; she has never had time for it. And this her life-chronicle, which, out of its very fulness, has taught her that the more one does, the more one finds to do – she will never flourish in your face, or the face of Heaven, as something uncommonly virtuous and extraordinary. She knows that, after all, she has simply done what it was her duty to do.

But – and when her place is vacant on earth, this will be said of her assuredly, both here and Otherwhere – '*She hath done what she could.*'[12]

CHAPTER II

SELF-DEPENDENCE

'If you want a thing done, go yourself; if not, send.'

This pithy axiom, of which most men know the full value, is by no means so well appreciated by women. One of the very last things we learn, often through a course of miserable helplessness, heart-burnings, difficulties, contumelies, and pain, is the lesson, taught to boys from their school-days, of self-dependence.

Its opposite, either plainly or impliedly, has been preached to us all our lives. 'An independent young lady' – 'a woman who can take care of herself' – and such-like phrases, have become tacitly suggestive of hoydenishness, coarseness, strong-mindedness, down to the lowest depth of bloomerism,[13] cigarette-smoking, and talking slang.

And there are many good reasons, ingrained in the very tenderest core of woman's nature, why this should be. We are 'the weaker vessel' – whether acknowledging it or not, most of us feel this: it becomes man's duty and delight to show us honour accordingly. And this honour, dear as it may be to him to give, is still dearer to us to receive.

Dependence is in itself an easy and pleasant thing: dependence upon one we love being perhaps the very sweetest thing in the world. To resign one's self totally and contentedly into the hands of another; to have no longer any need of asserting one's rights or one's personality, knowing that both are as precious to that other as they ever were to ourselves; to cease taking thought about one's self at all, and rest safe, at ease, assured that in great things and small we shall be guided and cherished, guarded and helped – in fact, thoroughly 'taken care of' – how delicious is all this! So delicious, that it seems granted to very few of us, and to fewer still as a permanent condition of being.

Were it our ordinary lot, were every woman living to have either father, brother, or husband, to watch over and protect her, then, indeed, the harsh but salutary doctrine of self-dependence need never be heard of. But it is not so. In spite of the pretty ideals of poets, the easy taken-for-granted truths of old-fashioned educators of female youth, this fact remains patent to any person of common-sense and experience, that in the present day, whether voluntarily or not, one-half of our women are *obliged* to take care of themselves – obliged to look solely to themselves for maintenance, position, occupation, amusement, reputation, life.

Of course I refer to the large class for which these Thoughts are meant – the single women; who, while most needing the exercise of self-dependence, are usually the very last in whom it is inculcated, or even permitted. From babyhood they are given to understand that helplessness is feminine and beautiful; helpfulness, – except in certain received forms of manifestation – unwomanly and ugly. The boys may do a thousand things which are 'not proper for little girls.'

And herein, I think, lies the great mistake at the root of most women's education, that the law of their existence is held to be, not Right, but Propriety; a certain received notion of womanhood, which has descended from certain excellent great-grandmothers, admirably suited for some sorts of their descendants, but totally ignoring the fact that each sex is composed of individuals, differing in character almost as much from one another as from the opposite sex. For do we not continually find womanish men and masculine women? and some of the finest types of character we have known among both sexes, are they not often those who combine the qualities of both? Therefore, there must be somewhere a standard of abstract right, including manhood and womanhood, and yet superior to either. One of the first of its common laws, or common duties, is this of self-dependence.

We women are, no less than men, each of us a distinct existence. In two out of the three great facts of our life[14] we are certainly independent agents, and all our life long we are accountable only, in the highest sense, to our own souls, and the Maker of them. Is it natural, is it right even, that we should be expected – and be ready enough, too, for it is much the easiest way – to hang our consciences, duties, actions, opinions, upon some one else – some individual, or some aggregate of individuals yclept Society? Is this Society to draw up a code of regulations as to what is proper for us to do, and what not? Which latter is supposed to be done for us; if not done, or there happens to be no one to do it, is it to be left undone? Alack, most frequently, whether or not it ought to be, it is!

Every one's experience may furnish dozens of cases of poor women suddenly thrown adrift – widows with families, orphan girls, reduced gentlewomen – clinging helplessly to every male relative or friend they have, year after year, sinking deeper in poverty or debt, eating the bitter bread of charity, or compelled to bow an honest pride to the cruellest humiliations, every one of which might have been spared them by the early practice of self-dependence.

I once heard a lady say – a tenderly-reared and tender-hearted woman – that if her riches made themselves wings, as in these times riches will, she did not know anything in the world that she could turn her hand to, to keep herself from starving. A more pitiable, and, in some sense, humbling confession, could hardly have been made; yet it is that not of hundreds, but of thousands, in England.

Sometimes exceptions arise: here is one:–

Two young women, well educated and refined, were left orphans, their father dying just when his business promised to realise a handsome provision for his family. It was essentially a man's business – in many points of view, decidedly an unpleasant one. Of course friends thought 'the girls' must give it up, go out as governesses, depend on relatives, or live in what genteel poverty the sale of the good-will might allow. But the 'girls' were wiser. They argued: 'If we had been boys, it would

have bene all right; we should have carried on the business, and
provided for our mother and the whole family. Being women,
we'll try it still. It is nothing wrong; it is simply disagreeable. It
needs common-sense, activity, diligence, and self-dependence.
We have all these; and what we have not, we will learn.' So
these sensible and well-educated young women laid aside their
pretty uselessness and pleasant idleness, and set to work. Happily, the trade was one that required no personal publicity; but
they had to keep the books, manage the stock, choose and
superintend fit agents – to do things difficult, not to say
distasteful, to most women, and resign enjoyments that, to
women of their refinement, must have cost daily self-denial. Yet
they did it; they filled their father's place, sustained their
delicate mother in ease and luxury, never once compromising
their womanhood by their work, but rather ennobling the work
by their doing of it.

Another case – different, and yet alike. A young girl, an elder
sister, had to receive for step-mother a woman who ought never
to have been any honest man's wife. Not waiting to be turned
out of her father's house, she did a most daring and 'improper'
thing – she left it, taking with her the brothers and sisters,
whom by this means only she believed she could save from
harm. She settled them in a London lodging, and worked for
them as a daily governess. 'Heaven helps those who help themselves.' From that day this girl never was dependent upon any
human being; while during a long life she has helped and
protected more than I could count – pupils and pupils' children,
friends and their children, besides brothers and sisters-in-law,
nephews and nieces, down to the slenderest tie of blood, or
even mere strangers. And yet she has never been anything but a
poor governess, always independent, always able to assist others
– because she never was and never will be indebted to any one,
except for love while she lives, and for a grave when she dies.
May she long possess the one and want the other!

And herein is answered the '*cui bono?*' of self-dependence,
that its advantages end not with the original possessor. In this
much-suffering world, a woman who can take care of herself

can always take care of other people. She not only ceases to be an unprotected female, a nuisance and a drag upon society, but her working-value therein is doubled and trebled, and society respects her accordingly. Even her kindly male friends, no longer afraid that when the charm to their vanity of 'being of use to a lady' has died out, they shall be saddled with a perpetual claimant for all manner of advice and assistance; the first not always followed, and the second often accepted without gratitude – even they yield an involuntary consideration to a lady who gives them no more trouble than she can avoid, and is always capable of thinking and acting for herself, so far as the natural restrictions and decorums of her sex allow. True, these have their limits, which it would be folly, if not worse, for her to attempt to pass; but a certain fine instinct, which, we flatter ourselves, is native to us women, will generally indicate the division between brave self-reliance and bold assumption.

Perhaps the line is most easily drawn, as in most difficulties, at that point where duty ends and pleasure begins. Thus, we should respect one who, on a mission of mercy or necessity, went through the lowest portions of St Giles' or the Gallowgate;[15] we should be rather disgusted if she did it for mere amusement or bravado. All honour to the poor sempstress or governess who traverses London streets alone, at all hours of day or night, unguarded except by her own modesty; but the strong-minded female who would venture on a solitary expedition to investigate the humours of Cremorne Gardens or Greenwich Fair,[16] though perfectly 'respectable,' would be an exceedingly condemnable sort of personage. There are many things at which, as mere pleasures, a woman has a right to hesitate; there is no single duty, whether or not it lies in the ordinary line of her sex, from which she ought to shrink, if it be plainly set before her.

Those who are the strongest advocates for the passive character of our sex, its claims, proprieties, and restrictions, are, I have often noticed, if the most sensitive, not always the justest or most generous. I have seen ladies, no longer either young or pretty, shocked at the idea of traversing a street's length at night, yet never hesitate at being 'fetched' by some female servant, who was both young and pretty, and to whom the danger of the expedition, or of the late return alone, was by far the greater of the two. I have known anxious mothers, who would not for worlds be guilty of the indecorum of sending their daughters unchaperoned to the theatre or a ball – and very right, too! – yet send out some other woman's young daughter, at eleven P.M., to the stand for a cab, or to the public-house for a supply of beer. It never strikes them that the doctrine for female dependence extends beyond themselves, whom it suits so easily, and to whom it saves so much trouble; that either every woman, be she servant or mistress, sempstress or fine lady, should receive the 'protection' suitable to her degree; or that each ought to be educated into equal self-dependence. Let us, at least, hold the balance of justice even, nor allow an over-consideration for the delicacy of one woman to trench on the rights, conveniences, and honest feelings of another.

We *must* help ourselves. In this curious phase of social history, when marriage is apparently ceasing to become the common lot, and a happy marriage the most uncommon lot of all, we must educate our maidens into what is far better than any blind clamour for ill-defined 'rights' – into what ought always to be the foundation of rights – duties. And there is one, the silent practice of which will secure to them almost every right they can fairly need – the duty of self-dependence. Not after any Amazonian fashion; no mutilating of fair woman-hood in order to assume the unnatural armour of men;[17] but simply by the full exercise of every faculty, physical, moral, and intellectual, with which Heaven has endowed us all, sev-erally and collectively, in different degrees; allowing no one to rust or lie idle, merely because their owner is a woman. And, above all, let us lay the foundation of all real womanliness by teaching our girls from their cradle that the priceless pearl of decorous beauty, chastity of mind as well as body, exists in themselves alone; that a single-hearted and pure-minded woman may go through the world, like Spenser's Una,[18] suffer-ing, indeed, but never defenceless; foot-sore and smirched, but never tainted; exposed, doubtless, to many trials, yet never either degraded or humiliated, unless by her own act she humiliates herself.

For heaven's sake – for the sake of 'womanhede,' the most heavenly thing next angelhood, (as men tell us when they are courting us, and which it depends upon ourselves to make them believe in all their lives) – young girls, trust yourselves; rely on yourselves! Be assured that no outward circumstances will harm you while you keep the jewel of purity in your bosom, and are ever ready with the steadfast, clean right hand, of which, till you use it, you never know the strength, though it be only a woman's hand.

Fear not the world: it is often juster to us than we are to ourselves. If in its harsh jostlings the 'weaker goes to the wall' – as so many allege is sure to happen to a woman – you will almost always find that this is not merely because of her sex, but from some inherent qualities in herself, which, existing either in woman or man, would produce just the same result, pitiful and blameable, but usually more pitiful than blameable. The world is hard enough, for two-thirds of it are struggling for the dear life – 'each for himself, and de'il tak the hindmost;' but it has a rough sense of moral justice after all. And whosoever denies that, spite of all hindrances from individual wickedness, *the right* shall not ultimately prevail, impugns not alone human justice, but the justice of God.

The age of chivalry, with all its benefits and harmfulnesses, is gone by, for us women. We cannot now have men for our knights-errant, expending blood and life for our sake, while we have nothing to do but sit idle on balconies, and drop flowers on half-dead victors at tilt and tourney. Nor, on the other hand, are we dressed-up dolls, pretty playthings, to be fought and scrambled for – petted, caressed, or flung out of the window, as our several lords and masters may please. Life is much more equally divided between us and them. We are neither goddesses nor slaves; they are neither heroes nor semi-demons: we just plod on together, men and women alike, on the same road, where daily experience illustrates Hudibras's keen truth, that

'The value of a thing
Is just as much as it will bring.'[19]

And our value is – exactly what we choose to make it.

Perhaps at no age since Eve's were women rated so exclusively at their own personal worth, apart from poetic flattery or
tyrannical depreciation; at no time in the world's history judged
so entirely by their individual merits, and respected according to
the respect which they earn for themselves. And shall we value
ourselves so meanly as to consider this unjust? Shall we not
rather accept our position, difficult indeed, and requiring from
us more than the world ever required before, but from its very
difficulty rendered the more honourable?

Let us not be afraid of men; for that, I suppose, lies at the root
of all these amiable hesitations. 'Gentlemen don't like such and
such things.' 'Gentlemen fancy so and so unfeminine.' My dear
little foolish cowards, do you think a man – a *good* man, in any
relation of life, ever loves a woman the more for reverencing her
the less? or likes her better for transferring all her burdens to his
shoulders, and pinning her conscience to his sleeve? Or, even
supposing he did like it, is a woman's divinity to be man – or God?

And here, piercing to the Foundation of all truth – I think we
may find the truth concerning self-dependence, which is only
real and only valuable when its root is not in self at all; when its
strength is drawn not from man, but from that Higher and
Diviner Source whence every individual soul proceeds, and to
which alone it is accountable. As soon as any woman, old or
young, once feels *that*, not as a vague sentimental belief, but as
a tangible, practical law of life, all weakness ends, all doubt
departs: she recognises the glory, honour, and beauty of her
existence; she is no longer afraid of its pains; she desires not to
shift one atom of its responsibilities to another. She is content to
take it just as it is, from the hands of the All-Father; her only
care being so to fulfil it, that while the world at large may
recognise and profit by her self-dependence, she herself, knowing that the utmost strength lies in the deepest humility, recognises, solely and above all, her dependence upon God.

CHAPTER III

FEMALE PROFESSIONS

Granted the necessity of something to do, and the self-dependence required for its achievement, we may go on to the very obvious question – *what* is a woman to do?'

A question more easily asked than answered; and the numerous replies to which, now current in book, pamphlet, newspaper, and review, suggesting everything possible and impossible, from compulsory wifehood in Australia to voluntary watchmaking at home, do at present rather confuse the matter than otherwise. No doubt, out of these 'many words,' which 'darken speech,' some plain word or two will one day take shape in action, so as to evolve a practical good.[20] In the meantime, it does no harm to have the muddy pond stirred up a little; any disturbance is better than stagnation.

These Thoughts – however desultory and unsatisfactory, seeing the great need there is for deeds rather than words – are those of a 'working' woman, who has been such all her life, having opportunities of comparing the experience of other working women with her own: she, therefore, at least escapes the folly of talking of what she knows nothing about.

Female professions, as distinct from what may be termed female handicrafts, which merit separate classification and discussion, may, I think, be thus divided: the instruction of youth; painting or art; literature; and the vocation of public entertainment – including actresses, singers, musicians, and the like.

The first of these, being a calling universally wanted, and the easiest in which to win, at all events, daily bread, is the great chasm into which the helpless and penniless of our sex generally plunge; and this indiscriminate Quintus Curtiusism,[21] so far from filling up the gulf, widens it every hour. It must be so, while young women of all classes and all degrees of capability rush into governessing, as many young men enter the church, – because they think it a 'respectable' profession to get on in, and are fit for nothing else. Thus the most important of ours, and the highest of all men's vocations, are both degraded – in so far as they can be degraded – by the unworthiness and incompetency of their professors.

If, in the most solemn sense, not one woman in five thousand is fit to be a mother, we may safely say that not two out of that number are fit to be governesses. Consider all that the office implies: very many of a mother's duties, with the addition of considerable mental attainments, firmness of character, good sense, good temper, good breeding; patience, gentleness, loving-kindness. In short, every quality that goes to make a perfect woman, is required of her who presumes to undertake the education of one single little child.

Does any one pause to reflect what a 'little child' is? Not sentimentally, as a creature to be philosophised upon, painted and poetised; nor selfishly, as a kissable, scoldable, sugar-plum-feedable plaything; but as a human soul and body, to be moulded, instructed, and influenced, in order that it in its turn may mould, instruct, and influence unborn generations. And yet, in face of this awful responsibility, wherein each deed and word of hers may bear fruit, good or ill, to indefinite ages, does nearly every educated gentlewoman thrown upon her own resources, nearly every half-educated 'young person' who wishes by that means to step out of her own sphere into the one above it, enter upon the vocation of a governess.

Whether it really is her vocation, she never stops to think; and yet, perhaps, in no calling is a personal bias more indispensable. For knowledge, and the power of imparting it intelligibly, are two distinct and often opposite qualities; the best student by no means necessarily makes the best teacher: nay, when both faculties are combined, they are sometimes neutralised by some fault of disposition, such as want of temper or of will. And allowing all these, granting every possible intellectual and practical competency, there remains still doubtful the moral influence, which, according to the source from which it springs, may ennoble or corrupt a child for life.

All these are facts so trite and so patent, that one would almost feel it superfluous to state them, did we not see how utterly they are ignored day by day by even sensible people; how parents go on lavishing expense on their house, dress, and entertainments – everything but the education of their children; sending their boys to cheap boarding-schools, and engaging for their daughters governesses at 20*l*. a year, or daily tuition at sixpence an hour; and how, as a natural result, thousands of incapable girls, and ill-informed, unscrupulous women, go on professing to teach everything under the sun, adding lie upon lie, and meanness upon meanness – often through no voluntary wickedness, but sheer helplessness, because they must either do that or starve!

Yet, all the while we expect our rising generation to turn out perfection; instead of which we find it – what?

I do solemnly aver, having seen more than one generation of young girls grow up into womanhood – that the fairest and best specimens of our sex that I have ever known have been among those who have never gone to school, or scarcely ever had a regular governess.

Surely such a fact as this – I put it to general experience, whether it is not a fact? – indicates some great flaw in the carrying out of this large branch of women's work. How is it to be remedied? I believe, like all reformations, it must begin at the root – with the governesses themselves.

Unless a woman has a decided pleasure and facility in teaching, an honest knowledge of everything she professes to impart, a liking for children, and above all, a strong moral sense of her responsibility towards them, for her to attempt to enrol herself in the scholastic order is absolute profanation. Better turn shopwoman, needlewoman, lady's-maid – even become a decent housemaid, and learn how to sweep a floor, than belie her own soul, and peril many other souls, by entering upon what is, or ought to be, a female 'ministry,' unconsecrated for, and incapable of the work.

'But,' say they, 'work we must have. Competition is so great, that if we did not profess to do everything, it would be supposed we could do nothing: and so we should starve.'

Yet, what is competition? A number of people attempting to do what most of them can only half do, and some cannot do at all – thereby 'cutting one another's throats,' as the saying is, so long as their incapacity is concealed; when it is found out, starving. There may be exceptions from exceeding misfortune and the like – but in the long run, I believe it will be found that few women, really competent to what they undertake, be it small or great, starve for want of work to do. So, in this case, no influence is so deeply felt in a house, or so anxiously retained, if only from self-interest, as the influence of a good governess over the children; among the innumerable throng of teachers, there is nothing more difficult to find – or more valuable when found, to judge by the high terms asked and obtained by many professors – than a lady who can teach only a single thing, solidly, conscientiously, and well.

In this, as in most social questions, where to theorise is easy and to practise very difficult, it will often be found that the silent undermining of an evil is safer than the loud outcry against it. If every governess, so far as her power extends, would strive to elevate the character of her profession by elevating its members, many of the unquestionable wrongs and miseries of governess-ship would gradually right themselves. A higher standard of capability would weed out much cumbersome mediocrity; and, competition lessened, the value of labour would rise. I say 'the value of labour,' because, when we women do work, we must learn to rate ourselves at no ideal and picturesque value, but simply as *labourers* – fair and honest competitors in the field of the world; and our wares as mere merchandise, where money's worth alone brings money, or has any right to expect it.

This applies equally to the two next professions, art and literature. I put art first, as being the most difficult – perhaps, in its highest form, almost impossible to women. There are many reasons for this; in the course of education necessary for a painter, in the not unnatural repugnance that is felt to women's drawing from 'the life,' attending anatomical dissections, and so on – all which studies are indispensable to one who would plumb the depths and scale the heights of the most arduous of the liberal arts. Whether any woman will ever do this, remains yet to be proved.[22] Meantime, many lower and yet honourable positions are open to female handlers of the brush.

But in literature we own no such boundaries; there we meet men on level ground – and, shall I say it? – we do often beat them in their own field. We are acute and accurate historians, clear explanators of science, especially successful in imaginative works, and within the last year *Aurora Leigh*[23] has proved that we can write as great a poem as any man among them all. Any publisher's list, any handful of weekly or monthly periodicals, can testify to our power of entering boldly on the literary profession, and pursuing it wholly, self-devotedly, and self-reliantly, thwarted by no hardships, and content with no height short of the highest.

So much for the best of us – women whose work will float down the ages, safe and sure; there is no need to speak of it or them. But there is another secondary class among us, neither 'geniuses' nor ordinary women – aspiring to both destinies, and usually achieving neither: of these it is necessary to say a word.

In any profession, there is nothing, short of being absolutely evil, which is so injurious, so fatal, as mediocrity. To the amateur who writes 'sweetly' or paints 'prettily' her work is mere recreation; and though it may be less improving for the mind to do small things on your own account, than to be satisfied with appreciating the greater doings of other people, still, it is harmless enough, if it stops there. But all who leave domestic criticism to plunge into the open arena of art – I use the word in its widest sense – must abide by art's severest canons. One of these is, that every person who paints a common-place picture, or writes a mediocre book, contributes temporarily – happily, only temporarily – to lower the standard of public taste, fills unworthily some better competitor's place, and without achieving any private good, does a positive wrong to the community at large.

One is often tempted to believe, in the great influx of small talents which now deluges us, that if half the books written, and pictures painted, were made into one great bonfire, it would be their shortest, easiest, and safest way of illuminating the world.[24]

Therefore, let men do as they will – and truly they are often ten times vainer and more ambitious than we! – but I would advise every woman to examine herself and judge herself, morally and intellectually, by the sharpest tests of criticism, before she attempts art or literature, either for abstract fame or as a means of livelihood. Let her take to heart, humbly, the telling truth, that

'Fools rush in where angels fear to tread,'[25]

and be satisfied that the smallest perfect achievement is nobler than the grandest failure. But having, after mature deliberation, chosen her calling, and conscientiously believing it is her calling – that in which she shall do most good, and best carry out the aim of her existence – let her fulfil to the last iota its solemn requirements.

These entail more, much more, than flighty young genius or easily-satisfied mediocrity ever dreams of; labour incessant, courage inexhaustible, sustained under difficulties, misfortunes, and rebuffs of every conceivable kind – added thereto, not unfrequently, the temperament to which these things come hardest. *Le génie c'est la patience;* and though there is a truth beyond it – since all the patience in the world will not serve as a substitute for genius, – still, never was a truer saying than this of old Buffon's.[26] Especially as applied to women, when engaged in a profession which demands from them, no less than from men, the fervent application, and sometimes the total devotion of a lifetime.

For, high as the calling is, it is not always, in the human sense, a happy one; it often results in, if it does not spring from, great sacrifices; and is full of a thousand misconstructions, annoyances, and temptations. Nay, since ambition is a quality far oftener deficient in us than in the other sex, its very successes are less sweet to women than to men. Many a 'celebrated authoress' or 'exquisite paintress' must have felt the heart-truth in *Aurora Leigh:*

> 'I might have been a common woman, now,
> And happier, less known and less left alone,
> Perhaps a better woman after all –
> With chubby children hanging round my neck,
> To keep me low and wise. Ah me! the vines
> That bear such fruit are proud to stoop with it –
> The palm stands upright in a realm of sand.'[27]

And, setting aside both these opposite poles of the female character and lot, it remains yet doubtful whether the maiden-aunt who goes from house to house, perpetually busy and useful – the maiden house-mother, who keeps together an orphan family, having all the cares, and only half the joys of maternity or mistress-ship – even the active, bustling 'old maid,' determined on setting everybody to rights, and having a finger in every pie that needs her, and a few that don't – I question whether each of these women has not a more natural, and therefore, probably, a happier existence, than any 'woman of genius' that ever enlightened the world.

But happiness is not the first nor the only thing on earth. Whosoever has entered upon this vocation in the right spirit, let her keep to it, neither afraid nor ashamed. The days of blue-stockings are over:[28] it is a notable fact, that the best house-keepers, the neatest needlewomen, the most discreet managers of their own and others' affairs, are ladies whose names the world cons over in library lists and exhibition catalogues. I could give them now – except that the world has no possible business with them, except to read their books and look at their pictures. It must imply something deficient in the women themselves, if the rude curiosity of this said well-meaning but often impertinent public is ever allowed to break in upon that dearest right of every woman – the inviolable sanctity of her home.

Without – in these books and by these pictures – let it always be a fair fight, and no quarter. To exact consideration merely on account of her sex, is in any woman the poorest cowardice. She has entered the neutral realm of pure intellect – has donned brain-armour, and must carry on with lawful, consecrated weapons a combat, of which the least reward in her eyes, in which she never can freeze up or burn out either the woman-tears or woman-smiles, will be that public acknowledgment called Fame.

This fame, as gained in art or literature, is certainly of a purer and safer kind than that which falls to the lot of the female *artiste*.

Most people will grant that no great gift is given to be hid under a bushel; that a Sarah Siddons, a Rachel, or a Jenny Lind,[29] being created, was certainly not created for nothing. There seems no reason why a great actress or vocalist should not exercise her talents to the utmost for the world's benefit, and her own; nor that any genius, boiling and bursting up to find expression, should be pent down, cruelly and dangerously, because it refuses to run in the ordinary channel of feminine development. But the last profession of the four which I have enumerated as the only paths at present open to women, is the one which is the most full of perils and difficulties, on account of the personality involved in its exercise.

We may paint scores of pictures, write shelvesful of books – the errant children of our brain may be familiar half over the known world, and yet we ourselves sit as quiet by our chimney-corner, live a life as simple and peaceful as any happy 'common woman' of them all. But with the *artiste* it is very different; she needs to be constantly before the public, not only mentally, but physically: the general eye becomes familiar, not merely with her genius, but her corporeality; and every comment of admiration or blame awarded to her, is necessarily an immediate personal criticism. This of itself is a position contrary to the instinctive something – call it reticence, modesty, shyness, what you will – which is inherent in every one of Eve's daughters. Any young girl, standing before a large party in her first *tableau vivant* – any singing-pupil at a public examination – any boy-lover of some adorable actress, at the moment when he first thinks of that goddess as *his wife*, will understand what I mean.

But that is by no means the chief objection; for the feeling of personal shyness dies out, and in the true *artiste* becomes altogether merged in the love and inspiration of her art – the inexplicable fascination of which turns the many-eyed gazing mass into a mere 'public,' of whose individuality the performer is no more conscious than was the Pythoness of her curled and scented Greek audience, when she felt on her tripod the afflatus of the unconquerable, inevitable god.[30] The saddest phase of *artiste*-life – which is, doubtless, the natural result of this constant appearance before the public eye, this incessant struggle for the public's personal verdict – is its intense involuntary egotism.

No one can have seen anything of theatrical or musical circles without noticing this – the incessant recurrence to '*my* part,' '*my* song,' 'what the public think of *me*.' In the hand-to-hand struggle for the capricious public's favour, this sad selfishness is apparently inevitable. 'Each for himself' seems implanted in masculine nature, for its own preservation; but when it comes to 'each for *herself*' – when you see the fairest Shakspeare heroines turn red or pale at the mention of a rival impersonator – when Miss This cannot be asked to a party for fear of meeting Madame That, or if they do meet, through all their smiling civility you perceive their backs are up, like two strange cats meeting at a parlour-door – I say, this is the most lamentable of all results, not absolutely vicious, which the world, and the necessity of working in it, effect on women.

And for this reason the profession of public entertainment, in all its gradation, from the inspired *tragédienne* to the poor chorus-singer, is, above any profession I know, to be marked with a spiritual Humane Society's pole, '*Dangerous.*' Not after the vulgar notion: we have among us too many chaste, matronly actresses, and charming maiden-vocalists, to enter now into the old question about the 'respectability' of the stage; but on account of the great danger to temperament, character, and mode of thought, to which such a life peculiarly exposes its followers.

But, if a woman has chosen it – I repeat in this as in any other – let her not forego it; for in every occupation the worthiness, like the 'readiness,' 'is all.' Never let her be moulded by her calling, but mould her calling to herself; being, as every woman ought to be, the woman first, the *artiste* afterwards. And, doubtless, so are many; doubtless one could find, not only among the higher ranks of this profession, where genius itself acts as a purifying and refining fire, but in its lower degrees, many who, under the glare of the footlights and the din of popular applause, have kept their freshness and singleness of character unfaded to the end. Ay, even among poor ballet-dancers, capering with set rouged smiles and leaden hearts – coarse screaming concert-singers, doing sham pathos at a guinea a-night – flaunting actresses-of-all-work, firmly believing themselves the best *Juliet* or *Lady Macbeth* extant, and yet condescending to take ever so small a part – even the big-headed '*princess*' of an Easter extrava-ganza, for the sake of the old parents, or the fiddler-husband and the sickly babies at home. No doubt, many of them live – let us rather say, endure – a life as pure, as patient, as self-denying, as that of hundreds of timid, daintily protected girls, and would-be correct matrons, who shrink in safe privacy from the very thought of these. But Heaven counts and cares for all.

Therefore, in this perilous road, double honour be unto those who walk upright, double pity unto those who fall!

Conning over again this desultory chapter, it seems to me it all comes to neither more nor less than this: that since a woman, by choosing a definite profession, must necessarily quit the kindly shelter and safe negativeness of a private life, and assume a substantive position, it is her duty not hastily to decide, and before deciding, in every way to count the cost. But having chosen, let her fulfil her lot. Let there be no hesitations, no regrets, no compromises – they are at once cowardly and vain. She may have missed or foregone much; – I repeat, our natural and happiest life is when we lose ourselves in the exquisite absorption of home, the delicious retirement of dependent love;

but what she has, she has, and nothing can ever take it from her. Nor is it, after all, a small thing for any woman – be she governess, painter, author, or *artiste* – to feel that, higher or lower, according to her degree, she ranks among that crowned band who, whether or not they are the happy ones, are elected to the heaven-given honour of being the Workers of the world.

CHAPTER IV

FEMALE HANDICRAFTS

While planning this chapter I chanced to read, in a late number of the *North British Quarterly*, a paper headed 'Employment of Women,' which expressed many of my ideas in forms so much clearer and better than any into which I can cast them, that I long hesitated whether it were worth-while attempting to set them down here at all; but afterwards, seeing that these Thoughts aim less at originality than usefulness – nay, that since they are but the repetition in one woman's written words of what must already have occurred to the minds of hundreds of other women, – if they were startlingly original, they would probably cease to be useful, – I determined to say my say. It matters little when, or how, or by how many, truth is spoken, if only it be truth.

Taking up the question of female handicrafts, in contradistinction to female professions, the first thing that strikes one is the largeness of the subject, and how very little one practically knows about it. Of necessity, it has not much to say for itself; it lives by its fingers rather than its brains; it cannot put its life into print. Sometimes a poet does this for it, and thrills millions with a *Song of the Shirt*; or a novelist presents us with some imaginary portrait – some *Lettice Arnold, Susan Hopley*, or *Ruth*,[31] idealised more or less, it may be, yet sufficiently true to nature to give us a passing interest in our shop-girls, sempstresses, and maid-servants, abstractedly, as a class. But of the individuals, of their modes of existence, feeling, and thought – of their sorrows and pleasures, accomplishments and defects – we 'ladies' of the middle and upper ranks, especially those who reside in great towns, know essentially nothing.

The whole working class is a silent class; and this division of it being a degree above the cottage visitations of ladies Bountiful, or the legislation of Ten-Hours'-Bill Committees in an enlightened British Parliament, is the most silent of all.[32] Yet it includes so many grades – from the West-end milliner, who dresses in silk every day, and is almost (often quite) a 'lady,' down to the wretched lodging-house 'slavey,' who seems to be less a woman than a mere working animal – that, viewing it, one shrinks back in awe of its vastness. What an enormous influence it must unconsciously exercise on society, this dumb multitude, which, behind counters, in work-rooms, garrets, and bazaars, or in service at fashionable, respectable, or barely decent houses, goes toiling, toiling on, from morning till night – often from night till morning – at anything and everything, just for daily bread and honesty!

Now, Society recognises this fact – gets up early-closing movements, makes eloquent speeches in lawn sleeves or peers' broadcloth at Hanover Square Rooms, or writes a letter to the *Times*, enlarging on the virtue of ordering court-dresses in time, so that one portion of Queen Victoria's female subjects may not be hurried into disease or death, or worse, in order that another portion may shine out brilliant and beautiful at Her Majesty's balls and drawing-rooms. All this is good; but it is only a drop in the bucket – a little oil cast on the top of the stream. The great tide of struggle and suffering flows on just the same; the surface may be slightly troubled, but the undercurrent seems to be in a state which it is impossible to change.

Did I say 'impossible?' No; I do not believe there is anything under heaven to which we have a right to apply that word.

Apparently, one of the chief elements of wrong in the class which I have distinguished as handicraftswomen, is the great and invidious distinction drawn between it and that of professional women. Many may repudiate this in theory; yet, practically, I ask lady-mothers whether they would not rather take for daughter-in-law the poorest governess, the most penniless dependant, than a 'person in business' – milliner, dressmaker, shop-woman, &c.? As for a domestic servant – a cook, or even a lady's-maid – I am afraid a young man's choice of such an one for his wife would ruin him for ever in the eyes of Society.

Society – begging her pardon! – is often a great fool. Why should it be less creditable to make good dresses than bad books? In what is it better to be at night a singing servant to an applauding or capriciously contemptuous public, than to wait on the said public in the day-time from behind the counter of shop or bazaar? I confess, I cannot see the mighty difference; when the question, as must be distinctly understood, concerns not personal merit or endowments, but external calling.

And here comes in the old warfare, which began worthily enough, in the respect due to mind over matter, head-work over hand-work, but has deteriorated by custom into a ridiculous and contemptible tyranny – the battle between professions and trades. I shall not enter into it here. Happily, men are now slowly waking up – women more slowly still – to a perception of the truth, that honour is an intrinsic and not extrinsic possession; that one means of livelihood is not of itself one whit more 'respectable' than another; that credit or discredit can attach in no degree to the work done, but to the manner of doing it, and to the individual who does it.

But, on the other hand, any class that, as a class, lacks honour, has usually, some time or other, fallen short in desert of it. Thus, among handicraftswomen, who bear to professional women the same relation as tradesmen to gentlemen, one often finds great self-assertion and equivalent want of self-respect, painful servility or pitiable impertinence – in short, many of those faults which arise in a transition state of partial education, and accidental semi-refinement. Also, since a certain amount of both refinement and education is necessary to create a standard of moral conscientiousness, this order of women is much more deficient than the one above it in that stern, steady uprightness which constitutes what we call elevation of character. Through the want of pride in their calling, and laxity or slovenliness of principle in pursuing it, they are at war with the class above them; which justly complains of those unconquerable faults and deficiencies that make patience the only virtue it can practise towards its inferiors.

How amend this lamentable state of things? How lessen the infinite wrongs, errors, and sufferings of this mass of woman-hood, out of which are glutted our churchyards, hospitals, prisons, penitentiaries; from which, more than from any other section of society, is taken that pest and anguish of our streets, the

> 'Eighty thousand women in one smile,
> Who only smile at night beneath the gas.'[33]

Many writers of both sexes are now striving to answer this question; and many others, working more by their lives than their pens, are practically trying to solve the problem. All honour and success attend both workers and writers! Each in their vocation will spur on society to bestir itself, and, by the combination of popular feeling, to achieve in some large form a solid social good.

But in these Thoughts I would fain address individuals. I want to speak, not to society at large, for as we well know, 'everybody's business' is often 'nobody's business,' but to each woman separately, appealing to her in her personal character as employer or employed.

And, first, as employer.

I am afraid it is from some natural deficiency in the constitu-tion of our sex that it is so difficult to teach us justice. It certainly was a mistake to make that admirable virtue a female; and even then the allegorist seems to have found it necessary to bandage her eyes. No; kindliness, unselfishness, charity, come to us by nature: but I wish I could see more of my sisters learning and practising what is far more difficult and far less attractive – common justice, especially towards one another.

In dealing with men, there is little fear but that they will take care of themselves. That 'first law of nature,' self-preservation, is – doubtless, for wise purposes – imprinted pretty strongly on the mind of the male sex. It is in transactions between women and women that the difficulty lies. Therein – I put the question to the aggregate conscience of us all – is it not, openly or secretly, our chief aim to get the largest possible amount of labour for the smallest possible price?

We do not mean any harm; we are only acting for the best – for our own benefit, and that of those nearest to us; and yet we are committing an act of injustice, the result of which fills slop-sellers' doors with starving sempstresses, and causes unlimited competition among incompetent milliners and dressmakers, while skilled labour in all these branches is lamentably scarce and extravagantly dear. Of course! so long as one continually hears ladies say: 'Oh, I got such and such a thing almost for half-price – such a bargain!' or: 'Do you know I have found out such a cheap dressmaker!' May I suggest to these the common-sense law of political economy, that neither labour nor material can possibly be got 'cheaply' – that is, below its average acknowledged cost, without *somebody's* being cheated? Consequently, these devotees to cheapness, when not victims – which they frequently are in the long run – are very little better than genteel swindlers.[34]

There is another lesser consideration, and yet not small either. Labour, unfairly remunerated, of necessity deteriorates in quality, and thereby lowers the standard of appreciation. Every time I pay a low price for an ill-fitting gown or an ugly tawdry bonnet – cheapness is usually tawdry – I am wronging not merely myself, but my *employée*, by encouraging careless work and bad taste, and by thus going in direct opposition to a rule from whence springs so much that is eclectic and beautiful in the female character, that 'whatever is worth doing at all is worth doing well.' If, on the contrary, I knowingly pay below its value for really good work, I am, as aforesaid, neither more nor less than a dishonest appropriator of other people's property – a swindler – a *thief*.

Humiliating as the confession may be, it must be owned that, on the whole, men are less prone to this petty vice than we are. You rarely find a gentleman beating down his tailor, cheapening his hosier, or haggling with his groom over a few shillings of wages. Either his wider experience has enlarged his mind, or he has less time for bargaining, or he will not take the trouble. It is among *us*, alas! that you see most instances of 'stinginess' – not the noble economy which can and does lessen its personal wants to the narrowest rational limit, but the mean parsimony which tries to satisfy them below cost-price, and consequently always at somebody else's expense rather than its own. Against this crying sin – none the less a sin because often masked as a virtue, and even corrupted from an original virtue – it becomes our bounden duty, as women, to protest with all our power. More especially, because it is a temptation peculiar to ourselves; engendered by many a cruel domestic narrowness, many a grinding struggle to 'make ends meet,' of which the sharpness always falls to the woman's lot, to a degree that men, in their grand picturesque pride and reckless indifference to expense, can rarely either feel or appreciate.

I do not here advance the argument, usually enforced by experience, that cheapness always comes dearest in the end, and that only a wealthy person can afford to make 'bargains;' because I wish to open the question – and leave it – on the far higher ground of moral justice. The celebrated sentiment of Benjamin Franklin,[35] 'Honesty is the best policy,' appears rather a mean and unchristian mode of inculcating the said virtue.

Another injustice, less patent, but equally harmful, is constantly committed by ladies – namely, the conducting of business relations in an unbusiness-like manner. Carelessness, irregularity, or delay in giving orders; needless absorption of time, which is money; and, above all, want of explicitness and decision, are faults which no one dare complain of in a customer, but yet which result in the most cruel wrong. Perhaps the first quality in an employer is to know her own mind; the second, to be able to state it clearly, so as to avoid the possibility of mistake; and no error caused by a blunder or irresolution on her part should ever be visited upon the person employed.

There is one injustice which I hardly need refer to, so nearly does it approach to actual dishonesty. Any lady who wilfully postpones payment beyond a reasonable time, or in any careless way prefers her convenience to her duty, her pleasure to her sense of right – who for one single day keeps one single person waiting for a debt which at all lies within her power to discharge

– is a creature so far below the level of true womanhood that I would rather not speak of her.

And now, as to the class of the employed. It resolves itself into so many branches that I shall attempt only to generalise, nor refer to distinctive occupations, which are dividing, sub-dividing, and extending from year to year. The world is slowly discovering that women are capable of far more crafts than was supposed, if only they are properly educated for them: that, here and abroad, they are good accountants, shopkeepers, drapers' assistants, telegraph clerks, watch-makers: and doubt-less would be better, if the ordinary training which almost every young man has a chance of getting, and which in any case he is supposed to have, were thought equally indispensable to young women. And well, indeed, if it were so: for there is no possible condition of life where business habits are not of the greatest value to any woman.

I have heard the outcry raised, that this educating of one sex to do the work and press into the place of the other lessens the value of labour, and so depreciates the chances of matrimony, to the manifest injury of both. Charming theory! which pays us the double-edged compliment of being so evidently afraid of our competitive powers, and so complacently satisfied, that the sole purpose and use of our existence is to be married!

But Nature, wiser than such theorists, contradicts them without any argument of ours. She has sufficiently limited our physique to prevent our being very fatal rivals in manual labour; she has given us instincts that will rarely make us prefer masculine occupations to sweeping the hearth and rocking the cradle – when such duties are possible. And if it were not so, would the case be any better? There is a certain amount of work to be done, and somebody must do it: a certain community to be fed, and it must be fed somehow. Would it benefit the male portion thereof to have all the burthen on their own shoulders? Would it raise the value of their labour to depreciate ours? or advantage them to keep us, forcibly, in idleness, ignorance, and incapacity? I trow not. Rather let each sex have a fair chance: let women, and single women above all, be taught to do all they can, and do it as well as they can. Little fear that there will not remain a sufficiently wide field open to competent men, and only men, in every handicraft: little fear that the natural *métier* of most women will not always be the cherished labours of the fireside.

One trade in all its branches, domestic or otherwise, is likely to remain principally our own – the use of the needle.

Who amongst us has not a great reverence for that little dainty tool; such a wonderful brightener and consoler; our weapon of defence against slothfulness, weariness, and sad thoughts; our thrifty helper in poverty, our pleasant friend at all times? From the first 'cobbled-up' doll's frock – the first neat stitching for mother, or hemming of father's pocket-handkerchief – the first bit of sewing shyly done for some one who is to own the hand and all its duties – most of all, the first strange, delicious fairy work, sewed at diligently, in solemn faith and tender love, for the tiny creature as yet unknown and unseen – truly, no one but ourselves can tell what the needle is to us women.

With all due respect for brains, I think women cannot be too early taught to respect likewise their own ten fingers.

It is a grand thing to be a good needlewoman, even in what is called in England 'plain sewing; and in Scotland, a 'white seam;' and any one who ever tried to make a dress knows well enough that skill, patience, and ingenuity, nay, a certain kind of genius, is necessary to achieve any good result. Of all artificers, the poor dressmaker is the last who ought to be grudged good payment. Instead of depreciating, we should rather try to inspire her with a sincere following of her art as an art – even a pleasant pride in it.

'The labour we delight in physics pain;' [36]

and it may be doubted whether any branch of labour can be worthily pursued unless the labourer take an interest in it beyond the mere hire. I know a dressmaker who evidently feels personally aggrieved when you decline to yield to her taste in costume; who never spares pains or patience to adorn her customers to the very best of her skill; and who, by her serious and simple belief in her own business, would half persuade you that the destinies of the whole civilised world hung on the noble but neglected art of mantua-making. One cannot but respect that woman!

Much has been said concerning justice from the employer to the employed, and as much might be said in behalf of the opposite side. For a person to undertake more work than she can finish, to break her promises, tell white lies, be wasteful, unpunctual, is to be scarcely less dishonest to her employer than if she directly robbed her. The want of conscientiousness, which is only too general among the lower order of shopkeepers and people in business, does more to brand upon trade the old stigma which the present generation is wisely endeavouring to efface, and to blacken and broaden the line, now fast vanishing, between tradesfolk and gentlefolk – more, tenfold, than all the narrow-minded pride of the most prejudiced aristocracy.

I should like to see working women – handicraftswomen – take up *their* pride, and wield it with sense and courage; I should like to see them educating themselves, for education is the grand motive power in the advancement of all classes. I do not allude to mere book-learning, but that combination of mental, moral, and manual attainments, the mere desire for and appreciation of which give a higher tone to the whole being. And there are few conditions of life, whether it be passed at the counter or over the needle, in the work-room or at home, where an intelligent young woman has not some opportunity of gaining information; little enough it may be – from a book snatched up at rare intervals, a print-shop window glanced at, as she passes along the street – a silent observation and imitation of whatever seems most pleasant and refined in those of her superiors with whom she may be thrown into contact. However small her progress may be, yet if she have a genuine wish for mental improvement, the true thirst after what is good and beautiful – the good being always the beautiful – for its own sake, there is little fear but that she will gradually attain her end.

There is one class which, from its daily and hourly familiarity with that above it, has perhaps more opportunities than any for this gradual self-cultivation – I mean the class of domestic servants; but these, though belonging to the ranks of women who live by hand-labour, form a body in so many points distinct, that they must form the subject of a separate chapter.

Cannot some one suggest a slight amendment on the usual cry of elevating the working classes – whether it be not possible to arouse in them the desire to elevate themselves? Every growth of nature begins less in the external force applied than the vital principle asserting itself within. It is the undercurrent that helps to break up the ice; the sap, as well as the sunshine, that brings out the green leaves of spring. I doubt if any class can be successfully elevated unless it has indicated the power to raise itself; and the first thing to make it worthy of respect is, to teach it to respect itself.

'In all labour there is profit' – ay, and honour too, if the toilers could but recognise it; if the large talk now current about 'the dignity of labour' could only be reduced to practice; if, to begin at the beginning, we could but each persuade the handful of young persons immediately around us and under our influence, that to make an elegant dress or pretty bonnet – nay, even to cook a good dinner, or take pride in a neatly kept house, is a right creditable, womanly thing in itself, quite distinct from the profit accruing from it. Also, since hope is the mainspring of excellence, as well as happiness, in any calling, let it be impressed on every one that her future advancement lies, spiritually as well as literally, in her own hands.

Seldom, with the commonest chance to start with, will a real good worker fail to find employment; seldomer still, with diligence, industry, civility, and punctuality, will a person of even moderate skill lack customers. Worth of any kind is rare enough in the world for most people to be thankful to get it – and keep it, too. In these days, the chief difficulty seems to consist, not in the acknowledgment of merit, but the finding of any merit that is worth acknowledging – above all, any merit that has the sense and consistency to acknowledge and have faith in itself, and to trust in its own power of upholding itself afloat in the very stormiest billows of the tempestuous world; assured with worthy old Milton, that

> 'If virtue feeble were
> Heaven itself would stoop to her.'[37]

But I am pulled down from this Utopia of female handicrafts by the distant half-smothered laughter of my two maid-servants, going cheerily to their bed through the silent house; and by the recollection that I myself must be up early, as my new sempstress is coming to-morrow. Well, she shall be kindly treated, have plenty of food and drink, light and fire; and though I shall be stern and remorseless as fate respecting the quality of her work, I shall give her plenty of time to do it in. No more will be expected from her than her capabilities seem to allow and her word promised; still, there will be no bating an inch of that: it would be unfair both to herself and me. In fact, the very reason I took her was from her honest look and downright sayings:– 'Ma'am, if you can't wait, or know anybody better, don't employ me; but, ma'am, when I say I'll come, I always do.' – (*P.S.* She didn't!!)

Honest woman! If she turns out fairly, so much the better for us both, in the future, as to gowns and crown-pieces. If she does not, I shall at least enjoy the satisfaction of having done unto her as, in her place, I would like others to do unto me – which simple axiom expresses and includes all I have been writing on this subject.

CHAPTER V

FEMALE SERVANTS[38]

Though female servants come under the category of handicrafts-women, yet they form a distinct class, very important in itself, and essential to the welfare of the community.

A faithful servant – next best blessing, and next rarest, after a faithful friend! – who among us has not had, or wanted, such an one? Some inestimable follower of the family, who has known all the family changes, sorrows, and joys; is always at hand to look after the petty necessities and indescribably small nothings which, in the aggregate, make up the sum of one's daily comfort; whom one can trust in sight and out of sight – call upon for help in season and out of season; rely on in absence, or sickness, or trouble, to 'keep the house going,' and upon whom one can at all times, and under all circumstances, depend for that conscientious fidelity of service which money can never purchase, nor repay.

And this, what domestic servants ought to be, might be, they are – alas, how seldom!

Looking round on the various households we know, I fear we shall find that this relation of master (or mistress) and servant – a relation so necessary, as to have been instituted from the foundation of the world, and since so hallowed by both biblical and secular chronicles, as to be, next to ties of blood and friendship, the most sacred bond that can exist between man and man – is, on the whole, as badly fulfilled as any under the sun.

Whose fault is this? – the superior's, who, in the march of intellect and education around him, losing somewhat the distinction of mere rank, yet tries to enforce it by instituting external distinctions impossible to be maintained between himself and his dependants? – or the inferior's, who, sufficiently advanced to detect the weaknesses of the class above him, though not to cure his own, abjures the blind reverence and obedience of ancient times, without attaining to the higher spirit of this our day – when the law of servitude has been remodelled, elevated, and consecrated by Christianity itself, in the person of its Divine Founder? *'He that is greatest among you, let him be your servant.'*[39]

This recognition of the sanctity of service, through the total and sublime equality on which, in one sense, are thus placed the server and the served, seems the point whereon all minor points ought to turn, and which, in the solemn responsibility it imposes on both parties, ought never to be absent from the mind of either; yet it is usually one of the very last things likely to enter there.

To tell Mrs Jones – who yesterday engaged her cook Betty for fourteen pounds a-year, having beaten her down from fourteen guineas by a compromise about the beer; and who, after various squabbles, finally turned out pretty Susan, the housemaid, into the ghastly Vanity-fair[40] of London, for gossiping on area steps with divers 'followers' – or the honourable Mrs Browne Browne, who keeps Victorine sitting up till daylight just to undo her mistress's gown, and last week threatened, though she did not dare, to dismiss the fine upper-nurse, because, during the brief minute or two after dessert, when Master Baby appeared, mamma, who rarely sees him at any other time, and never meddles with his education, physical or moral, was shocked to hear from his rosy lips a 'naughty word' – to say to these 'ladies' that the 'women' they employ are of the same feminine flesh and blood, would of course meet nominal assent. But to attempt to get them to carry that truth out practically – to own that they and their servants are of like passions and feelings, capable of similar elevation or deterioration of character, and amenable to the same moral laws – in fact, all 'sisters' together, accountable both to themselves and to the other sex for the influence they mutually exercise over one another, would, I fear, be held simply ridiculous. 'Sisters' indeed! Certainly not, under any circumstances – except when Death, the great Leveller, having permanently interposed, we may safely, over a few spadefuls of earth, venture to acknowledge 'our dear sister here departed.'

I have gone up and down the world a good deal, yet I have scarcely found one household, rich or poor, hard or benevolent, Christian or worldly, aristocratic or democratic, which, however correct in outward practice, could be brought to own as a guiding principle this, which is apparently the New-Testament principle with regard to service and servants.

This by no means implies or commands equality; of all shams, there is none so vain as the assertion of that which does not, and cannot exist in this world, and which the highest religious and social legislation never supposes possible.

For instance, my cook prepares and sends up dinner. From long practice, she does it a hundred times better than I could do; nay, even takes a pleasure and pride in it, for which I am truly thankful, and sincerely indebted to her, too: for a good cook is a household blessing, and no small contributor to health, temper, and enjoyment. Accordingly, I treat her with consideration, and even enter her domains with a certain respectful awe. But I do not invite her to eat her own dinner, or mingle in the society which to me is its most piquant sauce. She was not born to it, nor brought up for it. Good old soul! she would gape at the finest bon-mot, and doze over the most intellectual conversation. She is better left in peace by her kitchen-fire.

Also, though it is a real pleasure to me to watch my neat parlour-maid in and out of the drawing-room, to see by her bright intelligent face that she understands much of whatever talk is going on, and may learn something by it too sometimes; still, I should never think of asking her to take a seat among the guests. Poor little lass! she would be as unhappy and out of place here as I should be in the noisy Christmas party below-stairs, of which she is the very centre of attraction, getting more compliments and mistletoe-kisses than I ever got, or wished for, in my whole lifetime. And, by the same rule, though I like to see her prettily dressed, and never scruple to tell her when she sets my teeth on edge by a blue bow on a green-cotton gown, I do not deem it necessary, when she helps me on with my silk one, to condole with her over the said cotton, or to offer her the use of my toilet and my chaperonage at the conversazione to which I am going, where, in the scores I meet, there may be scarcely any face more pleasant, more kindly, or more necessary to me than her own.

Nevertheless, each is in her station. Providence fixed both where they are; and while they there remain, unless either individual is qualified to change, neither has the smallest right to overstep the barrier between them; recognised, perhaps, better tacitly than openly by either, but never by any ridiculous assumption of equality denied or set aside. Yet one meeting-point there is – far below, or above, all external barriers – the common womanhood in which all share. If anything were to happen to my little maid – if I caught her crying over 'father's' letter, or running in, laughing and rosy, after shutting the back gate on somebody, – I am afraid my heart would warm to her just as much as, though I never left my card at Buckingham Palace, it is prone to do to a certain Lady there, who takes early walks, and goes rides with her little children – apparently a better woman, wife, and mother than nine-tenths of her subjects. Is it not here, then, that true equality lies – in this recognition of a common nature; to the divinely-appointed law of which all external practice is to be referred? Would that both mistresses and servants could be brought to recognise this equality – not as a mere sentimental theory, but as a practical fact, the foundation and starting-point of all relations between them!

It concerns maids just as much as mistresses; and to them I wish to speak, in the earnest hope that every household which reads this book will do what is a practice, useful and excellent in itself, with all family books, – send it down of quiet evenings, Sundays and holidays, to be read in the kitchen, when work is done. For, work being done, no mental improvement that is

compatible with the duties of his or her calling ought to be
forbidden any human being.

I should like, first, to impress upon all women-servants how
very much society depends upon them for its well-being, physical and moral. And this, with no fear of thereby increasing their
self-conceit: it is not responsibility, but the want or loss of it,
which degrades character. To feel that you can or might be
something, is often the first step towards becoming it; and it is
safest, on the whole, to treat people as better than they are, if,
perchance, conscience may shame them into being what they
are believed, than to check all hope, paralyse all aspiration, and
irritate them, by the slow pressure of contemptuous incredulity,
into becoming actually as bad as they are supposed to be. Thus,
if the young women to whom has fallen the lot of domestic
service, of making homes comfortable, and especially of taking
care of children, could once be made to feel their own importance as a class – their infinite means of usefulness – I think it
would stimulate them into a far higher feeling of self-respect
and true respectability, and make them of double value to the
community at large.

What do you 'go to service' for? – Wages, of course: the
object being how much money you can earn, and how easy a
place you can get for it. Character is likewise indispensable to
you; so you seek out good families, and keep in them for a
certain length of time. Meanwhile, the most energetic and
sensible among you try to learn as much as lies in your way –
but only as a means of bettering yourselves. 'To better yourself,'
is usually held a satisfactory reason for quitting the most
satisfactory place and the kindest of mistresses.

On the whole, the bond between you and 'missis' is a mere
bargain – a matter of pounds, shillings, and pence; you do just
as much as she exacts, or as you consider your wages justify her
in expecting from you – not a particle more. As to rights,
privileges, and perquisites, it is not unfrequently either a daily
battle or a sort of armed treaty between kitchen and parlour.
The latter takes no interest in the former, except to see that you
do your work and keep your place; while you on your part,

except for gossip or curiosity, are comfortably indifferent to 'the family.' You leave or stay just as it suits them, or yourself, get through a prescribed round of work, are tolerably well-behaved, civil, honest – at least in great matters – and tell no lies, or only as many white ones as will answer your purposes. And so you go on, passing from 'place' to 'place,' resting nowhere, responsible nowhere; sometimes marrying, and dropping into a totally different sphere, but oftener still continuing in the same course from year to year, laying by little enough, either in wages or attachment; yet doing very well, in your own sense of the term, till sickness or old age overtakes you, and then – where are you?

I have read somewhere that in our hospitals and lunatic asylums there is, next to governesses, no class so numerous as that of female domestic servants.

Remember, I am referring not to the lower degrees, but to the respectable among you – those who can always command decent wages and good situations, so long as they are capable of taking them. Of the meaner class, ignorant, stupid, drifted from household to household, from pure incapacity to do or to learn anything, or expelled disgracefully thence for want of (poor wretches! were they ever taught it?) a sense of the common moral necessities of society, which objects to the open breach of at least the sixth, seventh, eighth, and ninth commandments[41] – of these unhappy dregs of your sisterhood, I cannot now venture to speak. I speak of those, born of respectable parents, starting in service with good prospects, able, generally, to read and write, and gifted with sufficient education and intelligence to make them a blessing to themselves and all about them, if their intelligence were not so often degraded into mere 'sharpness,' for want of that quality – rare in all classes, but rarest in yours – moral conscientiousness.

Why is it that, especially in large towns, a 'clever' servant is almost sure to turn out badly? Why do mistresses complain that, while one can get a decent servant, a good-natured servant, a servant who 'does her work pretty well, with plenty of looking after,' a conscientious servant is with difficulty, if at all, to be found?

By conscientious, I mean one who does her duty – that is, the general business of her calling – not merely for wages or a character, or even for the higher motive of 'pleasing missis,' but for the highest of all motives – because it *is* her duty. Because, to cook a dinner, with care and without waste; to keep a house clean and orderly in every corner, seen or not seen; to be scrupulously honest and truthful, in the smallest as in the greatest things; to abstain from pert answers in the parlour, squabbles in the kitchen, and ill-natured tittle-tattle about her fellow-servants or the family – concern not merely her position as a servant, but her conduct and character as a human being, accountable to God as much as the greatest woman that ever was born.

'Oh, that's fine talking!' you may say; 'but what can *I* do? what can be expected of *me* – only a poor servant?'

Only a poor servant! *Only* a person whom a whole household is obliged to trust, more or less, with its comfort, order, property, respectability, peace, health – I was going to add, life; who, in times of sickness or trouble, knows more of its secrets than nearest acquaintance; who is aware of all its domestic weaknesses, faults, and vexations; to whom the 'skeleton' said to be in every house must necessarily be a thing guessed at, if not only too familiar; on whom master, mistress, children, or friend must be daily dependent for numerous small comforts and attentions, scarcely known, perhaps, until they are missed. Only a poor servant! Why, no living creature has more opportunity of doing good or evil, and becoming to others either a blessing or a curse, than a 'poor servant!'

Not if she is a mere bird of passage, flitting from roof to roof, indifferent to everything save what she may pick up to feather her nest with by the way. Not if she starts with the notion that 'missis' and she are to be always at war, or on the alert against mutual encroachments, anxious only which can get the most out of the other. Not if she takes to fawning and flattering, humouring her mistress's weak points, and laughing at her behind her back; betraying the follies or misfortunes of one household into another; carrying on a regular system of double-faced hypocrisy, and fancying she is getting her revenge, and degrading her injurers, when, in fact, she more, much more, degrades herself.

These are the things which make servants despised; not because they are servants, but because the most of them, if they assume any moral standard at all, hold one so far below that of the class above them, that this class learns to regard and treat them as an inferior order of beings.

'What can you expect from a servant?' said to me a lady with whom I often used to argue the matter – a good and noble-minded woman, too, among whose few prejudices was this, fixed and immutable, against the whole race of domestics.

What do I expect from a servant? Why, precisely what I exact from myself – the same honesty of word and act, the same chastity and decency of behaviour, self-government in temper and speech, and propriety of dress and manner according to our respective stations.

Therefore, in any disputed point, I, as being probably the more educated, older, if not wiser of the two, feel bound as much as possible to put myself in her place, to try and under-stand her feelings and character, before I judge her, or legislate for her. I try in all things to set her an example to follow, rather than abuse her for faults and failings which she has sense enough to see I am just as liable to as she. I would rather help her in the right way, than drive her into it, whip in hand, and take another road myself. Reprove, I ought, and will, as often as she requires it; but reproof is one thing, scolding another: she should never see that I find fault merely from bad temper, or for the pleasure (?) of scolding. Authority I must have: it is for her good as well as mine that there should be only one mistress in the house, to whom obedience must be implicitly rendered, and whose domestic regulations will admit of no idleness, carelessness, or irregularity; but I would scorn to use my authority unjustly, or wantonly, or unkindly, simply for the sake of asserting it. If it is worth anything in itself, she will soon learn that it is not to be disputed.

And generally, rule, order, and even fair reproof, are among the last things that servants complain of. Selfishness, stinginess, want of consideration for others, are much oftener the fruitful source of all kinds of domestic rebellion, or the distrust which is worse than any open fight – the sense of gnawing injustice, which destroys all respect and attachment between 'upstairs' and 'down-stairs.'

And yet the servant is often very unjust, too. Cook, who has only to dress the dinner, and neither to work for it nor pay for it, turns up her nose at missis's 'meanness,' *i.e.* displeasure at waste or extravagance – cook, who, if any crash came, has only to look out for another place; while missis has her five children, whose little mouths must be filled, and little bodies must be clothed, and 'master,' whom it breaks her heart to see coming in from the City, haggard, tired, and cross – a crossness he cannot help, poor man! – or sitting down with a pitiful patience, sick and sad, almost wishing, save for her and the children, that he could lay his head on her shoulder and die! What does cook in the kitchen, fat and comfortable, know of all these things – of the agonised struggle for position and character – nay, mere bread – which makes the days and nights of thousands of the professional classes one long battle for life?

Also, the pretty housemaid, who has her regular work and periodical holiday, with her 'young man' coming faithfully on Sundays, about whom, should he turn out false, she rarely makes a fuss, but quickly takes up with another; she being essentially practical, and mental suffering being happily out of her line. Little she guesses of all the conflicts, torments, and endurances which fall to the lot of natures whom a different cultivation, if not a finer organisation, has rendered more alive to another sort of trouble – that anguish of spirit which is worse than any bodily pain. Little she knows, when she comes in singing to dust the parlour, of many a cruel scene transacted there; or of many an hour of mortal agony, bitter as death, yet sharpened by the full consciousness of youth and life, which has been spent in the pretty room, outside which she grumbles so, because 'miss *will* keep her door locked, and it'll be dinner time afore ever a body can get the beds made.'

Servants should make allowance for these things, and many more which they neither know nor understand. They should respect, not out of blind subservience, but mere common sense, the great difference which their narrower education and mode of thought often places between them and 'the family,' in its pleasures, tastes, and necessities, and, above all, in its sufferings. This difference must exist: in the happiest homes, cares and anxieties must be for ever arising, like sea-waves, to be breasted or avoided, or dashed against and broken, as may be; and against these the servant must bear her part as well as the mistress. But it is, and ought to be, something to know how often a word or look of respectful sympathy, a quiet little attention, an unofficious observance of one's comfort in trifles, will, in times of trouble, go direct to the mistress's heart, with a soothing influence of which the servant has not the slightest idea, and which is never afterwards forgotten.

'Better is a friend that is near than a brother afar off;' and better, many a time, is the silent kindness of some domestic, who, from long familiarity, understands one's peculiarities, than the sympathy of many an outside friend, who only rubs against one's angles, sharpened by sickness or pain, and often, unintentionally, hurts more by futile comforting than by total neglect.

A word on one branch of female service, undeniably the most important of all – the care and management of children.

I have always, from fond experience, held that child to be the happiest who never had a nursery-maid – only a mother. But this lot is too felicitous to fall to many, and perhaps, after all, would not be in reality so Utopian as in idea – particularly to the mothers. So let us grant hired nurses to be a natural necessity of civilisation.

Poor things! they certainly need consideration, for they have much to bear. Children are charming – in the abstract; but one sometimes sees the petted cherubs of the drawing-room the little fiends of the nursery, exhibiting, almost before they can speak, passions which would tempt one to believe in original sin, did not education commence with existence. Yet whatever the mysterious law of sin may be that Adam made us liable for, it is possible to bring even infants under the dominion of that law of love – given by the Second Adam[42] – to Whom little children came. And how? By *practising it ourselves.*

Ay; making allowance for the necessary shortcomings of all young things, just entered on the experience of life, from kittens to boys, the former being much the least troublesome of the two. I never once knew or heard of a case of irredeemably 'naughty' children, in regard to whom parents or nurses, or both, were not originally and principally to blame. I never saw a fretful, sullen girl, who had not been made so by selfishness and ill-humour on the part of others, or by tantalising restrictions and compelled submission, hard enough at any age, but especially in childhood. I never knew a revengeful boy, who had not first had the Cain-like spirit put into him by some taunting voice or uplifted hand – *not* a baby-hand; teaching him that what others did he might do, and that the blow he smarted from was exactly the same sort of pain, and dealt in the same spirit, as that he delighted to inflict on nurse or brother, feeling out of his fierce little heart that this was the sole consolation left him for his half-understood but intolerable wrongs.

Does ever any man or woman remember the feeling of being 'whipped' – as a child – the fierce anger, the insupportable ignominy, the longing for revenge, which blotted out all thought of contrition for the fault in rebellion against the punishment? With this recollection on their own parts, I can hardly suppose any parents venturing to inflict it – certainly not allowing its infliction by another, under any circumstances whatever. A nurse-maid or domestic of any sort, once discovered to have lifted up her hand against a child, ought to meet instant severe rebuke, and, on a repetition of the offence, instant dismissal.

A firm will the nurse must have – which the child will obey, knowing it must be obeyed; but it should be with her no less than with the parents, a loving will always. I will not suppose any young woman so mean and cowardly as to wreak her whims and tempers, or those of her mistress, on the helpless little sinner, who, however annoying, is after all such a very small sinner. I cannot believe she will find it so very hard to love the said sinner, who clings about her helplessly night and day, in the total dependence that of itself produces love. And surely, remembering her own childhood and its events – such nothings now, of such vast moment then, its unjust punishments, unremedied wrongs, and harshly-exacted sacrifices – things which in their results may have affected her temper for years, and even yet are unforgotten – she will strive as much as possible to put herself in her nursling's place, to look at the world from his point of view, and never, as people often do, to expect from him a degree of perfection which one rarely finds even in a grown person; above all, never to expect from him anything that she does not practise herself.

It will be seen that I hold this law of kindness as the Alpha and Omega of education. I once asked one – in his own house a father in everything but the name, his authority unquestioned, his least word held in reverence, his smallest wish obeyed – 'How did you ever manage to bring up these children?' He said: 'By *love*.'

That is the question. It is because people have so little love in them, so little purity and truth, self-control and self-denial, that they make such frightful errors in the bringing up of children. When I go from home to home of the middle classes, and see the sort of rule or misrule there, the countless evil influences, physical and spiritual, against which children have to struggle, I declare I often wonder that in the rising generation there should be any good men and women. And when I glance down the *Times* column of 'Want Places,' and speculate how few of these 'nurses,' upper and under 'girls,' and 'nursery-maids,' have the smallest knowledge of their responsibility, or care about fulfilling it, my wonder is, that the new generation should grow up to manhood and womanhood at all.

This responsibility – if the nurse ever reflects on it – how awful it is! To think that whatever the man may become, learned and great, worldly or wicked, he is at present only the child, courting her smile and coming to her for kisses, or hiding from her frown and sobbing on her neck, 'I will be good, I will be good!' That, be she old or young, clever or ignorant, ugly or

pretty, she has, next to the mother – sometimes before the
mother, though that is a sad thing to see – this all-powerful
influence over him, stronger than any he will afterwards allow
or own. That it rests with herself how she uses it, whether
wisely and tenderly, for the guidance and softening of his
nature, or harshly and capriciously, after a fashion which may
harden and brutalise him, and make him virtually disbelieve in
love and goodness for the remainder of his existence.

Truly, in this hard world, which they must only too soon be
thrust into, it is more essential even for boys than girls that, in
the dawn of life, while women solely have the management of
them, they should be accustomed to this law of love – love
paramount and never ceasing, clearly discernible in the midst of
restraint, reproof, and even punishment – love that tries to be
always as just as it is tender, and never exercises one of its rights
for its own pleasure and good, but for the child's. To the nurse,
unto whom it does not come by instinct, as it does to parents,
the practice of it may be difficult – very difficult – but God
forbid it should be impossible.

And what a reward there is in this, beyond any form of
service – to a woman! Respect and gratitude of parents; consideration from all in the house; affection, fresh, full, and free,
and sweet as only a child's love can be. Trying as the nurse-
maid's life is, countless as are her vexations and pains, how
many a childless wife or solitary old maid has envied her, playing
at romps for kisses, deafened with ever-sounding rills of delicious laughter all day, and lying down at night with a soft sleepy
thing breathing at her side, or wakened of a morning with two
little arms tight round her neck, smotheringly expressing a
wealth of love that kingdoms could not buy.

And when she grows an old woman, if, as often happens to
domestic servants, she does not marry, but remains in service all
her life, it must be her own fault if nurse's position is not an
exceedingly happy and honoured one. Not perhaps, in our
modern times, after the fashion of her order in novels and plays
– from *Juliet's* nurse downwards – but still abounding in comfort
and respect. Most likely, she still lives in the family – anyhow, it

will be strange if her grown-up 'children' do not now and then come and see her, to gossip over those old times, which grow the more precious the further we leave them behind. In time these children's children – with their other parent, who knew not nurse, and whom nurse still views with rather suspicious curiosity – come and chatter to her, eager to hear all about 'pa' or 'ma;' how 'ma' looked when she was a little baby; whether 'pa' was a good boy or a naughty boy, some thirty odd years ago. And – a remarkable moral fact! – the chances are that 'pa' will gravely confess to the latter; while old nurse, seeing all things through the softening glass of time, will protest that neither he nor any of the children ever gave her the least trouble since they were born!

I have said a good deal, and yet it seems as if I had almost left the subject where I found it, it is so wide. Let me end it in words which, coming into my mind now, transcend all mine, and yet, I trust, have been made the foundation of them; in which case I need not fear. Words open alike to master and servant – studied by how few, yet in which lies the only law of life for all:–

'Servants, obey in all things your masters according to the flesh; not with eye-service, as men-pleasers; but in singleness of heart, fearing God: and whatsoever ye do, do it heartily, as to the Lord, and not unto men; knowing that of the Lord ye shall receive the REWARD.'[43]

CHAPTER VI

THE MISTRESS OF A FAMILY

The *house-mother*! what a beautiful, comprehensive word it is! how suggestive of all that is wise and kindly, comfortable and good! Surely, whether the lot comes to her naturally, in the happy gradations of wifehood and motherhood – or as the maiden-mistress of an adopted family, – or, as one could find many instances in this our modern England, when the possession of a large fortune, received or earned, gives her, with all the cares and duties, many of the advantages of matronhood – every such woman must acknowledge that it is a solemn as well as a happy thing to be the mistress of a family.

Easy, pleasant, and beautiful as it is to obey, development of character is not complete when the person is fitted only to obey. There comes a time in most women's lives when they have to learn how to govern – first, themselves, then those about them. I say, to learn; because it has to be learned. Love of arbitrary power may come by instinct; as in the very youngest children you may see one fierce little spirit to which all the rest, whether older or younger, succumb: but to domineer and to rule are two distinct arts, proceeding often from totally opposite characters.

The most of women are, in their youth at least, by both habit and temperament, as I once heard it expressed by a very acute thinker – decidedly 'adjective.' Few of them have ever had the chance of becoming a 'noun substantive' – (whether or not that be a natural or enviable position). They have been accustomed all their lives hitherto to be governed, if not guarded; protected or unprotected, as may be; but rarely placed in circumstances where they had actively to assume the guardianship or rule of others. This then, if it falls to their lot, they have to acquire, difficultly, painfully: often with no preparation, or with what is worse than none, a complete ignorance that there is anything to be acquired! They expect all is to come quite naturally – the due arrangement and superintendence of a house – the regulation of an income – the guidance and control of servants.

And yet, every family is a little kingdom in itself: the members and followers of which are often as hard to manage as any of the turbulent governments whose discords convulse our world. 'Woe to thee, O land, when thy king is a child!' And woe to thee, O household, when thy mistress is – worse than a child – a foolish, ignorant, and incapable woman.

With families, as with kingdoms, one of the principal evidences of misgovernment is at the working root of the little community – the servants. Why is it that in one half of the families one knows, the grand burden of complaint is – servants? Is the fault altogether on one side? – which side, either party being left to decide: or is it a natural consequence of their relative positions, as ruler and ruled? a state of things equally hateful and inevitable, for which nobody is to blame?

Let us see – taking at random the most prominent specimens of mistresses of families, which present themselves to every one's notice who is at all familiar with middle-class society. These, I must distinctly state, are in every case generalisations of a class, and of no personal application; which, indeed, would mar the whole moral of these imaginary portraits, by giving results and unfairly omitting causes.

For instance, there is Mrs Smith. You will never once enter that lady's house without hearing of a change in its domestic arrangements; you will hardly knock at the door four successive weeks, without its being opened by a strange damsel. To count the number of servants Mrs Smith has had since her marriage, would puzzle her eldest boy, even though he is just going into his multiplication-table. Out of some scores, surely all could not have been so bad; yet, to hear her, no imps of Satan in female form could be worse than those with which her house has been haunted – cooks who sold the dripping, and gave the roast-meat to the policeman; housemaids who could only scrub and scour, and wait at table and clean plate, and keep tidy to answer the door, and who actually had never learned to sew neatly, or to get up fine linen! Nurses wickedly pretty, or thinking themselves so, who had the atrocious impudence to buy a bonnet 'just like my last new one,' with flowers inside! Poor Mrs Smith! Her whole soul is engrossed in the servant-question. Her whole life is a domestic battle – of the mean, scratch-and-snap, spit-and-snarl kind. She has a handsome house; she gives good wages – that is, her liberal husband does – but not a servant will stay with her.

And why? Because she is not fitted to be a mistress. She cannot rule – she can only order about; she cannot reprove – she can only scold. Possessing no real dignity, she is always trying to assert its semblance; having little or no education, she is the hardest of all judges upon ignorance. Though so tenacious of her prerogative, that she dismissed Sally Baines for imitating missis's bonnet – (Heaven forgive you, Mrs Smith! but do you know where you might find that poor pretty sixteen-year old child *now?*) – still, the more intelligent of her servants soon find out that she is 'not a lady;' that, in fact, if one were to strip off her satin gowns, and sell her carriage, and make her inhabit the basement-story instead of the drawing-room of her handsome house, Mrs Smith would be not one whit superior to her own cook. Her quick-witted parlour-maid is really her superior, and fully aware of it too, as you may see from the way in which she contrives to wind missis round her little finger, get her own way entirely, and rule the house-arrangements from attic to cellar. This being not unprofitable, she will probably outstay many of the other servants – not because she is any better than the rest, but merely cleverer.

Miss Brown's household is on quite a different plan. You will never hear the small domestic 'rows' – the petty squabbles between mistress and maid, injustice on one side and impertinence on the other. Miss Brown would never dream of quarrelling with 'a servant,' any more than with her dog or cat, or some other inferior animal. She strictly fulfils her duty as mistress;

gives regular wages, – very moderate, certainly, for her income is much below both her birth and her breeding; exacts no extra service; and is rigidly particular in allowing her servants the due holidays – namely, to church every other Sunday, and a day out once a-month. Her housekeeping is economical without being stingy; everything is expected to go on like clock-work; if otherwise, immediate dismissal follows, for Miss Brown dislikes to have to find fault, even in her own lofty and distant way. She is a conscientious, honourable lady, who exacts no more than she performs; and her servants respect her. But they stand in awe of her; they do not love her. There is a wide gulf between their humanity and hers – you never would believe that they and she shared the same flesh and blood of womanhood, and would end in the same dust and ashes. She is well served, well obeyed, and justly; but – and that is justice, too – she is neither sympathised with nor confided in. Perhaps this truth may have struck home to her sometimes; as when her maid, who had been ill unnoticed for months, in waiting on her one morning dropped down, and – died that night; or when, the day there came news of the battle of Inkermann,[44] she sat hour after hour with the *Times* in her lap, in her gloomy, lonely dining-room, and not a soul came nigh her to ask or learn from her speechless looks 'what of young Captain Brown?'

In the Jones's highly respectable family are most respectable servants, clever, quick, attentive, and fully conscious of their own value and capabilities. They dress quite as finely as 'the family,' go out with parasols on Sundays, and have their letters directed 'Miss.' They guard with jealousy all their perquisites and privileges – from the tradesmen's Christmas-boxes, and the talk outside the nearly-closed front-door with unlimited 'followers,' to the dearly-prized right of a pert answer to missis when she ventures to complain. And missis – a kind, easy soul – is rather afraid of so doing; and endures many an annoyance, together with a few real wrongs, rather than sweep her house with the besom of righteous destruction, and annihilate in their sprouting evils that will soon grow up like rampant weeds. This is no slight regret to Mrs Jones's friends, who see that a little judicious authority, steadily and unvaryingly asserted – a little quiet exercise of will, instead of fidgety or nervous fault-finding and needless suspiciousness, would make matters all straight, and reduce this excellent and liberal establishment, from the butler down to the little kitchen-maid, to the safe level of a limited monarchy. Instead of which there is a loose sway, which often borders upon that most dangerous of all governments – domestic republicanism.

This last is the government at Mrs Robinson's. She has long let the reins go – leaned back, and slumbered. Where her household will drive to, Heaven only knows! The house altogether takes care of itself. The mistress is too gentle to blame anybody for anything – too lazy to do anything herself, or show anybody else how to do it. I suppose she has eyes, yet you might write your name in dust-tracks on every bit of furniture in her house. She doubtless likes to wear a clean face and a decent gown, for she has tastes not unrefined; yet in Betty, her maid-of-all-work, both these advantages are apparently impossible luxuries. Mrs Robinson can't, or believes she can't, afford what is called a 'good' servant – that is, an efficient, responsible woman, who requires equivalent wages for valuable services; therefore she does with poor Betty, a very well-meaning girl, though quite incompetent for the duties she undertakes, and never likely to be instructed therein. For it never seems to strike Betty, or her mistress either, that though poverty may be inevitable, dirt and tatters are not – that a girl, if ever so ignorant, can generally be taught – a house, if ever so small and ill-furnished, can at least be clean – a dinner, if ever so plain, nay, scanty, may be well cooked and well arranged; and however the servants fall short, every mistress has always her own intelligent brain, and has, at the worst, her own pair of active hands. Did you ever consider that last possibility, my good Mrs Robinson? Would Betty honour you less if, every morning, she saw you dust a chair or two, or hunt out lurking ambushes of spiders – shaming her into knowledge and industry by the conviction, that what she left undone her mistress would certainly do? Would you be less amiable in your husband's eyes by the discovery, that it was you yourself who cooked, and then taught Betty to cook, his comfortable dinner? Would he have less pleasure in petting your dainty fingers for seeing on them a few needle-marks, caused by the sewing of tidy chair-covers, or the mending of clean threadbare carpets, so as to make the best of his plain, quiet home, where Heaven has at once denied the blessing and spared the responsibility of children? But you may be as ignorant as Betty herself. I am afraid you are. Let me give you a golden rule – 'Never expect a servant to do that which you cannot do, or, if necessary, will learn to do, yourself.'

Mrs Johnson, now, will be a very good illustration of this. I doubt if she is any richer than Mrs Robinson; for a few years after her marriage, I know it was very uphill-work indeed with the young couple; especially for the wife, who, married at nineteen, was as ignorant as any school-girl. She and her cook are reported to have studied Mrs Glass together.[45] To this day, I fancy the praise of any special dinner would be modestly received as conjointly due to 'missis and me.' So, doubtless would any grand effect in household arrangements, though, where all goes on so smoothly and orderly, that the most sudden visitor would only necessitate an extra knife and fork, and a clean pair of sheets in the spare room, there is not much opportunity for any *coup d'état* in the housemaid-line. As for the nursery-staff – but since her boys could walk alone, Mrs Johnson has abolished the nursery altogether. If she has no more children, these two lads will have the infinite blessing of never being 'managed' by any womenkind save their mother. Of course it is a busy, and often hard life for her; and her hand-maidens know it. They see her employed from morning to night, happy and merry enough, but always employed. They themselves would be ashamed to be lazy; they would do any-thing in the world to lighten things for missis. If little delicate Fred is ailing, Jane will sit up half the night with him, and still get up at five next morning. Mary, the cook, does not grumble at any accidental waiting, if missis, in her sewing, has the slightest need of Jane. Both would work their fingers to the bone any day to save her the least trouble or pain. Not a cloud comes across her path – not a day of illness – her own or her little ones' – shadows her bright looks, but is felt as an absolute grief in the kitchen. Jane's face, as she opens the front door, is a sufficient indication to all friends as how things are with 'the family;' and if you, being very intimate, make any chance inquiry of Mary in the street, ten to one she will tell you everything Mrs Johnson has done, and exactly how she has looked, for a week past, ending with a grave, respectful remark, ventured in right of her own ten years of eldership, that she 'is afraid missis is wearing herself out, and would you please to come and see her?'

And missis, on her side, returns the kindly interest. She likes to hear anything and everything that her damsels may have to tell, from the buying of a new gown to the birth of a new nephew. Any relatives of theirs who may appear in the kitchen, she generally goes to speak to, and welcomes always kindly. She is glad to encourage family affection, believing it to be quite as necessary and as beautiful in a poor housemaid as in a sentimental lady. Love, also. She has not the smallest objection to let that young baker come in to tea on Sundays, entering honestly at the front-door, without need of sneaking behind the area-railings. And if, on such Sundays, Jane is rather absent and awkward, with a tendency to forget the spoons, and put hot plates where cold should be, her mistress pardons all, and tempers master's indignation by reminding him of a certain summer, not ten years back when –, &c. Upon which he kisses his little wife, and grows mild.

Thus the family have no dread of 'followers,' no visions of burglarious sweethearts introduced by the kitchen-window, or tribes of locust 'cousins' creating a famine in the larder. Having always won confidence, Mrs Johnson has little fear of being deceived. When pretty Jane can make up her mind, doubtless there will occur that most creditable event to both parties – the maid being married from her mistress's house. Of course, Jane would be a great loss, or Mary either; but Mary is growing middle-aged, and is often seen secretly petting Master Fred, as only old maid-servants do pet the children of 'the family.' Freddy says, she has promised never to leave him; and her mistress, who probably knows as much of Mary's affairs as anybody, does not think it likely she ever will.

The Johnson household is the best example I know of the proper relation between kitchen and parlour. True, Jane and Mary are estimable women – might have been such in any 'place;' but I will do human nature the justice to believe, that the class of domestic servants contains many possible Janes and Marys, if only their good qualities could be elicited by a few more Mrs Johnsons.

It is an obvious law, that any movement for social advancement must necessarily commence in the higher class, and gradually influence the lower. By higher and lower, I mean simply as regards moral and intellectual cultivation, which, continued through generations and become a habit of life, makes, and is the only thing that does or ought to make, the difference between master and servant, patrician and plebeian. Mrs Thomson, descended from the clan Robertson, a very superior family, has a great deal more chance of being a lady than Peg Thompson her nursery-maid, whose father, grandfather, &c., have been farm-labourers. But if, by any of her not rare freaks, Dame Nature should have placed in Peg's uncouth body the soul of a gentlewoman, together with that rare quality of rising, which, in spite of circumstances, enables many refined minds to reach their natural level – if so, Mrs Thomson should not have the slightest objection to assist that desirable end in every possible way. Nay, finally, it might be rather a pleasure to her some day to sit at table with Miss Margaret Thompson; and she should altogether scorn the behaviour of that fine gentleman who once 'cut' honest Dodsley the publisher-footman – of whom the meek old fellow only observed: 'Yes, he knows me; I used to wait behind his chair.'

But since the laws of nature and of circumstance have made some to be mistresses and others servants – giving to the one incalculably more chances of superiority than the other, would it not be as well if more ladies would try to prove this superiority instead of resting content in the mere assertion thereof? The proverb asserts, 'A good mistress will make a good servant.'

Whether this is possible or not, all will agree that the best servant in the world cannot make a good mistress.

The reformatory process must necessarily commence with the superior.

Also the root of all improvement must be the mistress's own conviction, religious and sincere, of the truth, more than once already urged here, but which cannot be too often referred to, that she and her servants share one common womanhood: alike in its mental and physical weaknesses; in its capabilities of advancement and deterioration; in its tempers, passions, and prejudices: with aims, hopes, or interests distinctly defined, and pursued with equal eagerness; with a life here, meant as a school for the next life; with an immortal soul.

A lady who can once be made to feel that, so far as any human soul can be made responsible for another, she is responsible for that of every domestic who enters her house, has gained one step from which she is not likely ever to backslide. And if accountable for the soul – the better part, – so also for the body. Since, with advanced knowledge, we are all now beginning to recognise – some with the stolid assent of materialism, and some with the Christian's holy wonder at this human machine, made too wonderfully to be made for nothing, and by no one, – how mysteriously soul and body act and react upon one another; how one half of the shortcomings of the spirit springs from mere bodily causes; and how a healthy soul can stimulate even the poorest and most unsound dwelling-house of flesh and blood into something of its own beauty and divineness.

And yet there is a saying that one sometimes hears, and sees silently in action perpetually – 'Anything will do for the servants.' Kitchen and parlour are placed on quite a different footing; not only with regard to coarser food – reasonable enough sometimes, when the parlour has nice or sickly tastes, and the kitchen is blessed with the wholesome omnivorous appetite of hard work and an easy mind – but in the regular routine of daily life. 'Late to bed and early to rise,' yet still expected to be 'both healthy and wise;' compelled to sleep in damp, heat, uncleanliness, or ill-ventilation – anything is good enough for a 'servant's bedroom'; allowed no time for personal attention, sewing, or mending, yet required to be always 'tidy;' kept at work constantly, without regard to how much and what sort of work each person's strength can bear; yet supposed to be capable of working on for ever, without that occasional inter-mixture of 'play,' – not idleness, but wholesome amusement – without which every human being grows dull, dispirited, falls into ill-humour, and, finally into ill-health. Truly it often makes one's heart ache to think of the sort of life even well-meaning mistresses make their servants lead; and it would be curious, were it not so melancholy, to pause and consider, if in all one's acquaintance there are half-a-dozen ladies under whom, did fate compel, one would choose to 'go into service.'

My dear madam – who may be opening your eyes widely at this heterodox view of the question – you have no right to keep a servant at all unless you can keep her comfortable. You did not buy her, body and soul, like a negro slave; you only took her on hired service, to fulfil certain duties, which you must exact from her kindly and firmly, for her good as well as yours: but you have no right to any more. Except so far as nature and education have instituted a difference between you, you are not justified in placing either her enjoyments or necessities on a lower level than your own. The same sanitary laws, of physical and mental well-being, apply to you both; and neither can break them, or be allowed to break them, with impunity.

Moral laws, also. Mrs Smith thinks it is against her that poor Sally Baines sinned in the matter of the bonnet. Foolish Mrs Smith! Suppose you were to purchase at Swan and Edgar's that hundred-guinea Cachemire labelled 'the Queen's choice' – whom would you harm, her Majesty or yourself? So, when your Emma or Betsy buys a silk gown and a twelve-shilling parasol, she errs, and grievously, too: but it is against herself. She lowers her own self-respect by striving to maintain a false position; wastes in shabby showiness the money that she ought to lay up for sickness, old age, or marriage, and the happy duty of helping others; loses the simple neatness befitting the respectable maid-servant, and becomes ridiculous as the sham fine-lady.

But in this complaint, only too general, of servants 'dressing above their place,' the mistress's own example is the best warning and reproof: a thing, my poor Mrs Smith, which it would be vain to look for from you. Equally vain in another matter, which applies as stringently to that wretched Sally Baines – whom, if she now came drunk and flaunting to your area-gate, you would hustle away in charge of X 25[46] – as to your own little daughter, whom you hope one day to see Mrs Somebody, and will take all available maternal means to that desirable end.

You do not think it, but the kitchen is made of flesh and blood as well as the parlour. However you may insist upon 'No followers allowed,' Emma will meet her sweetheart round the corner, and cook will startle your nerves after five years' service with 'Please suit yourself marm, as I'm a-going to be married.' Happy for you if no worse occurs than this. For you are exacting an injustice – an impossibility: you are instituting a state of things which, from its very unnaturalness, gives a premium to deceit and immorality. Love – nay, I beg your pardon; you don't understand what that word means – but *courting*, which looks so pretty in the drawing-room, you treat as a crime in the kitchen; and therefore it is very likely to become such. An honest lover – as much Emma's right as your own when you took up with Mr Smith – you degrade into a 'follower,' who has to sneak about areas, hide in coal-cellars, and be gossiped with behind doors. Consequently, there can be no inquiry into his character, no open acknowledgment of an honourable attachment, which neither mistress nor maid need ever be ashamed of; everything goes on underhand, and if discovered at all, is generally in such a miserable form as to make prudent Mrs Smiths firmer than ever in their impossible edict, never obeyed. Whilst other women, accustomed to regard love and marriage according to the standard of the better classes, are shocked at the low tone of thought on such subjects, which inevitably results in that low tone of morals almost universally prevalent among the ranks from which female servants are recruited.

It is worth while trying whether – since dark deeds and ill

feelings can only be conquered by being brought to the light – mistresses should not make the experiment of saying, as every mother ought to say to her daughters – (alas, how few do! and what a train of horrible evils often results from that want of confidence between mother and child!) – 'Be honest with me. I don't expect from you more than human nature is capable of. I expect you to fall in love and be married: all I desire is that you should love worthily, and marry wisely. Only be honest. No falsehoods, no concealments of any kind. Let everything be plain, open, and above-board; tell the truth, and don't be afraid.'

Perhaps, then we should have less of these frightful cases of shame and sorrow, or those hasty marriages, of which one so often hears – when a decent, respectable girl, after a few months' wedlock, comes back to her old mistress, ragged and destitute, with a husband in jail for bigamy, or against whom she has to swear the peace, for that brutal ill-usage which makes us English disgraced abroad as 'the nation that beats its wives.'

In households as in states there must be one ruling head – and there ought to be but one. Every person knows what sort of system that is, which I have called domestic republicanism. Whether or not it is best for kingdoms, in families the only safe form of government is autocracy.

And the autocrat should decidedly be the lady, the mistress. The master, be he father, husband, or brother, has quite enough to do without-doors. He is the bread-winner; the woman, the bread-keeper, server, and expender. Nature as well as custom has – save in very exceptional cases – instituted this habit of life, and any alteration of it, making mamma attend the law-courts and Exchange, or drive about on a series of medical visits, while papa stays at home to cook the dinner and nurse the babies, would assuredly be very bad, if not for himself, for the dinner and the babies.

No. We of the 'softer' sex, though not by any means really so soft as we are complimented and coaxed into appearing, have no call, and, mostly, no desire to force ourselves into the province of men. We feel that we are not fitted for it. Female doctors – though all honour be to those heroic, self-sacrificing women, who are capable of undertaking such a profession – female missionaries, travellers, and life-long devotees to science, art, or philanthropy, are and always will be rare and peculiar cases, not to be judged by ordinary rules. The average number of us are content to leave to men their own proper place: but none the less resolutely ought we to keep our own – one of the first 'rights' of which is, the supreme rule in all domestic concerns.

A man has no business to meddle in the management of the house. No business, except through hard necessity, or the saddest incompetency on the part of others, to poke over the weekly bills, and insist on knowing what candles are per pound, whether the washing is done at home or abroad, and what he is going to have every day for dinner. He who voluntarily and habitually interferes in these things must be a rather small-minded gentleman, uncommonly inconvenient to his family and servants. Perhaps to more than they: since a man who is always 'muddling about' at home is rarely a great acquisition to the world outside.

I once heard a married lady say, with great glee and satisfaction: 'Oh, Mr —— saves me all trouble in housekeeping; he orders dinner, and goes to the butcher's to choose it, too: pays all the bills, and keeps the weekly accounts: he never wants me to do anything.' Thought I privately, 'My dear, if I were you I should be very much ashamed both of myself and Mr —— .'

When a house boasts both master and mistress, each should leave to the other the appointed work, and both qualify themselves rightly to fulfil the same, abstaining as much as possible from mutual interference. A man who can trust his wife or his housekeeper should no more meddle with her home concerns than she should pester him with questions about his business. No doubt, countless occasions will arise when he will be thankful and glad to take counsel with her in worldly cares; while she may have to remember all her life long, and never think of without a gush of gratitude and love, some season of sickness or affliction, when he filled his own place and hers too, ashamed of no womanish task, and neither irritated nor humiliated by ever such mean household cares.

A lady of my acquaintance gives it as her *sine qua non*[47] of domestic felicity, that the 'men of the family' should always be absent at least six hours in the day. And truly a mistress of a family, however strong her affection for the male members of it, cannot but acknowledge that this is a great boon. A house where 'papa' or 'the boys' are always 'pottering about,' popping in and out at all hours, everlastingly wanting something, or finding fault with something else, is a considerable trial to even feminine patience. And I beg to ask my sex generally – in confidence, of course – if it is not the greatest comfort possible when, the masculine half of the family being cleared out for the day, the house settles down into regular work and orderly quietness until evening?

Also, it is good for them, as well as for us, to have all the inevitable petty domestic 'bothers' got over in their absence; to effect which ought to be one of the principal aims of the mistress of a family. Let them, if possible, return to a quiet smiling home, with all its small annoyances brushed away like the dust and cinders from the grate – which, *en passant*, is one of the first requisites to make a fireside look comfortable. It might be as well, too, if the master himself could contrive to leave the worldly mud of the day at the scraper outside his door; however, as these chapters do not presume to lecture the lords of creation, I have nothing more to say on that score.

But she who, the minute an unfortunate man comes home, fastens upon him with a long tale of domestic grievances, real or imagined – how the butcher will never bring the meat in time, and the baker keeps a false account of loaves – how she is sure cook is given to drink, and that Mary's 'cousin' had his dinner off 'our' mutton yesterday; – why, such a lady deserves all she gets: cold looks, sharp speeches, hasty plunges into the convenient newspaper; perhaps an angry cigar – a walk, with no invitation for her company – or the club. Poor little woman! sitting crying over her lonely fire, not owning that she is wrong, but only that she is very unhappy, and very much ill-used, might one recommend to her notice one golden rule? – 'Never pester a man with things that he cannot remedy and does not

understand.' Also, for her own benefit as well as his, a harmless
rhyme, true enough of minor vexations, whatever it may be of
the greater griefs it so philosophically disposes of:–

'For every evil under the sun
There is a remedy – or there's none:
If there is one, try and find it;
If there isn't, never mind it.'

And when he comes in again, honest man! perhaps a little
repentant, too, there is but one course of conduct which I
recommend to all sensible women, viz. to put her arms round
his neck, and – hold her tongue.

But the house-mother has her troubles; ay, be she ever so
gifted with that blessed quality of taking them lightly and
cheerfully; weighing them at their just value and no more; never
tormenting herself and everybody else by that peculiarity of
selfish and narrow minds, which makes the breaking of a plate
as terrible a calamity as the crash of an empire. No one can hold
the reins of family government for ever so brief a time, without
feeling what a difficult position it is: how great its daily need of
self-control, as the very first means of controlling others; of
incessant individual activity, and a personal carrying out of all
regulations instituted for the ordering of the establishment,
which, unless faithfully observed by the mistress – the eye and
heart of the house – are no more than a dead letter to the rest
of the establishment.

No doubt this entails considerable self-sacrifice. It is not
pleasant for lazy ladies to get breakfast over at that regular early
hour, which alone sets a household fairly a-going for the day:
nor for unarithmetical ladies, who have always reckoned their
accounts by sixpences, to put down each item, and persevere in
balancing periodically receipts and expenditure: nor for weakly,
nervous, self-engrossed ladies, to rouse themselves sufficiently
to put their house in order, and keep it so; not by occasional
spasmodic 'setting to rights,' but by a general methodical over-
looking of all that is going on therein. Yet, unless all this is done,
it is in vain to insist on early rising, or grumble about waste, or

lecture upon neatness, cleanliness, and order. The servants get
to learn that 'missis is never in time;' and laugh at her com-
plaints of their unpunctuality. They see no use in good management, or avoidance of waste; – 'Missis never knows about
anything.' She may lecture till she is weary about neatness and
cleanliness; – 'Just put your head into her room and see!' For all
moral qualities, good temper, truth, kindliness, and, above all,
conscientiousness, if these are deficient in the mistress, it is idle
to expect them from servants, or children, or any members of
the family circle.

Yet this fact, so trite that readers may smile at its being urged
at all, is the last to be generally acted upon. Mistresses blame all
persons about them, and Providence above them; – for does it
not often virtually mean that? every thing and every body except
themselves. They will not see, that until a woman has done all
that is in her power to do, striving with antagonistic circumstances, great and small, and chiefly with her own self, her
errors of character, and weaknesses of temperament – until then
she has no right to begin blaming anybody. It is vain to attempt
showing them, what is plain enough to any unbiassed student of
life in the abstract – and this ought to strike solemnly upon the
mind of every woman who feels that where much is given much
is required – that, however fatally the conduct of the master
may affect the external fortunes of a family, there are very few
families whose internal mismanagement and domestic unhappiness are not mainly the fault of the mistress.

The *house-mother*! where could she find a nobler title, a more
sacred charge? All these souls, given into her hand to be cared
for, both in great things and small – if anything can be called
small on which rests the comfort of a family; and that to a
degree which can never be too much appreciated. For instance,
good temper is with many people dependent upon good health;
good health upon good digestion; good digestion upon wholesome, well-prepared food, eaten in peace and pleasantness. Ill-
cooked, untidy meals, are as great a cause of bad temper as
many a moral wrong; and a person of sensitive physique may be
nursed into settled hypochondria by living in close rooms,

where the sweet fresh air and sunshine are determinedly shut out, and the foul air as determinedly shut in. While those nervous, irritable temperaments, which, either from the slow deterioration of our race, or our modern error of cultivating the mind at the expense of the body, are getting so common now-a-days, are often driven almost into madness by the non-observance of those ordinary sanitary rules, ignorance or neglect of which, bad enough in anybody, is in the mistress of a family scarcely less than a crime.

Yet most of these short-comings in women, on whom this responsibility has fallen, are by no means intentional. A girl marries early, thinking only how pleasant it is to have a house of one's own, and never once how difficult it is to manage it: perhaps she makes a pride, and her young husband a joke, of her charming ignorance in common things – à la *David* and *Dora Copperfield*[48] – pretty enough while it lasts. But only picture these poor little silly *Doras* living, instead of, happily, dying! Drifting on to middle age – helpless, burdensome wives – lazy, feeble, many-childed mothers; meaning well enough, but incapable of acting upon their good intentions; either sinking into a hopeless indifference, which is not content, or wearing themselves out with weak complainings, which never result in any amendment. Poor dear women! we may pity and pardon, acknowledging their many gentle and estimable qualities; but all the passive sweetness in the world will not make up for active goodness; and there is many a 'most amiable woman,' who, whatever she might have been in an inferior position, when unhappily she is mistress of a family, by her over-kindness, lazy laxity, and general *laissez-faire*, does as much harm as the greatest shrew who ever embittered the peace of a household.

Power, of whatsoever kind and degree, so that it is just and lawful, is a glorious thing to have, a noble thing to use. But what shall be said for the woman who has had it and thrown it away, or retained it only to misuse it? Woe betide both her and all connected with her! for she has ceased to injure herself alone. Every life that was given her in charge for health of body and mind, peace, comfort, and enjoyment, will assuredly one day rise up in judgment against her. We can imagine such an one, suddenly waking up to the consciousness of all she has done and left undone – what those belonging to her are, and what she might, under God, have made them – crying out in her agony, 'Would that I had never been born!'

At present, the happiest thing for her – if there can be any happiness in a self-deception – is, that she really is unaware of her own position – that most humiliating position of a woman who is not mistress in her own family; whose servants disobey or despise her, whose children rule her, whose husband snubs her or neglects her, whose friends and neighbours criticise, compassionate, or laugh at her. Who, though anything but a bad woman, will slip through existence without dignity, effecting little or no real good: at best only patiently borne with and kindly treated while she lives, and her place filled up, some few regretting awhile, but none really missing her, as soon as ever she dies.

What a contrast to that portrait – standing out as true a photograph of nature in this our modern day, as it did in those ancient days, under the glowing sun of the East, 'the words of King Lemuel,' that '*his mother* taught him.'

'Who can find a virtuous woman? for her price is far above rubies.
The heart of her husband doth safely trust in her, so that she shall have no need of spoil.
She will do him good and not evil all the days of her life.
   *   *   *   *   *
She girdeth her loins with strength, and strengtheneth her arms.
She layeth her hands to the spindle, and her hands hold the distaff.
She stretcheth out her hand to the poor; yea, she reacheth forth her hands to the needy.
   *   *   *   *   *
Her husband is known in the gates, when he sitteth among the elders of the land.
   *   *   *   *   *
Strength and honour are her clothing; and she shall rejoice in time to come.
She openeth her mouth with wisdom; and in her tongue is the law of kindness.

She looketh well to the ways of her household, and eateth not the bread of idleness.

Her children arise up, and call her blessed; her husband also, and he praiseth her.

Many daughters have done virtuously, but thou excellest them all.

Favour is deceitful, and beauty is vain; but a woman that feareth the Lord, she shall be praised.

Give her of the fruit of her hands; and let her own works praise her in the gates.'[49]

CHAPTER VII

FEMALE FRIENDSHIPS

'And what is Friendship but a name,
A charm that lulls to sleep,
A shade that follows wealth and fame,
And leaves the wretch to weep?'

This remark, expressed too tersely and intelligibly to be considered 'poetry' now-a-days, must apply to the nobler sex. Few
observant persons will allege against ours, that even in its lowest
form our friendship is deceitful. Fickle it may be, weak, exaggerated, sentimental – the mere lath-and-plaster imitation of a
palace great enough for a demigod to dwell in – but it is rarely
false, parasitical, or diplomatic. The countless secondary motives
which many men are mean enough to have – nay, to own – are
all but impossible to us; impossible from the very faults of our
nature – our frivolity, irrationality, and incapacity to seize on
more than one idea at the same time. In truth, a sad proportion
of us are too empty-headed to be double-minded, too shallow to
be insincere. Nay, even the worst of us being more direct and
simple of character than men are, our lightest friendship – the
merest passing liking that we decorate with that name – is,
while it lasts, more true than the generality of the so-called
'friendships' of mankind.

But – and this 'but' will, I am aware, raise a whole nest of
hornets – from our very peculiarities of temperament, women's
friendships are rarely or never so firm, so just, or so enduring, as
those of men – *when* you can find them. Damon and Pythias,
Orestes and Pylades, Brutus and Cassius – last and loveliest,

David and Jonathan,[50] are pictures unmatched by any from our sex, down even to the far-famed ladies of Llangollen.[51] When such a bond really does exist, from its exception to general masculine idiosyncrasies – especially the enormous absorption in and devotion to Number One – from its total absence of sentimentality, its undemonstrativeness, depth, and power, a friendship between two men is a higher thing than between any two women – nay, one of the highest and noblest sights in the whole world. Precisely as, were comparisons not as foolish as they are odious, a truly good man, from the larger capacities of male nature both for virtue and vice, is, in one sense, more good than any good woman. But this question I leave to controversialists, who enjoy breaking their own heads, or one another's, over a bone of contention which is usually not worth picking after all.

Yet, though dissenting from much of the romance talked about female friendships, believing that two-thirds of them spring from mere idleness, or from that *besoin d'aimer* which, for want of natural domestic ties, makes this one a temporary substitute, Heaven forbid I should so malign my sex as to say they are incapable of an emotion which, in its right form and place, constitutes the strength, help, and sweetness of many, many lives; and the more so because it is one of the first sweetnesses we know.

Probably there are few women who have not had some first friendship, as delicious and almost as passionate as first love. It may not last – it seldom does; but at the time it is one of the purest, most self-forgetful and self-denying attachments that the human heart can experience: with many, the nearest approximation to that feeling called love – I mean love in its highest form, apart from all selfishnesses and sensuousnesses – which in all their after-life they will ever know. This girlish friendship, however fleeting in its character, and romantic, even silly, in its manifestations, let us take heed how we make light of, lest we be mocking at things more sacred than we are aware.

And yet, it is not the real thing – not *friendship*, but rather a kind of foreshadowing of love; as jealous, as exacting, as

unreasoning – as wildly happy and supremely miserable; ridicu-
lously so to a looker-on, but to the parties concerned, as vivid
and sincere as any after-passion into which the girl may fall; for
the time being, perhaps long after, colouring all her world. Yet
it is but a dream, to melt away like a dream when love appears;
or if it then wishes to keep up its vitality at all, it must change
its character, temper its exactions, resign its rights: in short, be
buried and come to life again in a totally different form.
Afterwards, should Laura and Matilda, with a house to mind
and a husband to fuss over, find themselves actually kissing the
babies instead of one another – and managing to exist for a year
without meeting, or a month without letter-writing, yet feel life
no blank, and affection a reality still – then their attachment has
taken its true shape as friendship, shown itself capable of
friendship's distinguishing feature – namely, tenderness without
appropriation; and the women, young or old, will love one
another faithfully to the end of their lives.

Perhaps this, which is the test of the sentiment, explains why
we thus seldom attain to it, in its highest phase, because nature
has made us in all our feelings so intensely personal. We have
instincts, passions, domestic affections, but friendship is, strictly
speaking, none of the three. It is – to borrow the phrase so
misused by that arch *im*-moralist, that high-priest of intellectual
self-worship, Goethe[52] – an elective affinity, based upon the
spiritual consanguinity, which, though frequently co-existent
with, is different from any tie of instinct or blood-relationship.
Therefore, neither the sanctities nor weaknesses of these rightly
appertain to it; its duties, immunities, benefits and pains, belong
to a distinct sphere, of which the vital atmosphere is perfect
liberty. A bond, not of nature but of choice, it should exist and
be maintained calm, free, and clear, having neither rights nor
jealousies; at once the firmest and most independent of all
human ties.

'Enough,' said Rasselas to Imlac; 'you convince me that no
man can ever be a poet.'[53] And truly, reviewing friendship in its
purest essence, one is prone to think that, in this imperfect
world of ours, no man – certainly no woman – ever can be a

friend. And yet we all own some dozens; from Mrs Granville Jones, who invites 'a few friends' – say two hundred – to pass with her a 'social evening' – to the poor costermonger, who shouts after the little pugilistic sweep the familiar tragico-comic saying: 'Hit him hard; he's got no friends!' And who that is not an utter misanthrope would refuse to those of his or her acquaintance that persist in claiming it, the kindly title, and the pleasant social charities which belong thereto?

'Love is sweet,
Given or returned;'

and so is friendship; when, be it ever so infinitesimal in quantity, its quality is unadulterated; springing, as, I repeat, women's friendship almost always does spring, out of that one-idea'd impulsiveness, often wrong-headed, but rarely evil-hearted, which makes us at once so charming and so troublesome, and which, I fear, never will be got out of us till we cease to be women, and become what men sometimes call us – and they well know they give us but too much need to be – angels.

Yes, with all our folly, we are not false: not even when Lavinia Smith adores with all her innocent soul the condescending Celestina Jones, though meeting twenty years after as fat Mrs Brown and vulgar Mrs Green, they may with difficulty remember one another's Christian names: not when Bessy Thompson, blessed with three particularly nice brothers, owns likewise three times three 'dearest' friends, who honestly persuade themselves and her that they come only to see dear Bessy; nevertheless, the fondness is real enough to outlast many bothers caused by said brothers, or even a cantankerous sister-in-law to end with. Nay, when Miss Hopkins, that middle-aged and strong-minded 'young lady' of blighted affections, and Mrs Jenkins, that woman of sublime aspirations, who has unluckily 'mated with a clown,' coalesce against the opposite sex, fall into one another's arms and vow eternal friendship – for a year; after which, for five more, they make all their acquaintances uncomfortable by their eternal enmity – even in this lamentable phase of the sentiment, it is more respectable than the time-serving, place-hunting, dinner-seeking devotion which Messrs. Tape and Tadpole choose to denominate 'friendship.'[54]

Men may laugh at us, and we deserve it: we are often egregious fools, but we are honest fools; and our folly, at least in this matter, usually ends where theirs begins – with middle life, or marriage.

It is the unmarried, the solitary, who are most prone to that sort of 'sentimental' friendship with their own or the opposite sex, which, though often most noble, unselfish, and true, is in some forms ludicrous, in others dangerous. For two women, past earliest girlhood, to be completely absorbed in one another, and make public demonstration of the fact, by caresses or quarrels, is so repugnant to common sense, that where it ceases to be silly it becomes actually wrong. But to see two women, whom Providence has denied nearer ties, by a wise substitution making the best of fate, loving, sustaining, and comforting one another, with a tenderness often closer than that of sisters, because it has all the novelty of election which belongs to the conjugal tie itself – this, I say, is an honourable and lovely sight.

Not less so the friendship – rare, I grant, yet quite possible – which subsists between a man and woman whom circumstances, or their own idiosyncrasies, preclude from the slightest chance of ever 'falling in love.' That such friendships can exist, especially between persons of a certain temperament and order of mind, and remain for a lifetime, utterly pure, interfering with no rights, and transgressing no law of morals or society, most people's observation of life will testify; and he must take a very low view of human nature who dares to say that these attachments, satirically termed 'Platonic,' are impossible. But, at the same time, common sense must allow that they are rare to find, and not the happiest always, when found; because in some degree they are contrary to nature. Nature's law undoubtedly is, that our nearest ties should be those of blood – father or brother, sister or mother – until comes the closer one of marriage; and it is always, if not wrong, rather pitiful, when any extraneous bond comes in between to forestall the entire affection that a young man ought to bring to his future wife, a young woman to her husband. I say *ought* – God knows if they ever do! But, however fate, or folly, or wickedness may interfere to prevent it, not the less true is the undoubted fact, that happy above all must be that marriage where neither husband nor wife ever had a friend so dear as one another.

After marriage, for either party to have or to desire a dearer or closer friend than the other, is a state of things so inconceivably deplorable – the more erring, the more deplorable – that it will not bear discussion. Such cases there are; but He who in the mystery of marriage prefigured a greater mystery still, alone can judge them, for He only knows their miseries, their temptations, and their wrongs.[55]

While allowing that a treaty of friendship, 'pure and simple,' can exist between a man and woman – under peculiar circumstances, even between a young man and a young woman – it must also be allowed that the experiment is difficult, often dangerous; so dangerous, that the matter-of-fact half of the world will not believe in it at all. Parents and guardians very naturally object to a gentleman's 'hanging up his hat' in their houses, or taking sentimental twilight rambles with their fair young daughters. They insist, and justly, that he ought to

'Come with a good will, or come not at all;'

namely, as a mere acquaintance, a pleasant friend of the family – the *whole* family, or as a declared suitor. And though this may fall rather hard upon the young man, who has just a hundred a-year, and, with every disposition towards flirting, a strong horror of matrimony – still, it is wisest and best. It may save both parties from frittering away, in a score of false sentimental likings, the love that ought to belong but to one; or, still worse, from committing or suffering what, beginning blamelessly on either side, frequently ends in incurable pain, irremediable wrong.

Therefore it is, generally speaking, those further on in life, with whom the love-phase is past, or for whom it never existed, who may best use the right, which every pure and independent heart undoubtedly has, of saying: 'I take this man or woman for my friend: only a friend – never either more or less – whom as such I mean to keep to the end of my days.' And if more of these, who really know what friendship is, would have the moral courage to assert its dignity against the sneers of society, which is loath to believe in anything higher and purer than itself, I think it would be all the better for the world.

Women's friendships with one another are of course free from all these perils, and yet they have their own. The wonderful law of sex – which exists spiritually as well as materially, and often independent of matter altogether; since we see many a man who is much more of a woman, and many a woman who would certainly be the 'better-half' of any man who cared for her – this law can rarely be withstood with impunity. In most friends whose attachment is specially deep and lasting, we can usually trace a difference – of strong or weak, gay or grave, brilliant or solid – answering in some measure to the difference of sex. Otherwise, a close, all-engrossing friendship between two women would seldom last long; or if it did, by their mutual feminine weaknesses acting and reacting upon one another, would most likely narrow the sympathies and deteriorate the character of both.

Herein lies the distinction – marked and inalienable – between friendship and love. The latter, being a natural necessity, requires but *the one*, whom it absorbs and assimilates till the two diverse, and often opposite characters, become a safe unity – according to divine ordinance, 'one flesh.' But friendship, to be friendship at all, must have an independent self-existence, capable of gradations and varieties; for though we can have but one dearest friend, it would argue small power of either appreciating or loving to have only one friend.

On the other hand, the 'hare with many friends' has passed into a proverb. Such a condition is manifestly impossible. The gentleman who, in answer to his servant's request to be allowed to go and 'see a friend,' cries:–

> 'Fetch me my coat, John! Though the night be raw,
> I'll see him too – the first I ever saw:'

this cynic, poor wretch! speaks wiser than he is aware of. One simple fact explains and limits the whole question – that those only can find true friends who have in themselves the will and capacity to be such.

A *friend*. Not perhaps until later life, until the follies, passions, and selfishnesses of youth have died out, do we – I mean especially we women – recognise the inestimable blessing, the responsibility awful as sweet, of possessing or of being a friend. And though, not willing to run counter to the world's kindly custom, we may give that solemn title to many who do not exactly own it; though year by year the fierce experience of life, through death, circumstance, or change, narrows the circle of those who do own it; still that man or woman must have been very unfortunate – perhaps, as there can be no result without a cause, worse than unfortunate – who, looking back on thirty, forty, or fifty years of existence, cannot say from the heart, 'I thank God for my friends.'

People rarely long keep what they do not deserve. If you find any who, in the decline of life, have few 'auld acquaintance,' and those few 'never brought to mind,' but in their stead a lengthy list of friends who are such no more, who have 'ill-treated' them, or with whom they have had a 'slight coolness;' if they are always finding fault with the friends they now have, and accusing them of ingratitude or neglect; if they tell you these friends' secrets, and expect you in return to tell them all *your* friends' secrets, and your own – beware of these people! They may have many good qualities; you may like them very much, and keep them as most pleasant society, but as for resting your heart upon them, you might as well rest it upon a burning rock or a broken reed.

But if you find people who through all life's vicissitudes and pangs have preserved a handful of real 'friends' – exclusive of you, for it takes years to judge the value of friendship towards ourselves – if on the whole they complain little either of these friends or of the world, which rarely misuses a good man or woman for ever; if they bestow no extravagant devotion on you, nor expect from you one whit more than you freely give; if they

never, under any excuse, however personally flattering, talk to
you about a third party, as you would shrink from their talking
to any third party about you – then, be satisfied;

> 'Those friends thou hast, and their adoption tried;
> Grapple them to thy soul with hoops of steel!'[56]

Never let them go; suffer no changing tide of fortune to sweep
them from you – no later friendships to usurp their place. Be
very patient with them; bear their little faults as they must bear
yours; make allowance for the countless unintentional slights,
neglects, or offences, that we all in the whirl of life must both
endure and commit towards those who form not a part, but an
adjunct of our existence – remembering, as I said before, that
the very element in which true friendship lives, and out of
which it cannot live at all, is perfect *liberty*.

Friendship once conceived should, like love, in one sense last
for ever. That it does not; that in the world's harsh wear and
tear many a very sincere attachment is slowly obliterated, or
both parties grow out of it and cast it, like a snake his last year's
skin – though that implies something of the snake-nature, I fear
– are facts too mournfully common to be denied. But there is a
third fact, as mournfully *un*common, which needs to be remembered likewise: we may lose the friend – the friendship we never
can or ought to lose. Actively, it may exist no more; but
passively, it is just as binding as the first moment when we
pledged it, as we believed, for ever. Its duties, like its delights,
may have become a dead-letter; but none of its claims or
confidences have we ever afterwards the smallest right to abjure
or to break.

And here is one accusation which I must sorrowfully bring
against women, as being much more guilty than men. We can
keep a secret – ay, against all satire, I protest we can – while the
confider remains our friend; but if that tie ceases, pop! out it
comes! and in the bitterness of invective, the pang of wounded
feeling, or afterwards in mere thoughtlessness, and easy forgetting of what is so easily healed, a thousand things are said and
done for which nothing can ever atone. The lost friendship,

which, once certain that it is past all revival, ought to be buried as solemnly and silently as a lost love, is cast out into the open street for all the snarling curs of society to gnaw at and mangle, and all the contemptuous misogynists who pass by to point the finger at – 'See what your grand ideals all come to!'

Good women – dear my sisters! be our friendships false or true, wise or foolish, living or dead – let us at least learn to keep them sacred! Men are far better than we in this. Rarely will a man voluntarily or thoughtlessly betray a friend's confidence, either at the time or afterwards. He will say, even to his own wife: 'I can't tell you this – I have no right to tell you:' and if she has the least spark of good feeling, she will honour and love him all the dearer for so saying. More rarely still will a man be heard, as women constantly are, speaking ill of some friend who a little while before, while the friendship lasted, was all perfection. What is necessary to be said he will say, but not a syllable more, leaving all the rest in that safe, still atmosphere, where all good fructifies and evil perishes – the atmosphere of silence.

Ay, above all things, what women need to learn in their friendships is the sanctity of silence – silence in outward demonstration, silence under wrong, silence with regard to the outside world, and often a delicate silence between one another. About the greatest virtue a friend can have, is to be able to hold her tongue; and though this, like all virtues carried to extremity, may grow into a fault, and do great harm, still, it never can do so much harm as that horrible laxity and profligacy of speech which is at the root of half the quarrels, cruelties, and injustices of the world.

And let every woman, old or young, in commencing a friendship, be careful that it is to the right thing she has given the right name. If so, let her enter upon it thoughtfully, earnestly, advisedly, as upon an engagement made for life, which in truth it is; since, whether its duration be brief or long, it is a tangible reality, and, as such, must have its influence on the total chronicle of existence, wherein no line can ever be quite blotted out. Let her, with the strength and comfort of it, prepare to take the burden; determined, whatever the other may do, to fulfil her own part, and act up to her own duty, absolutely and conscientiously, to the end. For truly, the greatest of all external blessings is it to be able to lean your heart against another heart, faithful, tender, true, and tried, and record with a thankfulness that years deepen instead of diminishing, 'I have got a friend!'

CHAPTER VIII

GOSSIP

One of the wisest and best among our English ethical writers, the author of *Companions of my Solitude*,[57] says, *àpropos* of gossip, that one half of the evil-speaking of the world arises, not from *malice prepense*, but from mere want of amusement. And I think we may even grant that in the other half, constituted small of mind or selfish in disposition, it is seldom worse than the natural falling back from large abstract interests, which they cannot understand, upon those which they can – alas! only the narrow, commonplace, and personal.

Yet they mean no harm; are often under the delusion that they both mean and do a great deal of good, take a benevolent watch over their fellow-creatures, and so forth. They would not say an untrue word, or do an unkind action – not they! The most barefaced slanderer always tells her story with a good motive, or thinks she does; begins with a harmless 'bit of gossip,' just to pass the time away – the time which hangs so heavy! and ends by becoming the most arrant and mischievous tale-bearer under the sun.

Ex. gratia[58] – Let me put on record the decline and fall, voluntarily confessed, of two friends of mine, certainly the last persons likely to take to tittle-tattle; being neither young nor elderly; on the whole, perhaps rather 'bright' than stupid; having plenty to do and to think of – too much, indeed, since they came on an enforced holiday out of that vortex in which London whirls her professional classes round and round, year by year, till at last often nothing but a handful of dry bones is cast on shore. They came to lodge at the village of X——, let me call it, as being an 'unknown quantity,' which the reader will vainly attempt to find out, since it is just like some hundred other villages – has its church and rector, great house and squire, doctor and lawyer (alas! poor village, I fear its *two* doctors and *two* lawyers); also its small select society, where everybody knows everybody – that is, their affairs: for themselves, one half the parish resolutely declines 'knowing' the other half – sometimes pretermittently, sometimes permanently. Of course, not a single soul would have ventured to know Bob and Maria – as I shall call the strangers – had they not brought an introduction to one family, under the shelter of whose respectability they meekly placed their own. A very worthy family it was, which showed them all hospitality, asked them to tea continually, and there, in the shadow of the pleasant drawing-room, which overlooked the street, indoctrinated them into all the mysteries of X——, something in this wise:

'Dear me! there's Mrs Smith; she has on that identical yellow bonnet which has been so long in Miss Miffin's shop-window. Got it cheap, no doubt: Mr Smith does keep the poor thing *so* close! Annabella, child, make haste; just tell me whether that isn't the same young man who called on the Joneses three times last week! Red whiskers and moustaches. One of those horrid officers, no doubt. My dear Miss Maria, I never do like to say a word against my neighbours; but before I would let my Annabella go about like the Jones's girls . . . . Bless my life! there's that cab at the corner house again – and her husband out! Well, if I ever could have believed it, even of silly, flirty Mrs Green! whom people do say old Mr Green married out of a London hosier's, where he went in to buy a pair of gloves. What a shocking place London must be . . .! But I beg your pardon, my dear . . .' And so on, and so on.

This, slightly varied, was the stock conversation, which seemed amply sufficient to fill the minds and hours of the whole family, and, indeed, of every family at X——.

Maria and Bob used to go home laughing, and thanking their stars that they *did* live in that shocking place London. Bob made harmless jokes at the expense of the unconscious household who,

'Pinnacled dim in the intense inane,'[59]

could drop down, hawk-like, upon reputations, bonnets, and beaus. Maria gave vent to a majestic but indignant pity; and both hugged themselves in the belief that never, under any circumstances, could *they* sink to such a dead-level of folly, vacuity, spite.

Weeks passed – rather slowly, especially when, of autumn evenings, they found themselves *minus* books, piano, theatre, concerts, society – in fact, in precisely the position of the inhabitants of X—— all year round. So, as daylight was less dull than candlelight, they used to rise at unearthly hours; dine – shall I betray the Goths? – at 11.30 A.M., take tea at 4 P.M., and go to bed as soon after dark as they could for shame. At last, from very dulness, Maria got into the habit of sitting at the window and telling Bob what was passing in the street, interspersed with little illustrative anecdotes she had caught up, 'just as bits of human nature.' One, the stock scandal of the place, interested them both so much, that they watched for the heroine's carriage every day for a week; and when at last Maria cried, 'There it is!' Bob jumped up with all the eagerness of Annabella herself, and missing the sight, retired grumbling: 'What nonsense! I declare you're getting just as bad a gossip as anybody here!' (*N.B.* – The masculine mind, in an accusative form, always prefers the second person of the verb.)

'Well,' observed Maria, 'shall I give up telling you any news I happen to hear?'

'Oh, no! You may tell what you like. As the man said when his wife beat him – it amuses you, and it doesn't harm me.'

Finally – I have it from Maria's own confession – coming in one afternoon absorbed in cogitations as to what possible motive Mrs Green could have in telling Mrs Elizabeth Jones she wished to call on her, Maria; and what on earth would be done if Annabella, whose mamma wouldn't allow her even to bow to Mrs Green, should happen to call at the same time – she was quite startled by Bob's springing up from the sofa to meet her, with an air of great relief.

'So you're back at last! Well, who did you see, and what did they say to you? Do sit down, and let's hear all the gossip going.'

'Gossip!' And meeting one another's eyes, they both burst into a hearty fit of laughter, declaring they never again would pride themselves on being a bit better than their neighbours.

Ay, fatal and vile as her progeny may be, 'the mother of mischief,' says the proverb, 'is no bigger than a midge's wing.' Nay, as many a vice can be traced back to an exaggerated virtue, this hateful propensity to tittle-tattle springs from the same peculiarity which, rightly guided, constitutes womanhood's chiefest strength and charm; blesses many a worthless man with a poor, fond, faithful wife, who loves him for nothing that he is or does, but merely because he is *himself*; forgives to many a scapegrace son or brother a hundred sins, and follows him to the grave or the scaffold, blind to everything except the fact that he is her own. Personal interests, personal attachments, personal prejudices, are, whether we own it or not, the ruling bias of us women: it is better to own it at once, govern, correct, and modify it, than to deny it in name, and betray it in every circumstance of our lives.

Men, whose habits of thought and action are at once more selfish and less personal than ours, are very seldom given to gossiping. They will take a vast interest in the misgovernment of India; or the ill-cooking of their own dinners; but any topic betwixt these two – such as the mismanagement of their neighbour's house, or the extravagance of their partner's wife – is a matter of very minor importance. They 'canna be fashed' with trifles that don't immediately concern themselves. It is the women – always the women – who poke about with undefended farthing candles in the choke-damp passages of this dangerous world; who put their feeble ignorant hands to the Archimedean lever that, slight as it seems, can shake society to its lowest foundations. For, though it irks me to wound with strong language the delicate sensibilities of my silver-tongued sisters, I would just remind them of what they may hear, certainly one Sunday in the year, concerning that same dainty little member, which is said to be 'a fire, a world of iniquity . . . and it is *set on fire of hell.*'[60]

Verily, the 'Silent Woman' – a lady without a head, who officiates as sign to many a country inn – had need to be so depicted. But it is not 'the gift of the gab,' the habit of using a dozen words where one would answer the purpose, which may arise from want of education, nervousness, or surplus but honest energy and earnest feeling – it is not that which does the harm; it is the lamentable fact, that whether from a superabundance of the imaginative faculty, carelessness of phrase, or a readiness to jump at conclusions, and represent facts not as they are but as they appear to the representers, very few women are absolutely and invariably veracious. Men lie wilfully, deliberately, on principle, as it were; but women quite involuntarily. Nay, they would start with horror from the bare thought of such a thing. They love truth in their hearts, and yet – and yet – they are constantly giving to things a slight colouring cast by their own individuality; twisting facts a little, a very little, according as their tastes, affections, or convenience indicate: never perhaps telling a direct lie, but merely a deformed or prevaricated truth.

And this makes the fatal danger of gossip. If all people spoke the absolute truth about their neighbours, or held their tongues, which is always a possible alternative, it would not so much matter. At the worst, there would be a few periodical social thunder-storms, and then the air would be clear. But the generality of people do *not* speak the truth: they speak what they see, or think, or believe, or wish. Few observant characters can have lived long in the world without learning to receive every fact communicated second-hand *with reservations* – reservations that do not necessarily stamp the communicator as a liar, but merely make allowance for certain inevitable variations, like the variations of the compass, which every circumnavigator must calculate upon as a natural necessity.

Thus, Miss A., in the weary small-talk of a morning call, not quite knowing what she says, or glad to say anything for the sake of talking, lets drop to Mrs B. that she heard Mrs C. say:

'She would take care to keep her boys out of the way of the little B's' – a very harmless remark, since, when it was uttered, the little B's were just recovering from the measles. But Miss A., an absent sort of woman, repeats it three months afterwards, forgetting all about the measles; indeed, she has persuaded herself that it referred to the rudeness of the B. lads, who are her own private terror, and she thinks it may probably do some good to give their over-indulgent mamma a hint on the subject. Mrs B., too well-bred to reply more than 'Indeed!' is yet mortally offended; declines the next dinner-party at the C's and confides her private reason for doing so to Miss D., a good-natured chatterbox, who, with the laudable intention of getting to the bottom of the matter, and reconciling the belligerents, immediately communicates the same. 'What have I done?' exclaims the hapless Mrs C. 'I never said any such thing!' 'Oh, but Miss A. protests she *heard* you say it.' Again Mrs C. warmly denies; which denial goes back directly to Miss A. and Mrs B., imparting to both them and Miss D. a very unpleasant feeling as to the lady's veracity. A few days after, thinking it over, she suddenly recollects that she really did say the identical words, with reference solely to the measles; bursts into a hearty fit of laughter, and congratulates herself that it is all right. But not so: the mountain cannot so quickly shrink into its original mole-hill. Mrs B., whose weak point is her children, receives the explanation with considerable dignity and reserve; is 'sorry that Mrs C. should have troubled herself about such a trifle;' shakes hands, and professes herself quite satisfied. Nevertheless, in her own inmost mind she thinks – and her countenance shows it – 'I believe you said it, for all that.' A slight coolness ensues, which everybody notices, discusses, and gives a separate version of; all which versions somehow or other come to the ears of the parties concerned, who, without clearly knowing why, feel vexed and aggrieved each at the other. The end of it all is a total estrangement.

Is not a little episode like this at the root of nearly all the family feuds, lost friendships, 'cut' acquaintanceships, so piti-fully rife in the world? Rarely any great matter, a point of principle or a violated pledge, an act of justice or dishonesty; it is almost always some petty action misinterpreted, some idle word repeated – or a succession of both these, gathering and gathering like the shingle on a sea-beach, something fresh being left behind by every day's tide. Not the men's doing – the fathers, husbands, or brothers, who have no time to bother themselves about such trifles, and who, if they see fit to quarrel over their two grand *causæ belli*, religion and politics, generally do it outright, and either abuse one another like pickpockets in newspaper columns, or, in revenge for any moral poaching on one another's property, take a horsewhip or a pair of pistols and so end the matter.

No. It is the women who are at the bottom of it all, who, in the narrowness or blankness of their daily lives, are glad to catch at any straw of interest – especially the unmarried, the idle, the rich, and the childless. As says the author I have before referred to: 'People not otherwise ill-natured are pleased with the misfortunes of their neighbours, solely because it gives them something to think about, something to talk about. They imagine how the principal actors and sufferers will bear it; what they will do; how they will look; and so the dull bystander forms a sort of drama for himself.'[61]

And what a drama! Such a petty plot – such small heroes and heroines – such a harmless villain! When we think of the contemptible nothings that form the daily scandal-dish of most villages, towns, cities, or communities, and then look up at the starry heaven which overshines them all, dropping its rain upon the just and the unjust – or look abroad on the world, of whose wide interests, miseries, joys, duties, they form such an infinitesimal part, one is tempted to blush for one's species. Strange, that while hundreds and thousands in this Britain have not a crust to eat, Mrs E. should become the town's talk for three days, because, owing a dinner-party to the F's, G's, H's, and J's, she clears accounts at a cheaper rate by giving a general tea-party instead. 'So mean! and with Mr E.'s large income, too!' – That while millions are living and dying without God in the world, despising Him, forgetting Him, or never having even heard His name, Miss K., a really exemplary woman, should not only refuse, even for charitable purposes, to associate with the L's, an equally irreproachable family, as to morals and benevolence, but should actually forbid her district poor to receive their teaching or their Bibles, because they refuse to add thereto the Church of England Catechism. As to visiting them – 'Quite impossible; they are Dissenters, you know.'[62]

The gossip of opposing religionism – I will not even call it religion, though religion itself is often very far from pure 'godliness' – is at once the most virulent and the saddest phase of the disease; and our sex, it must be confessed, are the more liable to it, especially in the provinces. There, the parish curate may at times be seen walking with the Unitarian or Independent minister, if they happen to be well-educated young men of a social turn; even the rector, worthy man! will occasionally have the sense to join with other worthy men of every denomination in matters of local improvement. But oh! the talk that this gives rise to among the female population! till the reverend objects of it, who in their daily duties have usually more to do with women than with men – another involuntary tribute to those virtues which form the bright under-side of every fault that can be alleged against us – are often driven to give in to the force of public opinion, to that incessant babble of silvery waters which wears through the rockiest soil.

The next grand source of gossip – and this, too, curiously indicates how true must be the instinct of womanhood, even in its lowest forms so evidently a corruption from the highest – is love, and with or without that preliminary, matrimony. What on earth should we do if we had no matches to make, or mar; no 'unfortunate attachments' to shake our heads over; no flirtations to speculate about and comment upon with knowing smiles; no engagements 'on' or 'off' to speak our minds about, nosing out every little circumstance, and ferreting our game to their very hole, as if all their affairs, their hopes, trials, faults, or wrongs, were being transacted for our own private and peculiar entertainment! Of all forms of gossip – I speak of mere gossip, as distinguished from the carrion-crow and dunghill-fly system of scandal-mongering – this tittle-tattle about love-affairs is the most general, the most odious, and the most dangerous.

Every one of us must have known within our own experience many an instance of dawning loves checked, unhappy loves made cruelly public, happy loves embittered, warm, honest loves turned cold, by this horrible system of gossiping about young or unmarried people – 'evening' to one another folk who have not the slightest mutual inclination, or if they had, such an idea put into their heads would effectually smother it; setting down every harmless free liking as 'a case,' or 'a flirtation;' and if anything 'serious' does turn up, pouncing on it, hunting it down, and never letting it go till dismembered and ground to the bone. Should it ever come to a marriage – and the wonder is, considering all these things, that any love-affair ever does come to that climax at all, or that any honest-hearted, delicate-minded young people, ever have the courage to indulge the world by an open attachment or engagement – heavens and earth! how it is talked about! How one learns every single item of what 'he' said and 'she' said, and what all the relations said, and how it came about, and how it never would have come about at all but for So-and so, and what they have to live upon, and how capable or incapable they are of living upon it, and how very much better both parties would have done if they had only each left the choosing of the other to about four-and-twenty anxious friends, all of which were quite certain the affianced pair never would suit one another, but would have exactly suited somebody else, &c. &c., *ad libitum* and *ad infinitum*.

Many women, otherwise kindly and generous, have in this matter no more consideration towards their own sex or the other, no more sense of the sanctity and silence due to the relation between them, than if the divinely instituted bond of marriage were no higher or purer than the natural instincts of the beasts that perish. It is most sad, nay, it is sickening, to see the way in which, from the age of fourteen upwards, a young woman, on this one subject of her possible or probable matrimonial arrangements, is quizzed, talked over, commented upon, advised, condoled with, lectured, interrogated – until, if she has

happily never had cause to blush for herself, not a week passes
that she does not blush for her sex, out of utter contempt,
disgust, and indignation.

Surely all right-minded women ought to set their faces
resolutely against this desecration of feelings, to maintain the
sanctity of which is the only preservative of our influence – that
is, our rightful and holy influence, over men. Not that, after the
school of Mesdames Barbauld, Hannah More,[63] and other excellent but exceedingly prosy personages, love should be exorcised
out of young women's lives and conversations – query, *if*
possible? – but let it be treated of delicately, earnestly, ration-
ally, as a matter which, if they have any business with it at all, is
undoubtedly the most serious business of their lives. There can
be – there ought to be – no medium course; a love-affair is
either sober earnest or contemptible folly, if not wickedness: to
gossip about it is, in the first instance, intrusive, unkind, or
dangerous; in the second, simply silly. Practical people may
choose between the two alternatives.

Gossip, public, private, social – to fight against it either by
word or pen seems, after all, like fighting with shadows. Everybody laughs at it, protests against it, blames and despises it; yet
everybody does it, or at least encourages others in it: quite
innocently, unconsciously, in such a small, harmless fashion –
yet, we do it. We must talk about something, and it is not all of
us who can find a rational topic of conversation, or discuss it
when found. Many, too, who in their hearts hate the very
thought of tattle and tale-bearing, are shy of lifting up their
voices against it, lest they should be ridiculed for Quixotism, or
thought to set themselves up as more virtuous than their
neighbours. Others, like our lamented friends, Maria and Bob,
from mere idleness and indifference, long kept hovering over
the unclean stream, at last drop into it, and are drifted away by
it. Where does it land them? Ay, where?

If I, or any one, were to unfold on this subject only our own
experience and observation – not a tittle more – what a volume
it would make!

Families set by the ears, parents against children, brothers against brothers – not to mention brothers and sisters-in-law, who seem generally to assume, with the legal title, the legal right of interminably squabbling. Friendships sundered, betrothals broken, marriages annulled – in the spirit, at least, while in the letter kept outwardly, to be a daily torment, temptation, and despair. Acquaintances that would otherwise have maintained a safe and not unkindly indifference, forced into absolute dislike – originating how they know not; but there it is. Old companions, that would have borne each other's little foibles, have forgiven and forgotten little annoyances, and kept up an honest affection till death, driven at last into open rupture, or frozen into a coldness more hopeless still, which no afterwarmth will ever have power to thaw.

Truly, from the smallest Little Peddlington that carries on, year by year, its bloodless wars, its harmless scandals, its daily chronicle of interminable nothings, to the great metropolitan world, fashionable, intellectual, noble, or royal, the blight and curse of civilised life is gossip.

How is it to be removed? How are scores of well-meaning women, who in their hearts really like and respect one another – who, did trouble come to any one of them, would be ready with countless mutual kindnesses, small and great, and among whom the sudden advent of death would subdue every idle tongue to honest praise, and silence, at once and for ever, every bitter word against the neighbour departed – how are they to be taught to be every day as generous, considerate, liberal-minded – in short, womanly, as they would assuredly be in any exceptionable day of adversity? How are they to be made to feel the littleness, the ineffably pitiful littleness, of raking up and criticising every slight peculiarity of manner, habits, temper, character, word, action, motive – household, children, servants, living, furniture, and dress: thus constituting themselves the amateur rag-pickers, *chiffonnières*[64] – I was going to say, scavengers, but they do *not* leave the streets clean – of all the blind alleys and foul by-ways of society; while the whole world lies free and open before them, to do their work and choose their innocent pleasure therein – this busy, bright, beautiful world?

Such a revolution is, I doubt, quite hopeless on this side of Paradise. But every woman has it in her power personally to withstand the spread of this great plague of tongues, since it lies within her own volition what she will do with her own.

'All the king's horses and all the king's men'

cannot make us either use or bridle that little member. It is our never-failing weapon, double-edged, delicate, bright, keen; a weapon not necessarily either lethal or vile, but taking its character solely from the manner in which we use it.

First, let every one of us cultivate, in every word that issues from her mouth, absolute truth. I say cultivate, because to very few people – as may be noticed of most young children – does truth, this rigid, literal veracity, come by nature. To many, even who love it and prize it dearly in others, it comes only after the self-control, watchfulness, and bitter experience of years. Let no one conscious of needing this care be afraid to begin it from the very beginning; or in her daily life and conversation fear to confess: 'Stay, I said a little more than I meant' – 'I think I was not quite correct about such a thing' – 'Thus it was; at least, thus it seemed to me personally,' &c. &c. Even in the simplest, most everyday statements, we cannot be too guarded or too exact. The 'hundred cats' that the little lad saw 'fighting on our back-wall,' and which afterwards dwindled down to 'our cat and another,' is a case in point, not near so foolish as it seems.

'Believe only half of what you see, and nothing that you hear,' is a cynical saying, and yet less bitter than at first appears. It does not argue that human nature is false, but simply that it is human nature. How can any fallible human being with two eyes, two ears, one judgment, and one brain – all more or less limited in their apprehensions of things external, and biassed by a thousand internal impressions, purely individual – how can we possibly decide on even the plainest actions of another, to say nothing of the words, which may have gone through half-a-dozen different translations and modifications, or the motives, which can only be known to the Omniscient Himself?

In His name, therefore, let us 'judge not, that we be not

judged.' Let us be 'quick to hear, slow to speak;' slowest of all
to speak any evil, or to listen to it, about anybody. The good we
need be less careful over; we are not likely ever to hear too
much of that.

'But,' say some – very excellent people, too – 'are we never
to open our mouths? – never to mention the ill things we see or
hear; never to stand up for the right, by proclaiming, or by
warning and testifying against the wrong?'

Against wrong – in the abstract, yes: but against individuals –
doubtful. All the gossip in the world, or the dread of it, will
never turn one domestic tyrant into a decent husband or father;
one light woman into a matron leal[65] and wise. Do your
neighbour good by all means in your power, moral as well as
physical – by kindness, by patience, by unflinching resistance
against every outward evil – by the silent preaching of your own
contrary life. But if the only good you can do him is by talking
at him or about him – nay, even *to* him, if it be in a self-satisfied,
super-virtuous, style – such as I earnestly hope the present
writer is not doing – you had much better leave him alone. If he
be foolish, soon or late he will reap the fruit of his folly; if
wicked, be sure his sin will find him out. If he has wronged you,
you will neither lessen the wrong nor increase his repentance by
parading it. And if – since there are two sides to every subject,
and it takes two to make a quarrel – you have wronged him,
surely you will not right him or yourself by abusing him. In
Heaven's name, let him alone.

CHAPTER IX

WOMEN OF THE WORLD

The world! It is a word capable of as diverse interpretations or misinterpretations as the thing itself – a thing by various people supposed to belong to heaven, man, or the devil, or alternately to all three. But this is not the place to argue the pros and cons of that doctrinal theology which views as totally evil the same world which its Creator pronounced to be 'very good,' the same world in and for which its Redeemer lived as well as died; nor, taking it at its present worst, a sinful, miserable, mysterious, yet neither wholly comfortless, hopeless, nor godless world, shall I refer further to that strange Manichaeanism[66] which believes that anything earth possesses of good can have sprung from any other source than the All-good, that any happiness in it could exist for a moment, unless derived from Infinite Perfection.

'A woman of the world' – 'Quite a woman of the world' – 'A mere woman of the world' – with how many modifications of tone and emphasis do we hear the phrase; which seems inherently to imply a contradiction. Nature herself has apparently decided for women, physically as well as mentally, that their natural destiny should be *not* of the world. In the earlier ages of Judaism and Islamism, nobody ever seems to have ventured a doubt of this. Christianity alone raised the woman to her rightful and original place, as man's one help-meet, bone of his bone and flesh of his flesh, his equal in all points of vital moment, yet made suited to him by an harmonious something which is less inferiority than difference. And this difference will for ever exist. Volumes written on female progress; speeches interminable, delivered from the public rostrum in female treble, which from that very publicity and bravado would convert the most obvious 'rights' into something very like a wrong; biographies numberless of great women – ay, and good – who, stepping out of their natural sphere, have done service in courts, camps, or diplomatic bureaus: all these exceptional cases will never set aside the universal law, that woman's proper place is home.[67] Not merely

'To suckle fools and chronicle small-beer,'[68]

– Shakspeare, who knew us well, would never have made any but an *Iago* say so – but to go hand-in-hand with man on their distinct yet parallel roads, to be within-doors what he has to be in the world without – sole influence and authority in the limited monarchy of home.

Thus, to be a 'woman of the world,' though not essentially a criminal accusation, implies a state of being not natural, and therefore not happy. Without any sentimental heroics against the hollowness of such an existence, and putting aside the religious view of it altogether, I believe most people will admit that no woman living entirely in and for the world ever was, ever could be, a happy woman; that is, according to the definition of happiness, which supposes it to consist of having our highest faculties most highly developed, and in use to their fullest extent. Any other sort of happiness, either dependent on externally favourable circumstances, or resting on safe negations of ill, we must be considered to possess in common with the oyster; indeed, that easy-tempered and steadfast mollusk, if not 'in love,' probably has it in much greater perfection than we.

Starting with the proposition that a woman of the world is not a happy woman; that if she had been, most likely she never would have become what she is – I do not think it necessary to nail her up, poor painted jay, as a 'shocking example' over Society's barn-door, around which strut and crow a great many fowls quite as mean and not half so attractive. For she is very charming in her way – that is, the principal and best type of her class; she wears *à merveille* that beautiful mask said to be 'the homage paid by vice to virtue.' And since the successful imitation of an article argues a certain acquaintance with the original, she may once upon a time have actually believed in many of those things which she now so cleverly impersonates – virtue, heroism, truth, love, friendship, honour, and fidelity. She is like certain stamped-out bronze ornaments, an admirable imitation of real womanhood – till you walk round her to the other side.

The woman of the world is rarely a very young woman. It stands to reason, she could not be. To young people, the world is always a paradise – a fool's paradise, devoutly believed in: it is not till they have found out its shams that they are able to assume them. By that time, however, they have ceased to be fools: it takes a certain amount of undoubted cleverness to make any success, or take any rule in the world.

By the world, I do not mean the aristocratic Vanity-fair – let those preach of it who move up and down or keep stalls therein – but the world of the middle classes; the 'society' into which drift the homeless, thoughtless, ambitious, pleasure-loving among them; those who have no purpose in life except to get through it somehow, and those who never had any interest in it except their own beloved selves.

A woman of the sort I write of may in one sense be placed at the lowest deep of womanhood, because her centre of existence is undoubtedly herself. You may trace this before you have been introduced to her five minutes: in the sweet manner which so well simulates a universal benevolence, being exactly the same to everybody – namely, everybody worth knowing; in the air of interest with which she asks a dozen polite or kindly questions, of which she never waits for the answer; in the instinctive consciousness you have that all the while she is talking agreeably to you, or flatteringly listening to your talented conversation, her attention is on the *qui vive*[69] after every body and every thing throughout the room – that is, everything that concerns herself. As for yourself, from the moment you have passed out of her sight, or ceased to minister to her amusement or convenience, you may be quite certain you will have as completely slipped out of her memory as if you had vanished into another sphere. Her own sphere cannot contain you; for though it seems so large, it has no real existence: it is merely a reflection of so much of the outer world as can be received into the one small drop of not over-clear water, which constitutes this woman's soul.

Yet waste not your wrath upon her – she is as much to be pitied as blamed. Do not grow savage at hearing her, in that softly-pitched voice of hers, talk sentiment by the yard, while you know she snubs horribly in private every unlucky relative she has; whose only hours of quiet are when they joyfully deck her and send her out to adorn society. Do not laugh when she criticises pictures, and goes into raptures over books, which you are morally certain she has never either seen or read; or if she had, from the very character of her mind, could no more understand them than your cat can appreciate Shakspeare. Contemn her not, for her state might not have been always thus; you know not the causes which produced it; and – stay till you see her end.

There is a class of worldly women which, to my mind, is much worse than this; because their shams are less cleverly sustained, and their ideal of good (for every human being *must* have one – the conqueror his crown, and the sot his gin-bottle) is far lower and more contemptible. The brilliant woman of society has usually her pet philanthropies, her literary, learned, or political penchants, in which the good she thirsts after, though unreal, is the imitation of a vital reality; and as such is often, in some degree, useful to others. But this pseudo-woman of the world has no ideal beyond fine dresses, houses, carriages, acquaintances; and even these she does not value for their own sakes, only because they are superior to her neighbour's.

You will find her chiefly among the half-educated *nouveaux riches* of the professional classes, vainly striving to attain their level – the highest point visible on her horizon. And this is no happy altitude of learning, or intelligence, or refinement; but merely a certain 'position' – a place at a dinner-party, or a house in a square.

While the first kind of woman always has a degree of sway in society, this one is society's most prostrate slave. She dares not furnish her house, choose her servants, eat her food, pay her visits, or even put the gown on her back and the bonnet on her head, save by rule and precedent. She will worry herself and you about the veriest trifles of *convenance* – such as whether it is most genteel to leave one card with the corner turned down, or to expend a separate card upon each member of the family. To find herself at a full-dress soirée in demi-toilette would make this poor lady miserable for a month; and if by any chance you omitted paying her the proper visit of inquiry after an entertainment, she would consider you meant a personal insult, and, if she dared – only she seldom ventures on any decisive proceedings – would cut your acquaintance immediately.

The celebrated Mrs Grundy[70] keeps her in a state of mortal servitude. Even in London, which to a lady of medium age, established character, and decent behaviour, is the most independent place in the world; where, as I once heard said: 'My dear, be assured you are not of the least importance to anybody – may go anywhere, dress anyhow, and, in short, do anything you like except stand on your head' – even here she is for ever pursued by a host of vague adjectives, 'proper,' 'correct,' 'genteel,' which hunt her to death like a pack of rabid hounds.

True, the world, like its master, is by no means so black as it is sometimes painted: it often has a foundation of good sense and right feeling under its most ridiculous and wearisome forms; but this woman sees only the forms, among which she blunders like one of those quack-artists who pretend to draw the human figure without the smallest knowledge of anatomy. Utterly ignorant of the framework on which society moves, she is perpetually straining at gnats and swallowing camels, both in manners and morals. To her, laborious politeness stands in the stead of kindliness; show, of hospitality; etiquette, of decorum. *Les bienséances*,[71] which are only valuable as being the index and offering of a gentle, generous, and benevolent heart, are to this unfortunate woman the brazen altar upon which she immolates her own comfort and that of everybody connected with her.

How often do we hear the phrases, – 'What will the world say?' – 'Perhaps; but, then, we live in the world.' – 'A good soul enough, but totally ignorant of the world.' – It is worth while pausing a moment to consider of what this 'world' really consists, that women seem at once so eagerly to run after, and to be so terribly afraid of.

Not the moral world, which judges their sins – with, alas, how short-sighted and unevenly balanced a judgment, often! – but the perpetually changing world of custom, which regulates their clothes, furniture, houses, manner of living, sayings, doings, and sufferings. Take it to pieces, and what is it? Nothing but a floating atmosphere of common-place people surrounding certain congeries of people a little less ordinary, the nucleus of which is generally one person decidedly extra-ordinary, who, by force of will, position, intellect, or character, or by some un-questionable magnitude of virtue or vice, stands out distinctly from the average multitude, and rules it according to his or her individual choice. All the rest are, as I said, a mere atmosphere of nobodies; which atmosphere can be cloven any day – one sees it done continually – by a single flesh-and-blood arm: yet in it the woman of the world allows herself to sit and suffocate; dare not dress comfortably, act and speak straightforwardly, live naturally, or sometimes even honestly. For will she not rather run in debt for a bonnet, than wear her old one a year behind the *mode*? give a ball and stint the family dinner for a month after? take a large house, and furnish handsome reception-rooms, while her household huddle together anyhow in untidy attic bed-chambers, and her servants swelter on shake-downs beside the kitchen fire? She prefers this a hundred times to stating plainly, by word or manner: 'My income is so much a-year – I don't care who knows it – it will not allow me to live beyond a certain rate, it will not keep comfortably both my family and acquaintance; therefore, excuse my preferring the comfort of my family to the entertainment of my acquaintance. And, Society, if you choose to look in upon us, you must just take us as we are, without any pretences of any kind; or you may shut the door, and – good by!'

And Society, in the aggregate, is no fool. It is astonishing what an amount of 'eccentricity' it will stand from anybody who takes the bull by the horns, too fearless or too indifferent to think of consequences. How respectfully it will follow a clever woman who is superior to the weakness of washing her hands or combing her hair properly, whose milliner and dress-maker must evidently have lived in the last century, and who, in her manners and conversation, often breaks through every rule of even the commonest civility! How the same thoroughly respectable set, which would be shocked to let its young daughters take a morning shopping in Regent Street unprotected by a tall footman, will carry them at night to a soirée given by a Lady Somebody, of rather more than doubtful reputation, till some rich marriage, which in its utter lovelessness and hypocrisy may have been, in the sight of Heaven, the foulest of all her sins, in the sight of man obliterated every one of them at once!

Yet this 'world' which, when we come to look at it, seems nothing – less than nothing – a chimera that no honest heart need quail at for a moment – is at once the idol and the *bête noire* of a large portion of women-kind during their whole existence. Ay, from the day when baby's first wardrobe must be of the most extravagant description, costing in lace, braiding, and embroidery almost as much as mamma's marriage outfit – which was a deal too fine for her station – when all the while unfortunate baby would be quite as pretty and twice as comfortable in plain muslin and lawn; down to the last day of our subjugation to fashion, when we must needs be carried to our permanent repose under a proper amount of feathers, and followed by a customary number of mourning coaches – after being coaxed to it – useless luxury! by a satin-lined coffin, stuffed pillow, and ornamented shroud.

In the intermediate stage, marriage, we are worse off still, because the world's iron hand is upon us at a time and under circumstances when we can most keenly feel its grinding weight.

'Do you think,' said a young lady once to me, 'that Henry and I ought to marry upon less than four hundred a-year?'

'No certainly, my dear; because you marry for so many people's benefit besides your own. How, for instance, could your acquaintance bear to see moreen[72] curtains, instead of the blue-and-silver damask you were talking of! And how could you give those charming little dinner-parties which, you say, are indispensable to one in your position, without three servants, or a boy in buttons as well? Nay, if you went into society at all, of the kind you now keep, a fifth of Henry's annual income would melt away in dresses, bouquets, and white kid-gloves. No, my dear girl, I can by no means advise *you* to marry upon less than four hundred a-year.'

My young friend looked up, a little doubtful if I were in jest or earnest; and Mr Henry gave vent to an impatient sigh. I thought – 'Poor things!' for they were honestly in love, and there was no earthly reason why they should not marry. How many hundreds more are thus wasting the best years of their life, the best hopes of their youth, love, home, usefulness, energy – and God only knows how much besides – and for what? Evening-parties, dresses, and gloves, a fine house, and blue-and-silver curtains!

Yet a woman of the world would have said that this couple were quite right; that if they had married and lived afterwards with the careful prudence that alone would have been possible to a young man of Mr Henry's independent character, they must infallibly have gone down in society, have dropped out of their natural circle, to begin life – as their parents did, – as most middle-class parents have done, – narrowly and humbly. Though without much fear of positive starvation, they must have given up many luxuries, have had to learn and practise many domestic economies which probably never had come into the head of either the lady or the gentleman; and yet love might have taught them, as it teaches the most ignorant. They would undoubtedly have had to live, for the next few years at least, not for society at large, but for their own two selves and their immediate connexions.

And very likely Henry would have done it, for a young fellow in love will do mightily heroic things; some, especially hard-worked professional men, being weak enough to believe that a snug fire-side, where a cheerful-faced little wife has warmed his slippers and sits pouring out his tea – even if obliged to make sundry intermediate rushes up-stairs to quiet something which obstinately refuses to go to sleep – is preferable to a handsome solitary club-dinner, a wine-and-cigar party, or a ball, at which he revels till 3 A.M. in the smiles of a tarlatane[73] angel, whom he may ask to waltz *ad libitum,* but dare not for his life – or his honour, which is dearer – ask any other question, until he has got grey hairs and a thousand a-year. Dares not, for the worldly fathers, the still more worldly mothers, nay, the young daughters themselves, whose hearts, under their innocent muslins, are slowly hardening into those of premature women of the world, would stand aghast at the idea; 'Love in a cottage' – such an out-of-date, absurdly romantic, preposterous thing! Which it decidedly is – for people who bring to the said cottage the expectations and necessities of Hyde Park Gardens or Belgrave Square.

Yet, on the other hand, it is hardly possible to over-calculate the evils accruing to individuals and to society in general from this custom, gradually increasing, of late and ultra-prudent marriages. Parents bring up their daughters in luxurious homes, expecting and exacting that the home to which they transfer them should be of almost equal ease; forgetting how next to impossible it is for such a home to be offered by any young man of the present generation, who has to work his way like his father before him. Daughters, accustomed to a life of ease and laziness, are early taught to check every tendency towards 'a romantic attachment' – the insane folly of loving a man for what he is, rather than for what he has got; of being content to fight the worldly battle hand-in-hand – with a hand that is worth clasping, rather than settle down in comfortable sloth, protected and provided for in all external things. Young men ... But words fail to trace the lot of enforced bachelorhood, hardest when its hardship ceases to be consciously felt. An unmarried woman, if a good woman, can always make herself happy; find innumerable duties, interests, amusements; live a pure, cheerful, and useful life. So can some men – but very, very few.

Scarcely any sight is more pitiable than a young man who has

drifted on to past thirty, without home or near kindred; with
just income enough to keep him respectably in the position
which he supposes himself bound to maintain, and to supply
him with the various small luxuries – such as thirty guineas per
annum in cigars, &c. – which have become habitual to him. Like
his fellow-mortals, he is liable enough to the unlucky weakness
of falling in love, now and then; but he somehow manages to
extinguish the passion before it gets fairly alight; knowing he
can no more venture to ask a girl in his own sphere to marry
him, or be engaged to him, than he can coax the planet Venus
out of her golden west into the dirty, gloomy, two-pair-back
where his laundress cheats him, and his landlady abuses him:
whence, perhaps, he occasionally emerges gloriously, all studs
and white necktie – to assist at some young beauty's wedding,
where he feels in his heart he might once have been the happy
bridegroom – if from his silence she had not been driven to go
desperately and sell herself to the old fool opposite, and is fast
becoming, nay, is already become, a fool's clever mate – a mere
woman of the world. And he – what a noble ideal he has gained
of our sex, from this and other similar experiences! with what
truth of emotion will he repeat, as he gives the toast of 'The
bridesmaids,' the hackneyed quotation about pain and sorrow
wringing the brow, and smile half-adoringly, half-pathetically, at
the 'ministering angels' who titter around him. They, charming
innocents! will doubtless go home avouching 'What a delightful
person is Mr So-and-So. I wonder he never gets married.' While
Mr So-and-So also goes home, sardonically minded, to his dull
lodgings, his book and his cigar, or – he best knows where. And
in the slow process of inevitable deterioration, by forty he learns
to think matrimomy a decided humbug; and hugs himself in the
conclusion that a virtuous, high-minded, and disinterested
woman, if existing at all, exists as a mere *lusus naturae*[74] – not to
be met with by mortal man now-a-days. Relieving his feelings
with a grunt – half-sigh, half-sneer – he dresses and goes to the
opera – or the *ballet,* at all events – or settles himself on the sofa
to a French novel, and ends by firmly believing us women to be
– what we are painted there![75]

Good God! – the exclamation is too solemn to be profane – if this state of things be true, and it is true, and I have barely touched the outer surface of its unfathomably horrible truth – what will the next generation come to? What will they be – those unborn millions who are to grow up into our men and our women? The possible result, even in a practical, to say nothing of a moral light, is awful to think upon.

Can it not be averted? Can we not – since, while the power of the world is with men, the influence lies with women – can we not bring up our girls more usefully and less showily – less dependent on luxury and wealth? Can we not teach them from babyhood that to labour is a higher thing than merely to enjoy; that even enjoyment itself is never so sweet as when it has been earned? Can we not put into their minds, whatever be their station, principles of truth, simplicity of taste, helpfulness, hatred of waste; and, these being firmly rooted, trust to their blossoming up in whatever destiny the young maiden may be called to? We should not then have to witness the terrors that beset dying beds when a family of girls will be left unprovided for; nor the angry shame when some thoughtless young pair commit matrimony, and rush ignorantly into debt, poverty, and disgrace, from which – *facilis descensus Averni*[76] – all the efforts of too-late compassionate relatives can never altogether raise them.

Nevertheless – and I risk this declaration without fear of its causing a general rush to the register-offices, or the publication, at every out-of-the-way church in the three kingdoms, of surreptitious bans between all the under-aged simpletons who choose to fly in the face of Providence by marrying upon

'Nothing a week, and that uncertain – very!'

– nevertheless, taking life as a whole, believing that it consists not in what we have, but in our power of enjoying the same; that there are in it things nobler and dearer than ease, plenty, or freedom from care – nay, even than existence itself; surely it is not Quixotism, but common-sense and Christianity, to protest that love is better than outside show, labour than indolence, virtue than mere respectability. Truly, in this present day –

putting aside those cases where duty and justice have claims higher than either love or happiness – there is many an instance of cowardly selfishness, weakness and falsehood, committed by young people of both sexes, under the names of prudence, honourable feeling, or obedience to parents; there is many an act, petted under the name of a virtue, which is a much blacker crime before God, and of far more fatal result to society at large, than the worst of these so-called improvident marriages.

Strange how much people will sacrifice – ay, even women will – to this Moloch of the world! It reminds me of an infantile worship, which a certain friend of mine confessed to have instituted, and officiated as high-priestess of, at the age of three-and-a-half. She used to collect from her own store, and levy from unwilling co-idolaters, all sorts of childish dainties, together with turnips, apple-parings, &c., and lay them in a remote corner of the farmyard, as an offering to a mysterious invisible being called Dor, who came in the night and feasted thereon – at least, the sacrifice was always gone the next morning. A pious relative, finding her out, stopped with great horror the proceedings of this earnest little heathen; but for years after, nothing would have persuaded my deluded young friend that the awful Dor was, in fact, only a chance-wind, a hen and her chickens, or a hungry old sow. So, often, it is not till half a life-time has been expended on this thankless service, that we come to find out – if we ever do find out – that the invisible Daimon who swallows up the best of our good things – time, ease, wealth, money, comfort, peace, and well if no more than these – is, after all, a combination of the merest accidents, or perhaps one individual brute beast.

Yet, there is a fascination, hard to account for, but idle to gainsay, in this miserable Eleusinia,[77] this blind worship of a self-invented god. Who does not know the story of the wise old nanny-goat, which painted to her dear daughter that horrible wild beast, the leopard, giving him every conceivable ugliness, a ghastly wide mouth and fiery eyes; so that when the fair Miss Kid saw a beautiful animal with shiny spotted skin and graceful motions, sporting innocently after his own tail in the forest shadow, how could she ever identify him with the portrait her mother drew? What could she do, but approach, and wonder, and admire, then fall right into his clutches, and have her poor little bones crunched between his dazzling jaws? Would not many a mother do well in laying to heart this old fable?

Yes, the world is doubtless very pleasant in its way. Delicious, almost to deliriousness, is a young girl's first step into the enchanted circle called 'good society;' to feel herself in her best attire and best looks, charming and charmed, for the behoof of the entire company; or, as it usually soon comes to, poor little fool! for the sake of one particular person therein. And for a long time after, though the first magic of the cup is gone, though it intoxicates rather than exhilarates, it is by no means the poison-cup that frigid moralists would make us believe. It has a little of the narcotic; and the young woman begins to take it as such, feeling rather ashamed of herself for so doing; and, like all opiates, it leaves a slight bitterness in the mouth. But what of that?

Now and then our young lady wonders, during 'slow' evening-parties and prosy morning-calls, whether her whistle is worth quite as much as she has daily to pay for it – whether the agreeable circles in which she moves are not, if they would but avow it, for the chief part of the time that they spend together, a very great bore to themselves and to one another – whether, after all, one handful of the salt of common-sense would not purify society as well as a bushel of idle ceremonies, and one ounce of kind feeling, tact, and thoughtfulness for others, be worth a cart-load of ponderous etiquette. And perhaps she sets to work on this grand, new, and original system of hers, which every young heart thinks it is the very first to discover and practise –

> 'Like one who tries in little boat
> To tug to him the ship afloat.'[78]

Most likely she fails – fails totally, angrily, miserably; only gets herself misjudged and laughed at, and resolves no more to remodel the world – which may be a wise determination; or settles into stolid indifference, and believes that, after all, right and wrong do not much matter; it will all be the same a hundred years hence: so drops slowly into the current, and is drifted with the rest, along, along – whither?

Or else, having just penetration enough left to distinguish a truth from its *eidolon,* its *doppel-gänger,*[79] which almost always walks alongside of it, and mimics it, in this strange world of ours, she gradually perceives the sense, beauty, and fitness which may be traced under the most exaggerated forms and customs. She sees also that these

> 'Nice customs courtesy to great kings,'[80]

as saith Henry of England when he kisses his French Katherine; and that any woman is unworthy of the just empery of her sex when she gives up to either fashion or ceremony her common-sense, comfort, or good taste: when, for instance, she condescends to make of herself a silk-draped walking butter-tub, or a female

> 'Whose head
> Does grow beneath her shoulders;'[81]

when she suffers herself to waste hour after hour, day after day, year after year, in the company of frivolous folk, whom she can do no good to, and receive no good from, and whom, she is fully aware, if she dropped out of their smiling circle to-morrow, to die in a ditch, in the hospital close by, or were even to create a temporary sensation by jumping from Waterloo Bridge, would merely remark: 'Dear me, how shocking! Who would have thought it? – Well, as I was saying . . .'

No doubt, this conviction, when it fairly breaks upon her, strikes her poor weakened eyes with a painful glare, which throws into harder outline than is natural the cruel angles of this would-be palace – that for a time seems to her little better than a grim dungeon, from which she only seeks to escape –

> 'Anywhere, anywhere, out of the world.'[82]

This is the crisis of her life. She either ends by a tacit,

hopeless acquiescence in what she both despises and disbelieves, or herself sinking to their level, accepts them as realities after all. Or else, by a desperate struggle, she creeps from chaos into order, from darkness into clear day, learns slowly and temperately to distinguish things, and people, in their true colours and natural forms; taking them just as they are, no better and no worse, and trying to make the best of them: to use the world, in short, as its Maker doth – after the example of Him who himself said that the tares and wheat *must* 'grow together until the harvest.'[83]

Such an one – and I ask those of my sex who read this page, if I have not painted her according to nature? if many weary, dissatisfied hearts, beating heavily with pulses they do not understand, will not confess, that in some poor way I have spoken out their already half-recognised feelings? – such an one will escape that end to which all must come who fix their pleasures alone in this life: the woman of fashion, after the pattern of *Mrs Skewton* and *Lady Kew:*[84] the woman of 'mind,' fluttering her faded plumage in the face of a new generation, which recognises her not, or recognises only to make game of her: or the ordinary woman of the world.

This latter – in her day of decline, who has not encountered her some time or another? Dependent on the pity of those who remember what she was, or might have been; invited out, because there is a certain agreeableness about her still, and because, 'poor thing, she likes a little society;' yet made irritable by a perpetual need of excitement, which drives her to prefer anybody's company to her own. Painfully jealous over every fragment of the affection which she herself has never disinterestedly shown to anybody, but has spread it, like school bread and butter, over so wide a surface, that tastelessness is the natural consequence of its extreme tenuity.

Friendships she has none: she never either desired or deserved them. In all her long career, she has never been able to take root in any human heart. As for the Heart Divine, the chances are that she has never once sought it, or believed in it. She has believed in a cushioned pew, in a velvet prayer-book with a gilt cross on the back; in certain religious thoughts, words, and deeds, proper for Sundays and holidays, and possibly suitable for that 'convenient season' when she means to 'make her peace with Heaven,' as the judge tells the criminal who is 'turned off' to seek in another existence that hope which man denies. But for all else her soul – contradistinguished from her intellect, which may be vivid and brilliant still – is a blank, a darkness, a death in life.

And yet the woman of the world will one day have to *die*! We can but leave her to Infinite Mercy then.

CHAPTER X

HAPPY AND UNHAPPY WOMEN

I give fair warning that this is likely to be a 'sentimental' chapter. Those who object to the same, and complain that these 'Thoughts' are 'not practical,' had better pass it over at once; since it treats of things essentially unpractical, impossible to be weighed and measured, handled and analysed, yet as real in themselves as the air we breathe and the sunshine we delight in – things wholly intangible, yet the very essence and necessity of our lives.

Happiness! Can any human being undertake to define it for another? Various last-century poets have indulged in 'Odes' to it, and good Mrs Barbauld wrote a 'Search' after it – a most correct, elegantly phrased, and genteel little drama, which, the *dramatis personæ* being all females, and not a bit of love in the whole, is, I believe, still acted in old-fashioned boarding-schools, with great *éclat*.[85] The plot, if I remember right, consists of an elderly lady's leading four or five younger ones on the immemorial search, through a good many very long speeches; but whether they ever found happiness, or what it was like when found, I really have not the least recollection.

Let us hope that excellent Mrs Barbauld is one of the very few who dare venture upon even the primary question – What is Happiness? Perhaps, poor dear woman! she is better able to answer it now.

I fear, the inevitable conclusion we must all come to is, that in this world happiness is quite indefinable. We can no more grasp it than we can grasp the sun in the sky or the moon in the water. We can feel it interpenetrating our whole being with

warmth and strength; we can see it in a pale reflection shining
elsewhere; or in its total absence, we, walking in darkness, learn
to appreciate what it is by what it is not. But I doubt whether
any woman ever craved for it, philosophised over it, or –
pardon, shade of Barbauld! – commenced the systematic search
after it, and ever attained her end. For happiness is not an end
– it is only a means, an adjunct, a consequence. The Omnipotent
Himself could never be supposed by any, save those who out of
their own human selfishness construct the attributes of Divinity,
to be absorbed throughout eternity in the contemplation of His
own ineffable bliss, were it not identical with His ineffable
goodness and love.

Therefore, whosoever starts with 'to be happy' as the *summum
bonum*[86] of existence, will assuredly find out she has made as
great a mistake as when in her babyhood she cried, as most of
us do, for the moon, which we cannot get for all our crying.
And yet it is a very good moon, notwithstanding: a real moon,
too, who will help us to many a poetical dream, light us in many
a lovers' walk, till she shine over the grass of our graves upon a
new generation ready to follow upon the immemorial quest.
Which, like the quest of the Sangreal, is only possible to pure
hearts, although the very purest can never fully attain it, except,
like Sir Galahad, through the gates of the Holy City – the New
Jerusalem.[87]

Happy and unhappy women – the adjectives being applied
less with reference to circumstances than character, which is the
only mode of judgment possible – to judge them and discourse
of them is a very difficult matter at best. Yet I am afraid it
cannot be doubted that there is a large average of unhappiness
existent among women: not merely unhappiness of circumstances, but unhappiness of soul – a state of being often as
unaccountable as it is irrational, finding vent in those innumerable faults of temper and disposition which arise from no
inherent vice, but merely because the individual is not happy.

Possibly, women more than men are liable to this dreary
mental eclipse – neither daylight nor darkness. A man will go
poetically wretched or morbidly misanthropic, or any great

misfortune will overthrow him entirely, drive him to insanity, lure him to slip out of life through the terrible by-road of suicide; but he rarely drags on existence from year to year, with 'nerves,' 'low spirits,' and the various maladies of mind and temper that make many women a torment to themselves, and a burden to all connected with them.

Why is this? and is it inevitable? Any one who could in the smallest degree answer this question, would be doing something to the lessening of a great evil – greater than many other evils which, being social and practical, show more largely on the aggregate census of female woe.

Most assuredly, however unpoetical may be such a view of the matter, the origin of a great deal of unhappiness is physical disease; or rather, the loss of that healthy condition of body, which in the present state of civilisation, so far removed from a state of nature, can only be kept up in any individual by the knowledge and practice of the ordinary laws of hygiene – generally the very last knowledge that women seem to have. The daily necessities of water, fresh air, proper clothing, food, and sleep, with the due regulation of each of these, without which no human being can expect to live healthily or happily, are matters in which the only excuse for lamentable neglect is still more lamentable ignorance.

An ignorance the worse, because it is generally quite unac-knowledged. If you tell a young girl that water, the colder the better, is essential to every pore of her delicate skin every morning; that moderate out-door exercise, and regularity in eating, sleeping, employment, and amusement, are to her a daily necessity; that she should make it a part of her education to acquire a certain amount of current information on sanitary science, and especially on the laws of her own being, physical and mental: tell her this, and the chances are she will stare at you uncomprehendingly, or be shocked, as if you were saying to her something 'improper,' or answer flippantly: 'Oh, yes; I know all that.'

But of what use is the knowledge? – when she lies in bed till ten o' the clock, and sits up till any hour the next morning; eats all manner of food at all manner of irregular intervals; is horrified at leaving her bed-room window two inches open, or at being caught in a slight shower; yet will cower all day over the fire in a high woollen dress, and put on a low muslin one in the evening. When she wears all winter thin boots, gossamer stockings, a gown open at the chest and arms, and a loose mantle that every wind blows under, yet wonders that she always has a cold! – and weighs herself down in summer-time with four petticoats heaped one over the other, yet is quite astonished that she gets hot and tired so soon! Truly any sensible, old-fashioned body, who knows how much the health, happiness, and general well-being of this generation – and, alas! not this generation alone – depend upon these charming, lovable, fascinating young fools, cannot fail to be 'aggravated' by them every day.

However humiliating the fact may be to those poetical theorists who, in spite of all the laws of nature, wish to make the soul entirely independent of the body – forgetting, that if so, its temporary probation in the body at all, would have been quite unnecessary – I repeat, there can be no really sanitary state of mind without a similar condition of body; and that one of the first requisites of happiness is *good health*. But as this is not meant to be an essay on domestic hygiene, I had better here leave the subject.

Its corresponding phase opens a gate of misery so wide that one almost shrinks from entering it. Infinite, past human counting or judging, are the causes of mental unhappiness. Many of them spring from a real foundation, of sorrows varied beyond all measuring or reasoning upon: of these, I do not attempt to speak, for words would be idle and presumptuous; I only speak of that frame of mind – sometimes left behind by a great trouble, sometimes arising from troubles purely imaginary – which is called 'an unhappy disposition.'

Its root of pain is manifold; but, with women, undoubtedly can be oftenest traced to something connected with the affections: not merely the passion called *par excellence* love, but the entire range of personal sympathies and attachments, out of which we draw the sweetness and bitterness of the best part of our lives. If otherwise – if, as the phrase goes, an individual happens to have 'more head than heart,' she may be a very clever, agreeable personage, but she is not properly *a woman* – not the creature who, with all her imperfections, is nearer to heaven than man, in one particular – she 'loves much.' And loving is so frequently, nay, inevitably, identical with suffering, either with, or for, or from, the object beloved, that we need not go further to find the cause of the many anxious, soured faces, and irritable tempers, that we meet with among women.

Charity cannot too deeply or too frequently call to mind how very difficult it is to be good, or amiable, or even commonly agreeable, when one is inwardly miserable. This fact is not enough recognised by those very worthy people who take such a world of pains to make other people virtuous, and so very little to make them happy. They sow good seed, are everlastingly weeding and watering, give it every care and advantage under the sun – except sunshine – and then they wonder that it does not flower!

One may see many a young woman who has, outwardly speaking, 'everything she can possibly want,' absolutely withering in the atmosphere of a loveless home, exposed to those small ill-humours by which people mean no harm – only *do* it; chilled by reserve, wounded by neglect, or worried by anxiety over some thoughtless one, who might so easily have spared her it all; safe from either misfortune or ill-treatment, yet harassed daily by petty pains and unconscious cruelties, which a stranger might laugh at; and she laughs herself, when she counts them up, they are so very small – yet they are there.

'I can bear anything,' said to me a woman, no longer very young or very fascinating, or particularly clever, who had gone through seas of sorrow, yet whose blue eyes still kept the dewiness and cheerfulness of their youth; 'I can bear anything, except unkindness.'

She was right. There are numberless cases where gentle creatures, who would have endured bravely any amount of real trouble, have their lives frozen up by those small unkindnesses

which copy-books avouch to be 'a great offence;' where an
avalanche of worldly benefits, an act of undoubted generosity,
or the most conscientious administering of a friendly rebuke,
has had its good effects wholly neutralised by the manner in
which it was done. It is vain to preach to people unless you also
love them – Christianly love them; it is not the smallest use to
try to make people good, unless you try at the same time – and
they feel that you are trying – to make them happy. And you
rarely can make another happy, unless you are happy yourself.

Naming the affections as the chief source of unhappiness
among our sex, it would be wrong to pass over one phase of
them, which must nevertheless be touched tenderly and delicately, as one that women instinctively hide out of sight and
comment – I mean what is usually termed 'a disappointment.'
Alas! – as if there were no disappointments but those of love!
and yet, until men and women are made differently from what
God made them, it must always be, from its very secretness and
inwardness, the sharpest of all pangs, save that of conscience.

A lost love. Deny it who will, ridicule it, treat it as mere
imagination and sentiment, the thing is and will be; and women
do suffer therefrom, in all its infinite varieties: loss by death, by
faithlessness or unworthiness, and by mistaken or unrequited
affection. Of these, the second is beyond all question the worst.
There is in death a consecration which lulls the sharpest personal anguish into comparative calm; and in time there comes,
to all pure and religious natures, that sense of total possession of
the objects beloved, which death alone gives – that faith, which
is content to see them safe landed out of the troubles of this
changeful life, into the life everlasting. And an attachment which
has always been on one side only, has a certain incompleteness
which prevents its ever knowing the full agony of having and
losing, while at the same time it preserves to the last a dreamy
sanctity which sweetens half its pain. But to have loved and lost,
either by that total disenchantment which leaves compassion as
the sole substitute for love which can exist no more, or by the
slow torment which is obliged to let go day by day all that
constitutes the diviner part of love – namely, reverence, belief,

and trust, yet clings desperately to the only thing left it, a long-suffering apologetic tenderness – this lot is probably the hardest any woman can have to bear.

> 'What is good for a bootless bene? –
> And she made answer, Endless sorrow.'[88]

No. There is no sorrow under heaven which is, or ought to be, endless. To believe or to make it so, is an insult to Heaven itself. Each of us must have known more than one instance when a saintly or heroic life has been developed from what at first seemed a stroke like death itself; a life full of the calmest and truest happiness – because it has bent itself to the Divine will, and learned the best of all lessons, to endure. But how that lesson is learned, through what bitter teaching, hard to be understood or obeyed, till the hand of the Great Teacher is recognised clearly through it all, is a subject too sacred to be entered upon here.

It is a curious truth – and yet a truth forced upon us by daily observation – that it is *not* the women who have suffered most who are the unhappy women. A state of permanent unhappiness – not the morbid, half-cherished melancholy of youth, which generally wears off with wiser years, but that settled, incurable discontent and dissatisfaction with all things and all people, which we see in some women, is, with very rare exceptions, at once the index and the exponent of a thoroughly selfish character. Nor can it be too early impressed upon every girl that this condition of mental *mal-aise,* whatever be its origin, is neither a poetical nor a beautiful thing, but a mere disease, and as such ought to be combated and medicined with all remedies in her power, practical, corporeal, and spiritual. For though it is folly to suppose that happiness is a matter of volition, and that we can make ourselves content and cheerful whenever we choose – a theory that many poor hypochondriacs are taunted with till they are nigh driven mad – yet, on the other hand, no sane mind is ever left without the power of self-discipline and self-control, in a measure, which measure increases in proportion as it is exercised.

Let any sufferer be once convinced that she has this power – that it is possible by careful watch, or, better, by substitution of subjects and occupations, to abstract her mind from dwelling on some predominant idea, which otherwise runs in and out of the chambers of the brain like a haunting devil, at last growing into the monomania which, philosophy says, every human being is affected with, on some one particular point – only, happily, he does not know it; only let her try if she has not, with regard to her mental constitution, the same faculty which would prevent her from dancing with a sprained ankle, or imagining that there is an earthquake because her own head is spinning with fever, and she will have at least taken the first steps towards cure. As many a man sits wearying his soul out by trying to remedy some grand flaw in the plan of society, or the problem of the universe, when perhaps the chief thing wrong is his own liver, or overtasked brain; so many a woman will pine away to the brink of the grave with an imaginary broken heart, or sour to the very essence of vinegar on account of everybody's supposed ill-usage of her, when it is her own restless, dissatisfied, selfish heart, which makes her at war with everybody.

Would that women – and men, too, but that their busier and more active lives save most of them from it – could be taught from their childhood to recognise as an evil spirit this spirit of causeless melancholy – this demon which dwells among the tombs, and yet, which first shows itself in such a charming and picturesque form, that we hug it to our innocent breasts, and never suspect that it may enter in and dwell there till we are actually 'possessed;' cease almost to be accountable beings, and are fitter for a lunatic asylum than for the home-circle, which, be it ever so bright and happy, has always, from the inevitable misfortunes of life, only too much need of sunshine rather than shadow, or permanent gloom.

Oh, if such women did but know what comfort there is in a cheerful spirit! how the heart leaps up to meet a sunshiny face, a merry tongue, an even temper, and a heart which either naturally, or, what is better, from conscientious principle, has learned to take all things on their bright side, believing that the

Giver of life being all-perfect Love, the best offering we can make to Him is to enjoy to the full what He sends of good, and bear what He allows of evil! – like a child who, when once it thoroughly believes in its father, believes in all his dealings with it, whether it understands them or not.

And here, if the subject were not too solemn to be more than touched upon, – yet no one dare avoid it who believes that there are no such distinctions as 'secular' and 'religious,' but that the whole earth with all therein is, not only on Sundays, but all days, continually 'the LORD's' – I will put it to most people's experience, which is better than a hundred homilies, whether, though they may have known sincere Christians who, from various causes, were not altogether happy, they ever knew one *happy* person, man or woman, who, whatever his or her form of creed might be, was not in heart, and speech, and daily life, emphatically a follower of Christ – a Christian?

Among the many secondary influences which can be employed either by or upon a naturally anxious or morbid temperament, there is none so ready to hand, or so wholesome, as that one incessantly referred to in the course of these pages, – constant employment. A very large number of women, particularly young women, are by nature constituted so exceedingly restless of mind, or with such a strong physical tendency to nervous depression, that they can by no possibility keep themselves in a state of even tolerable cheerfulness, except by being continually occupied. At what, matters little; even apparently useless work is far better for them than no work at all. To such I cannot too strongly recommend the case of

> 'Honest John Tomkins, the hedger and ditcher,
> Who, though he was poor, didn't want to be richer,'

but always managed to keep in a state of sublime content and superabundant gaiety; and how?

> 'He always had something or other to do,
> If not for himself – for his neighbour.'

And that work for our neighbour is perhaps the most useful

and satisfactory of the two, because it takes us out of ourselves; which, to a person who has not a happy self to rest in, is one good thing achieved: this, quite apart from the abstract question of benevolence, or the notion of keeping a balance-sheet with Heaven for work done to our fellow-creatures – certainly a very fruitless recipe for happiness.

The sufferer, on waking in the morning – that cruel moment when any incurable pain wakes up too, sharply, so sharply! and the burden of a monotonous life falls down upon us, or rises like a dead blank wall before us, making us turn round on the pillow longing for another night, instead of an insupportable day – should rouse herself with the thought: 'Now, what have I got to do to-day?' (Mark, not to enjoy or to suffer, only *to do*.) She should never lie down at night without counting up, with a resolute, uncompromising, unexcusing veracity, 'How much have I done to-day?' 'I can't be happy,' she may ponder wearily; ''tis useless trying – so we'll not think about it: but how much have I done this day? how much can I do to-morrow?' And if she has strength steadily to fulfil this manner of life, it will be strange if, some day, the faint, involuntary thrill that we call 'feeling happy' – something like that with which we stop to see a daisy at our feet in January – does not come and startle into vague, mysterious hope, the poor wondering heart.

Another element of happiness, incalculable in its influence over those of sensitive and delicate physical organisation, is Order. Any one who has just quitted a disorderly household, where the rooms are untidy and 'littery,' where meals take place at any hour and in any fashion, where there is a general atmosphere of noise, confusion, and irregularity; of doing things at all times and seasons, or not doing anything in particular all day over; who, emerging from this, drops into a quiet, busy, regular family, where each has an appointed task, and does it; where the day moves on smoothly, subdivided by proper seasons of labour, leisure, food, and sleep – oh, what a Paradise it seems! How the restless or anxious spirit nestles down in it, and, almost without volition, falls into its cheerful round, recovering tone, and calm, and strength.

'Order is Heaven's first law,'[89]

and a mind without order can by no possibility be either a healthy or a happy mind. Therefore, beyond all sentimental sympathy, or contemptuous blame, should be impressed upon all women inclined to melancholy, or weighed down with any irremediable, grief, this simple advice – to make their daily round of life as harmoniously methodical as they possibly can; leaving no odd hours, scarcely an odd ten minutes, to be idle and dreary in; and by means of orderly-arranged, light, airy rooms, neat dress, and every pleasant external influence that is attainable, to leave untried none of these secondary means which are in the power of every one of us, for our own benefit or that of others, and the importance of which we never know until we have proved them.

There is another maxim – easy to give, and hard to practise –. Accustom yourself always to look at the bright side of things, and never make a fuss about trifles. It is pitiful to see what mere nothings some women will worry and fret over – lamenting as much over an ill-made gown as others do over a lost fortune; how some people we can always depend upon for making the best, instead of the worst, of whatever happens, thus greatly lessening our anxieties for themselves in their troubles; and, oh! how infinitely comforting when we bring to them any of our own. For we all of us have – wretched, indeed, if we have not! – some friends, or friend, to whom we instinctively carry every one of our griefs or vexations, assured that, if any one can help us, they can and will, while with others we as instinctively 'keep ourselves to ourselves,' whether sorrowing or rejoicing; and many more there are whom we should never dream of burdening with our cares at all, any more than we would think of putting a butterfly in harness.

The disposition which can bear trouble; which, while passing over the lesser annoyances of life, as unworthy to be measured in life's whole sum, can yet meet real affliction steadily, struggle with it while resistance is possible; conquered, sit down patiently, to let the storms sweep over; and on their passing, if they pass, rise up, and go on its way, looking up to that region of blue calm which is never long invisible to the pure of heart – this is the blessedest possession that any woman can have. Better than a house full of silver and gold, better than beauty, or high fortunes, or prosperous and satisfied love.

While, on the other hand, of all characters not radically bad, there is none more useless to herself and everybody else, who inflicts more pain, anxiety, and gloom on those around her, than the one who is often deprecatingly or apologetically described as being 'of an unhappy temperament.' You may know her at once by her dull or vinegar aspect, her fidgety ways, her proneness to take the hard or ill-natured view of things and people. Possibly she is unmarried, and her mocking acquaintance insult woman-hood by setting down that as the cause of her disagreeableness. Most wicked libel! There never was an unhappy old maid yet who would not have been equally unhappy as a wife – and more guilty, for she would have made two people miserable instead of one. It needs only to count up all the unhappy women one knows – women whom one would not change lots with for the riches of the Queen of Sheba – to see that most of them are those whom fate has apparently loaded with benefits, love, home, ease, luxury, leisure; and denied only the vague fine something, as indescribable as it is unattainable, – the capacity to enjoy them all.

Unfortunate ones! You see by their countenances that they never know what it is to enjoy. That thrill of thankful gladness, oftenest caused by little things – a lovely bit of nature, a holiday after long toil, a sudden piece of good news, an unexpected face, or a letter that warms one's inmost heart – to them is altogether incomprehensible. To hear one of them in her rampant phase, you would suppose the whole machinery of the universe, down even to the weather, was in league against her small individual-ity; that everything everybody did, or said, or thought was with one sole purpose – her personal injury. And when she sinks to the melancholy mood, though your heart may bleed for her, aware how horribly real are her self-created sufferings, still your tenderness sits uneasily, more as a duty than a pleasure; and you often feel, and are shocked at feeling, that her presence acts upon you like the proverbial wet-blanket, and her absence gives you an involuntary sense of relief.

For, though we may pity the unhappy ever so lovingly and sincerely, and strive with all our power to lift them out of their grief, – when they hug it, and refuse to be lifted out of it, patience sometimes fails. Human life is so full of pain, that once past the youthful delusion that a sad countenance is interesting, and an incurable woe the most delightful thing possible, the mind instinctively turns where it can get rest, and cheer, and sunshine. And the friend who can bring to it the largest portion of these is, of a natural necessity, the most useful, the most welcome, and the most dear.

The 'happy woman' – in this our world, which is apparently meant to be the road to perfection, never its goal – you will find too few specimens to be ever likely to mistake her. But you will recognise her presence the moment she crosses your path. Not by her extreme liveliness – lively people are rarely either happy or able to diffuse happiness; but by a sense of brightness and cheerfulness that enters with her – as an evening sunbeam across your parlour wall. Like the fairy Order in the nursery tale, she takes up the tangled threads of your mind, and reduces them to regularity, till you distinguish a clear pattern through the ugly maze. She may be neither handsome, nor clever, nor entertaining, yet somehow she makes you feel 'comfortable,' because she is so comfortable herself. She shames you out of your complainings, for she makes none. Yet, mayhap, since it is the divine law that we should all, like our Master, be 'made perfect through suffering,'[90] you are fully aware that she has had far more sorrow than ever you had; that her daily path, had you to tread it, would be to you as gloomy and full of pitfalls as to her it is safe and bright. She may have even less than the medium lot of earthly blessings, yet all she has she enjoys to the full; and it is so pleasant to see any one enjoy! For her sorrows, she neither hypocritically denies, nor proudly smothers them – she simply bears them; therefore they come to her, as sorrows were meant to come, naturally and wholesomely, and passing over, leave her full of compassion for all who may have to endure the same.

Thus, whatever her fate may be, married or single, rich or poor, in health or sickness – though a cheerful spirit has twice as much chance of health as a melancholy one – she will be all her days a living justification of the ways of Providence, Who makes the light as well as the darkness, nay, makes the light out of the darkness. For not only in the creation of a world, but in that which is equally marvellous, the birth and development of every human soul, there is a divine verity symbolised by the one line, –

'And GOD said, Let there be light! and *there was light.*'[91]

CHAPTER XI

LOST WOMEN

I enter on this subject with a hesitation strong enough to have prevented my entering on it at all, did I not believe that to write for or concerning women, and avoid entirely that deplorable phase of womanhood which, in country cottages as in city streets, in books, newspapers, and daily talk, meets us so continually that no young girl can long be kept ignorant of it, is to give a one-sided and garbled view of life, which, however pretty and pleasant, would be false, and being false, useless. We have not to construct human nature afresh, but to take it as we find it, and make the best of it: we have no right, not even the most sensitive of us women, mercifully constituted with less temptation to evil than men, to treat as impure what God has not made impure, or to shrink with sanctimonious ultra-delicacy from the barest mention of things which, though happy circumstances of temperament or education have shielded us from ever being touched or harmed thereby, we must know to exist. If we do not know it, our ignorance – quite a different thing from innocence – is at once both helpless and dangerous: narrows our judgment, exposes us to a thousand painful mistakes, and greatly limits our power of usefulness in the world.

On the other hand, a woman who is for ever paddling needlessly in the filthy puddles of human nature, just as a child delights in walking up a dirty gutter when there is a clean pavement alongside, deserves, like the child, whatever mud she gets. And there is even a worse kind of woman still, only too common among respectable matrons, talkative old maids, and even worldly, fascinating young ones, who is ready to rake up every scandalous tale, and titter over every vile *double entendre,* who degrades the most solemn mysteries of holy Nature into vehicles for disgraceful jokes, whose mind, instead of being a decent dwelling-house, is a perfect Augean stable of uncleanness.[92] Such a one cannot be too fiercely reprobated, too utterly despised. However intact her reputation, she is as great a slur upon womanhood, as great a bane to all true modesty, as the most unchaste Messalina who ever disgraced her sex.[93]

I beg to warn these foul grubbers in the dark places of the earth – not for purposes of cleansing, but merely because it amuses them – that they will not find anything entertaining in this article. They will only find one woman's indignant protest against a tone of thought and conversation which, as their consciences will tell them, many other women think it no shame to pursue when among their own sex; and which, did the other sex know it, would be as harmful, as fatal, as any open vice, by making men disbelieve in virtue – disbelieve in *us.* For its vileness in the sight of Heaven – truly, if we think of that, many a well-reputed British lady is as much a 'lost' woman as any poor, seduced creature whose child is born in a workhouse, or strangled at a ditch-side.

It is to the latter class, who have fallen out of the ranks of honest women, without sinking to a lower depth still, that I chiefly refer: because with them, those for whom this book is meant – namely, the ordinary middle ranks of unmarried females – are more likely to have to do. That other class, awful in its extent and universality, of women who make a trade of sin, whom philanthropists and political economists are for ever discussing, and can come to no conclusion about – I leave to the wise and generous of both sexes who devote their lives to the subject; to the examination and amelioration of a fact so terrible that, were it not a fact, one would hardly be justified in alluding to it here. Wretched ones! whom even to think of turns any woman's heart cold, with shame for her own sex, and horror at the other: outcasts to whom happiness and love are things unknown, God and heaven mere words to swear with, and to whom this earth must be a daily hell:

'Non ragionam di lor, ma guarda, e passa.'[94]

But the others cross our path continually. No one can have taken any interest in the working-classes without being aware how frightfully common among them is what they term 'a misfortune' – how few young women come to the marriage-altar at all, or come there just a week or two before maternity; or having already had several children, often only half brothers and sisters, whom no ceremony has ever legalised. Whatever be the causes of this – and I merely skim over the surface of a state of things which the *Times* and Sanitary Commissioners have plumbed to sickening depths – it undoubtedly exists;[95] and no single woman who takes any thought of what is going on around her, no mistress or mother who requires constantly servants for her house, and nurse-maids for her children, can or dare blind herself to the fact. It is easy for tenderly reared young ladies, who study human passions through Miss Austen or Miss Edgeworth, or the *Loves of the Angels*,[96] to say: 'How shocking! Oh, it can't be true!' but it is true; and they will not live many more years without finding it to be true. Better face truth at once, in all its bareness, than be swaddled up for ever in the folds of a silken falsehood.

Another fact, stranger still to account for, is, that the women who thus fall are by no means the worst of their station. I have heard it affirmed by more than one lady – by one in particular, whose experience is as large as her benevolence – that many of them are of the very best; refined, intelligent, truthful, and affectionate.

'I don't know how it is,' she would say – 'whether their very superiority makes them dissatisfied with their own rank – such brutes or clowns as labouring men often are! – so that they fall easier victims to the rank above them; or whether, though this theory will shock many people, other virtues can exist and flourish, entirely distinct from, and after the loss of, that which we are accustomed to believe the indispensable prime virtue of our sex – chastity. I cannot explain it; I can only say that it is so: that some of my most promising village-girls have been the first

to come to harm; and some of the best and most faithful
servants I ever had, have been girls who have fallen into shame,
and who, had I not gone to the rescue, and put them on the way
to do well, would infallibly have become "lost" women.'

There, perhaps, is one clue caught. Had she not 'come to the
rescue.' Rescue, then, is possible; and they were capable of being
rescued.

I read lately an essay, and from a pure and good woman's
pen, too, arguing, what licentious materialists are now-a-days
unblushingly asserting, that chastity is *not* indispensable in our
sex; that the old chivalrous boast of families – 'all their men
were brave, and all their women virtuous' – was, to say the
least, a mistake, which led people into worse ills than it remedied, by causing an extravagant terror at the loss of these good
qualities, and a corresponding indifference to evil ones much
more important.

While widely differing from this writer – for God forbid that
our Englishwomen should ever come to regard with less horror
than now the loss of personal chastity! – I think it cannot be
doubted that even this loss does not indicate total corruption or
entail permanent degradation; that after it, and in spite of it,
many estimable and womanly qualities may be found existing,
not only in our picturesque *Nell Gwynnes* and *Peg Woffingtons,*[97]
but our poor every-day sinners: the servant obliged to be
dismissed without a character and with a baby; the sempstress
quitting starvation for elegant infamy; the illiterate village lass,
who thinks it so grand to be made a lady of – so much better to
be a rich man's mistress than a working-man's ill-used wife, or
rather slave.

Till we allow that no one sin, not even this sin, necessarily
corrupts the entire character, we shall scarcely be able to judge
it with that fairness which gives hope of our remedying it, or
trying to lessen in ever so minute a degree, by our individual
dealing with any individual case that comes in our way, the
enormous aggregate of misery that it entails. This it behoves us
to do, even on selfish grounds, for it touches us closer than
many of us are aware – ay, in our hearths and homes – in the

sons and brothers that we have to send out to struggle in a world of which we at the fireside know absolutely nothing; if we marry, in the fathers we give to our innocent children, the servants we trust their infancy to, and the influences to which we are obliged to expose them daily and hourly, unless we were to bring them up in a sort of domestic Happy Valley, which their first effort would be to get out of as fast as ever they could. And supposing we are saved from all this; that our position is one peculiarly exempt from evil; that if pollution in any form comes nigh us, we just sweep it hastily and noiselessly away from our doors, and think we are all right and safe. Alas! we forget that a refuse-heap outside her gate may breed a plague even in a queen's palace.

One word, before continuing this subject. Many of us will not investigate it because they are afraid: afraid, not so much of being, as of being thought to be, especially by the other sex, incorrect, indelicate, unfeminine; of being supposed to know more than they ought to know, or than the present refinement of society – a good and beautiful thing when real – concludes that they do know.

O women! women! why have you not more faith in your-selves – in that strong inner purity which alone can make a woman brave! which, if she knows herself to be clean in heart and desire, in body and soul, loving cleanness for its own sake, and not for the credit that it brings, will give her a freedom of action and a fearlessness of consequences which are to her a greater safeguard than any external decorum. To be, and not to seem, is the amulet of her innocence.

Young women, who look forward to marriage and mother-hood, in all its peace and dignity, as your natural lot, have you ever thought for a moment what it must be to feel that you have lost innocence, that no power on earth can ever make you innocent any more, or give you back that jewel of glory and strength, having which, as the old superstition says,

> 'Even the lion will turn and flee
> From a maid in the pride of her purity?'

That, whether the world knows it or not, *you* know yourself to be – not this? The free, happy ignorance of maidenhood is gone for ever; the sacred dignity and honour of matronhood is not, and never can be attained. Surely this consciousness alone must be the most awful punishment to any woman; and from it no kindness, no sympathy, no concealment of shame, or even restoration to good repute, can entirely free her. She must bear her burden, lighter or heavier as it may seem at different times, and she must bear it to the day of her death. I think this fact alone is enough to make a chaste woman's first feeling towards an unchaste that of unqualified, unmitigated pity.

This, not in the form of exaggerated sentimentalism, with which it has of late been the fashion to treat such subjects, laying all the blame upon the seducer, and exalting the seduced into a paragon of injured simplicity, whom society ought to pet, and soothe, and treat with far more interest and consideration than those who have not erred. Never, as it seems to me, was there a greater mistake than that into which some writers have fallen, in fact and fiction, but especially in fiction, through their generous over-eagerness to redeem the lost. These are painted – one heroine I call to mind now – as such patterns of excellence, that we wonder, first, how they ever could have been led astray, and secondly, whether this exceeding helplessness and simplicity of theirs did not make the sin so venial, that it seems as wrong to blame them for it as to scold a child for tumbling into an open well. Consequently, their penitence becomes unnecessary and unnatural; their suffering disproportionably unjust. You close the book, inclined to arraign society, morality, and, what is worse, Providence; but for all else, feeling that the question is left much as you found it; that angelic sinners such as these, if they exist at all, are such exceptions to the generality of their class, that their example is of very little practical service to the rest.[98]

To refine away error till it is hardly error at all, to place vice under such extenuating circumstances that we cannot condemn it for sheer pity, is a fault so dangerous that Charity herself ought to steel her heart against it. Far better and safer to call

Crime by its right name, and paint it in its true colours – treating it even as the Ragged Schools did the young vagabonds of our streets[99] – not by persuading them and society that they were clean, respectable, ill-used, and maligned individuals; or by waiting for them to grow decent before they dealt with them at all, but by simply saying: 'Come, just as you are – ragged, dirty, dishonest. Only come, and we will do our best to make you what you ought to be.'

Allowing the pity, which, as I said, ought to be a woman's primary sentiment towards her lost sisterhood, what is the next thing to be done? Surely there must be some light beyond that of mere compassion to guide her in her after-conduct towards them?

Where shall we find this light? In the world and its ordinary code of social morality, suited to social convenience? I fear not. The general opinion, even among good men, seems to be that this great question is a very sad thing, but a sort of unconquerable necessity; there is no use in talking about it, and indeed the less it is talked of the better. Good women are much of the same mind. The laxer-principled of both sexes treat the matter with philosophical indifference, or with the kind of laugh that makes the blood boil in any truly virtuous heart.

Then, where are we to look? –

> 'I came not to call the righteous, but *sinners* to repentance.'
> 'Neither do I condemn thee: go and *sin no more.*'
> 'Her *sins, which are many,* are forgiven; because she loved much.'[100]

These words, thus quoted here, may raise a sneer on the lips of some, and shock others who are accustomed to put on religion with their Sunday clothes, and take it off on Monday, as quite too fine, maybe too useless for every-day wear. But I must write them, because I believe them. I believe there is no other light on this difficult question than that given by the New Testament. There, clear and plain, and everywhere repeated, shines the doctrine – of which, until then, there was no trace; either in external or revealed religion – that for every crime, being repented of and forsaken, there is forgiveness with Heaven; and if with Heaven, there ought to be with men. This, without entering at all into the doctrinal question of atonement, but simply taking the basis of Christian morality, as contrasted with the natural morality of the savage, or even of the ancient Jew, which without equivalent retribution pre-supposes no such thing as pardon.

All who have had any experience among criminals – from the poor little 'black sheep' of the family, who is always getting into trouble, and is told continually by everybody that, strive as he will, he never can be a good boy, like brother Tommy, down to the lowest, most reprobate convict, who is shipped off to the colonies because the mother-country cannot exactly hang him, and does not know what else to do with him – unite in stating that, when you shut the door of hope on any human soul, you may at once give up all chance of its reformation. As well bid a man eat without food, see without light, or breathe without air, as bid him mend his ways, while at the same time you tell him that, however he amends, he will be in just the same position – the same hopelessly degraded, unpardoned, miserable sinner.

Yet this is practically the language used to fallen women, and chiefly by their own sex: 'God may forgive you, but we never can!' – a declaration which, however common, in spirit if not in substance, is, when one comes to analyse it, unparalleled in its arrogance of blasphemy.

That for a single offence, however grave, a whole life should be blasted, is a doctrine repugnant even to Nature's own dealings in the visible world. There, her voice clearly says – 'Let all these wonderful powers of vital renewal have free play: let the foul flesh slough itself away; lop off the gangrened limb; enter into life maimed, if it must be:' but never, till the last moment of total dissolution, does she say: 'Thou shalt not enter into life at all.'

Therefore, once let a woman feel that, in moral as in physical disease, 'while there is life there is hope' – dependent on the one only condition that she shall *sin no more,* and what a future you open for her! what a weight you lift off from her poor miserable spirit, which might otherwise be crushed down to the lowest deep, to that which is far worse than any bodily pollution, ineradicable corruption of soul!

The next thing to be set before her is courage. That intolerable dread of shame, which is the last token of departing modesty, to what will it not drive some women! To what self-control and ingenuity, what resistance of weakness and endurance of bodily pain, which, in another cause, would be called heroic – blunting every natural instinct, and goading them on to the last refuge of mortal fear – infanticide.

Surely, even by this means, many a woman might be saved, if there were any one to save her, any one to say plainly: 'What are you afraid of – God or man? your sin or its results?' Alas! it will be found almost invariably the latter: loss of position, of character, and consequently the means of livelihood. Respectability shuts the door upon her; mothers will not let their young folks come into contact with her; mistresses will not take her as a servant. Nor can one wonder at this, even while believing that in many cases the fear is much more selfish than virtuous, and continued long after its cause has entirely ceased to exist. It is one of the few cases in which – at least at first – the sufferers cannot help themselves; they must suffer for a season: they must bear patiently the working out of that immutable law which makes sin, sooner or later, its own Nemesis.

But not for ever – and it is worth while, in considering this insane terror of worldly opinion, to ask: 'Which half of the world are you afraid of, the good or the bad?' For it may often be noticed, the less virtuous people are, the more they shrink away from the slightest whiff of the odour of un-sanctity. The good are ever the most charitable, the pure are the most brave. I believe there are hundreds and thousands of Englishwomen who would willingly throw the shelter of their stainless repute around any poor creature who came to them and said honestly: 'I have sinned – help me that I may sin no more.' But the unfortunates will not believe this. They are like the poor Indians, who think it necessary to pacify the evil principle by a greater worship than that which they offer to the Good Spirit;

because, they say, the Bad Spirit is the stronger. Have we not, even in this Britain, far too many such tacit devil-worshippers?

Given a chance, the smallest chance, and a woman's redemption lies in her own hands. She cannot be too strongly impressed with this fact, or too soon. No human power could have degraded her against her will; no human power can keep her in degradation unless by her will. Granted the sin, howsoever incurred, wilfully or blindly, or under circumstances of desperate temptation; capable of some palliations, or with no palliation at all – take it just as it stands, in its whole enormity, and – there leave it. Set it aside, at once and altogether, and begin anew. Better beg, or hunger, or die in a ditch – except that the people who die in ditches are not usually the best of even this world's children – than live a day in voluntary unchastity.

This may sound fine and romantic – far too romantic, forsooth, to be applied to any of the cases that we are likely to meet with. And yet it is the plain truth: as true of a king's mistress as of a ruined servant-maid. No help from without can rescue either, unless she wishes to save herself.

She has more power to do this than at first appears; but it must be by the prime agent, Truth.

After the first false step, the principal cause of women's further downfall is their being afraid of truth – truth, which must of necessity be the beginning and end of all attempts at restoration to honour. For the wretched girl, who, in terror of losing a place, or of being turned from an angry father's door, fabricates tale after tale, denies and denies till she can deny no longer, till all ends in a jail and a charge of child-murder; for the fashionable lady whose life is a long deceit, exposed to constant fear lest a breath should tear her flimsy reputation to rags; and for all the unnumerable cases between these two poles of society, there is but one warning – No virtue ever was founded on *a lie*.

The truth, then, at all risks and costs – the truth from the beginning. Make a clean breast to whomsoever you need to make it, and then – face the world.

This must be terrible enough – no denying that; but it must be done: there is no help for it. Perhaps, in many a case, if it

were done at once, it would save much after-misery, especially
the perpetual dread and danger of exposure, which makes the
sin itself quite a secondary consideration compared with the
fear of its discovery. This once over, with all its paralysing
effects, the worst has come to the worst, and there is a chance
of hope.

Begin again. Put the whole past life aside as if it had never
been, and try what you can do with the future. This, I think,
should be the counsel given to all erring women not irretriev-
ably 'lost.'

It would be a blessed thing if our honourable women,
mothers and matrons, would consider a little more what could
be done with such persons: any openings for useful employment; any positions sufficiently guarded to be safe, and yet free
enough to afford trial, without drawing too harshly the line –
always harsh enough – between these, and those who are of un-
blemished reputation. Reformatories, Magdalen Institutions,[101]
and the like, are admirable in their way; but there are numberless cases in which individual judgment and help alone are
possible. It is this – the train of thought that shall result in act,
and which I desire to suggest to individual minds, in the hope of
arousing that imperceptibly small influence of the many, which
forms the strongest lever of universal opinion.

I said in a former paper, that the only way to make people
good, is to make them happy. Strange that this truth should
apply to circumstances like these now written of! and yet it
does; and it would be vain to deny it. Bid a woman lift up her
head and live; tell her that she can and ought to live, and you
must give her something to live for. You must put into her poor
sore heart, if you can, a little more than peace – comfort. And
where is she to find it?

Heterodox as the doctrine may appear to some, it seems to
me that Heaven always leaves its sign of hope and redemption
on any woman when she is left with a child. Some taste of the
ineffable joy, the solemn consecration of maternity, must come
even to the most wretched and guilty creature thinking of the
double life she bears, or the helpless life to which she has given

birth – that life for which she is as responsible to God, to itself, and to the world, as any married mother of them all.

And the sense of responsibility alone conveys a certain amount of comfort and hope. One can imagine many a sinful mother, who, for the very child's sake, would learn to hate the sin, and to make to the poor innocent the only atonement possible, by giving it what is better even than stainless birth – a virtuous bringing-up. One can conceive such a woman taking her baby in her arms, and starting afresh to face the world – made bold by a love which has no taint in it, and cheered by the knowledge that no human being can take from her either this love, or its duties, or its rewards.

For it rests with herself alone, the comfort she may derive from, and the honour in which she may be held by, her child. A mother's subsequent conduct and character might give a son as much pride in her, and in the nameless parentage which he owes her, as in any long lawful line

> 'Whose ignoble blood
> Has crept through scoundrels ever since the flood.'[102]

Even a daughter might live to say: 'Mother, do not grieve; I had rather have had you, just as you are, than any mother I know. It has been better, for me at least, than if you had married my father.'

I have written thus much, and yet, after all, it seems but 'words, words, words.' Everywhere around us we see women falling, fallen, and we cannot help them; we cannot make them feel the hideousness of sin, the peace and strength of that cleanness of soul which is not afraid of anything in earth or heaven; we cannot force upon their minds the possibility of return, after ever so long wanderings, to those pleasant paths out of which there is no peace and no strength for either man or woman; and in order to this return is needed – for both alike – not so much outside help, as inward repentance.

All I can do – all, I fear, that any one can do by mere speech – is to impress upon every woman, and chiefly on those who, reared innocently in safe homes, view the wicked world without,

somewhat like gazers at a show or spectators at a battle –
shocked, wondering, perhaps pitying a little, but not understanding at all – that this repentance is possible. Also, that once
having returned to a chaste life, a woman's former life should
never once be 'cast up' against her; that she should be allowed
to resume, if not her pristine position, at least one that is full of
usefulness, pleasantness, and respect – a respect, the amount of
which must be determined by her own daily conduct. She
should be judged – as, indeed, human wisdom alone has a right
to judge, in all cases – solely by what she is now, and not by
what she has been. That judgment may be, ought to be, stern
and fixed as justice itself with regard to her present, and even
her past, so far as concerns the crime committed; but it ought
never to take the law into its own hands towards the criminal,
who, for all it knows, may have long since become less a
criminal than a sufferer. Virtue degrades herself, and loses every
vestige of her power, when her dealings with Vice sink into a
mere matter of individual opinion, personal dislike, or selfish
fear of harm. For all offences, punishment, retributive and
inevitable, must come; but punishment is one thing, revenge is
another. ONE only, who is Omniscient as well as Omnipotent,
can declare, 'Vengenance is *Mine*.'

CHAPTER XII

GROWING OLD

'"Do ye think of the days that are gone, Jeanie,
  As ye sit by your fire at night?
Do ye wish that the morn would bring back the time,
  When your heart and your step were so light?"
"I think of the days that are gone, Robin,
  And of all that I joyed in then;
But the brightest that ever arose on me,
  I have never wished back again."'

Growing old! A time we talk of, and jest or moralise over, but find almost impossible to realise – at least to ourselves. In others, we can see its approach clearer: yet even then we are slow to recognise it. 'What, Miss So-and-so looking old, did you say? Impossible! she is quite a young person: only a year older than I – and that would make her just ... Bless me! I am forgetting how time goes on. Yes,' – with a faint deprecation which truth forbids you to contradict, and politeness to notice, – 'I suppose we are neither of us so young as we used to be.'

Without doubt, it is a trying crisis in a woman's life – a single woman's particularly – when she begins to suspect she is 'not so young as she used to be;' that, after crying 'Wolf' ever since the respectable maturity of seventeen – as some young ladies are fond of doing, to the extreme amusement of their friends – the grim wolf, old age, is actually showing his teeth in the distance; and no courteous blindness on the part of these said friends, no alarmed indifference on her own, can neutralise the fact that he is, if still far off, in sight. And, however charmingly poetical he may appear to sweet fourteen-and-a-half, who writes melancholy verses about 'I wish I were again a child,' or merry three-and-twenty, who preserves in silver paper 'my first grey hair,' old age, viewed as a near approaching reality, is – quite another thing.

To feel that you have had your fair half at least of the ordinary terms of years allotted to mortals; that you have no right to expect to be any handsomer, or stronger, or happier than you are now; that you have climbed to the summit of life, whence the next step must necessarily be decadence; – ay, though you do not feel it, though the air may be as fresh, and the view as grand – still, you know that it is so. Slower or faster, you are going down-hill. To those who go 'hand-in-hand,'

> 'And sleep thegither at the foot,'

it may be a safer and sweeter descent; but I am writing for those who have to make the descent alone.

It is not a pleasant descent at the beginning. When you find at parties that you are not asked to dance as much as formerly, and your partners are chiefly stout, middle-aged gentlemen, and slim lads, who blush terribly and require a great deal of drawing out; – when you are 'dear'-ed and patronised by stylish young chits, who were in their cradles when you were a grown woman; or when some boy, who was your plaything in petticoats, has the impertinence to look over your head, bearded and grand, or even to consult you on his love-affairs; – when you find your acquaintance delicately abstaining from the term 'old maid' in your presence, or immediately qualifying it by an eager panegyric on the solitary sisterhood; – when servants address you as 'Ma'am,' instead of 'Miss;' and if you are at all stout and comfortable-looking, strange shopkeepers persist in making out your bills to 'Mrs Blank,' and pressing upon your notice toys and perambulators.

Rather trying, too, when, in speaking of yourself as a 'girl' – which, from long habit, you unwittingly do – you detect a covert smile on the face of your interlocutor; or, led by chance excitement to deport yourself in an ultra-youthful manner, some instinct warns you that you are making yourself ridiculous.

Or catching in some strange looking-glass the face that you are too familiar with to notice much, ordinarily, you suddenly become aware that it is *not* a young face; that it will never be a young face again, that it will gradually alter and alter, until the known face of your girlhood, whether plain or pretty, loved or disliked, admired or despised, will have altogether vanished – nay, is vanished: look as you will, you cannot see it any more.

There is no denying the fact, and it ought to silence many an ill-natured remark upon those unlucky ones who insist on remaining 'young ladies of a certain age,' – that with most people the passing from maturity to middle age is so gradual, as to be almost imperceptible to the individual concerned. It is very difficult for a woman to recognise that she is growing old; and to many – nay, to all, more or less – this recognition cannot but be fraught with considerable pain. Even the most frivolous are somewhat to be pitied, when, not conducting themselves as *passées,* because they really do not think it, they expose them-selves to all manner of misconstructions by still determinedly grasping that fair sceptre of youth, which they never suspect is now the merest 'rag of sovereignty' – sovereignty deposed.

Nor can the most sensible woman fairly put aside her youth, with all it has enjoyed, or lost, or missed; its hopes and interests, omissions and commissions, doings and sufferings; satisfied that it is henceforth to be considered entirely as a thing gone by – without a momentary spasm of the heart. Young people forget this as completely as they forget that they themselves may one day experience the same, or they would not be so ready to laugh at even the foolishest of those foolish old virgins who deems herself juvenile long after everybody else has ceased to share in the pleasing delusion, and thereby makes both useless and ridiculous that season of early autumn which ought to be the most peaceful, abundant, safe, and sacred time in a woman's whole existence. They would not, with the proverbial harsh judgment of youth, scorn so cruelly those poor little absurdities, of which the unlucky person who indulges therein is probably quite unaware – merely dresses as she has always done, and carries on the harmless coquetries and *minauderies* of her teens, unconscious how exceedingly ludicrous they appear in a lady of – say forty! Yet in this sort of exhibition, which society too often sees and enjoys, any honest heart cannot but often feel, that of all the actors engaged in it the one who plays the least objectionable and disgraceful part is she who only makes a fool of *herself*.

Alas! why should she do it? Why cling so desperately to the youth that will not stay? and which, after all, is not such a very precious or even a happy thing. Why give herself such a world of trouble to deny or conceal her exact age, when half her acquaintance must either know it or guess it, or be supremely indifferent about it? Why appear dressed – *un*dressed, cynics would say – after the pattern of her niece, the belle of the ball; annoying the eye with beauty either half withered or long overblown, and which in its prime would have been all the lovelier for more concealment?

In this matter of dress, a word or two. There are two styles of costume which ladies past their *première jeunesse* are most prone to fall into: one hardly knows which is the worst. Perhaps, though, it is the ultra-juvenile – such as the insane juxtaposition of a yellow skin and white tarlatane, or the anomalous adorning of grey hair with artificial flowers. It may be questioned whether at any age beyond twenty a ball-costume is really becoming; but after thirty, it is the very last sort of attire that a lady can assume with impunity. It is said that you can only make yourself look younger by dressing a little older than you really are; and truly I have seen many a woman look withered and old in the customary evening-dress which, being unmarried, she thinks necessary to shiver in, who would have appeared fair as a sunshiny October day if she would only have done Nature the justice to assume, in her autumn time, an autumnal livery. If she would only have the sense to believe that grey hair was meant to soften wrinkles and brighten faded cheeks, giving the same effect for which our youthful grandmothers wore powder; that flimsy, light-coloured dresses, fripperied over with trimmings, only suit airy figures and active motions; that a sober-tinted substantial gown and a pretty cap will any day take away ten years from a lady's appearance; – above all, if she would observe this one grand rule of the toilet, always advisable, but after youth indispensable – that though good personal 'points' are by no means a warrant for undue exhibition thereof, no point that is positively unbeautiful ought ever, by any pretence of fashion or custom, to be shown.

The other sort of dress, which, it must be owned, is less frequent, is the dowdy style. People say – though not very soon – 'Oh, I am not a young woman now; it does not signify what I wear.' Whether they quite believe it is another question; but they say it – and act upon it when laziness or indifference prompts. Foolish women! they forget, that if we have reason at any time more than another to mind our 'looks,' it is when our looks are departing from us. Youth can do almost anything in the toilet – middle-age cannot; yet is none the less bound to present to her friends and society the most pleasing exterior she can. Easy is it to do this when we have those about us who love us, and take notice of what we wear, and in whose eyes we would like to appear gracious and lovely to the last, so far as nature allows: not easy when things are otherwise. This, perhaps, is the reason why we see so many unmarried women grow careless and 'old-fashioned' in their dress – 'What does it signify? – nobody cares.'

I think a woman ought to care a little – a very little – for herself. Without preaching up vanity, or undue waste of time over that most thankless duty of adorning one's self for nobody's pleasure in particular – is it not still a right and becoming feeling to have some respect for that personality which, as well as our soul, Heaven gave us to make the best of? And is it not our duty – considering the great number of uncomely people there are in the world – to lessen it by each of us making herself as little uncomely as she can?

Because a lady ceases to dress youthfully, she has no excuse for dressing untidily; and though having found out that one general style suits both her person, her taste, and her conveni-ence, she keeps to it, and generally prefers moulding the fashion to herself, rather than herself to the fashion, – still, that is no reason why she should try the risible nerves of one generation by showing up to them the out-of-date costume of another. Neatness invariable; hues carefully harmonised, and as time advances, subsiding into a general unity of tone, softening and darkening in colour, until black, white, and grey alone remain, as the suitable garb for old age: these things are every woman's bounden duty to observe as long as she lives. No poverty, grief, sickness, or loneliness – those mental causes which act so strongly upon the external life – can justify any one (to use a phrase probably soon to be obsolete, when charity and common-sense have left the rising generation no Fifth of November) in thus voluntarily 'making a Guy of herself.'

That slow, fine, and yet perceptible change of mien and behaviour, natural and proper to advancing years, is scarcely reducible to rule at all. It is but the outer reflection of an inward process of the mind. We only discover its full importance by the absence of it, as noticeable in a person 'who has such very "young" manners,' who falls into raptures of enthusiasm, and expresses loudly every emotion of her nature. Such a character, when real, is unobjectionable, nay, charming, in extreme youth; but the great improbability of its being real makes it rather ludicrous, if not disagreeable, in mature age, when the passions die out or are quieted down, the sense of happiness itself is calm, and the fullest, tenderest tide of which the loving heart is capable, may be described by those 'still waters' which 'run deep.'

To 'grow old gracefully,' as one, who truly has exemplified her theory, has written and expressed it, is a good and beautiful thing; to grow old worthily, a better. And the first effort to that end is not only to recognise, but to become personally recon-ciled to the fact of youth's departure; to see, or, if not seeing, to have faith in, the wisdom of that which we call change, yet which is in truth progression; to follow openly and fearlessly, in ourselves and our daily life, the same law which makes spring pass into summer, summer into autumn, autumn into winter, preserving an especial beauty and fitness in each of the four.

Yes, if women could only believe it, there is a wonderful

beauty even in growing old. The charm of expression arising from softened temper or ripened intellect, often amply atones for the loss of form and colouring; and, consequently, to those who never could boast either of these latter, years give much more than they take away. A sensitive person often requires half a lifetime to get thoroughly used to this corporeal machine, to attain a wholesome indifference both to its defects and perfections, and to learn at last, what nobody would acquire from any teacher but experience, that it is the mind alone which is of any consequence; that with a good temper, sincerity, and a moderate stock of brains – or even the two former only – any sort of body can in time be made useful, respectable, and agreeable, as a travelling-dress for the soul. Many a one, who was absolutely plain in youth, thus grows pleasant and well-looking in declining years. You will hardly ever find anybody, not ugly in mind, who is repulsively ugly in person after middle life.

So with the character. If a woman is ever to be wise or sensible, the chances are that she will have become so somewhere between thirty and forty. Her natural good qualities will have developed; her evil ones will have either been partly subdued, or have overgrown her like rampant weeds; for, however we may talk about people being 'not a whit altered' – 'just the same as ever' – not one of us is, or can be, for long together, exactly the same; no more than that the body we carry with us is the identical body we were born with, or the one we supposed ours seven years ago. Therein, as in our spiritual self which inhabits it, goes on a perpetual change and renewal: if this ceased, the result would be, not permanence, but corruption. In moral and mental, as well as physical growth, it is impossible to remain stationary; if we do not advance, we retrograde. Talk of 'too late to improve' – 'too old to learn,' &c.! Idle words! A human being should be improving with every day of a lifetime; and will probably have to go on learning throughout all the ages of immortality.

And this brings me to one among the number of what I may term 'the pleasures of growing old.'

At our outset, 'to love' is the verb we are most prone to

conjugate; afterwards we discover, that though the first, it is by no means the sole verb in the grammar of life, or even the only one that implies (*vide* Lennie or Murray)[103] 'to be, to do, or to suffer.' To know – that is, to acquire, to find out, to be able to trace and appreciate the causes of things, gradually becomes a necessity, an exquisite delight. We begin to taste the full meaning of that promise which describes the other world as a place where 'we shall know even as we are known.'[104] Nay, even this world, with all its burdens and pains, presents itself in a phase of abstract interest entirely apart from ourselves and our small lot therein, whether joyful or sorrowful. We take pleasure in tracing the large workings of all things – more clearly apprehended as we cease to expect, or conduct ourselves as if we expected, that Providence will appear as *Deus ex machina* for our own private benefit. We are able to pass out of our own small daily sphere, and take interest in the marvellous government of the universe; to see the grand workings of cause and effect, the educing of good out of apparent evil, the clearing away of the knots in tangled destinies, general or individual, the wonderful agency of time, change and progress in ourselves, in those surrounding us, and in the world at large. We have lived just long enough to catch a faint tone or two of the large harmonies of nature and fate – to trace the apparent plot and purpose of our own life and that of others, sufficiently to make us content to sit still and see the play played out. As I once heard said, 'We feel we should like to go on living, were it only out of curiosity.'

In small minds, this feeling expends itself in meddling, gossiping, scandal-mongering; but such are only the abortive developments of a right noble quality, which, properly guided, results in benefits incalculable to the individual and to society. For, undoubtedly, the after-half of life is the best working-time. Beautiful is youth's enthusiasm, and grand are its achievements; but the most solid and permanent good is done by the persistent strength and wide experience of middle age.

A principal agent in this is a blessing which rarely comes till then – contentment: not mere resignation, a passive acquiescence in what cannot be removed, but active contentment; bought, and cheaply, too, by a personal share in that daily account of joy and pain, which the longer one lives the more one sees is pretty equally balanced in all lives. Young people are happy – enjoy ecstatically, either in prospect or fruition, 'the top of life;' but they are seldom contented. It is not possible. Not till the cloudy maze is half travelled through, and we begin to see the object and purpose of it, can we be really content.

One great element in this – nor let us think shame to grant that which God and nature also allow – consists in the doubtful question, 'To marry or not to marry?' being by this time generally settled; the world's idle curiosity or impertinent meddling therewith having come to an end; which alone is a great boon to any woman. Her relations with the other sex imperceptibly change their character, or slowly decline. Though there are exceptions, of old lovers who have become friends, and friends whom no new love could make swerve from the fealty of years, still it usually happens so. If a woman wishes to retain her sway over mankind – not an unnatural wish, even in the good and amiable, who have been long used to attention and admiration in society – she must do it by means quite different from any she has hitherto employed. Even then, be her wit ever so sparkling, her influence ever so pure and true, she will often find her listener preferring bright eyes to intellectual conversation, and the satisfaction of his heart to the improvement of his mind. And who can blame him?

Pleasant as men's society undoubtedly is; honourable, well-informed gentlemen, who meet a lady on the easy neutral ground of mutual esteem, and take more pains to be agreeable to her than, unfortunately, her own sex frequently do; they are, after all, but men. Not one of them is really necessary to a woman's happiness, except *the* one whom, by this time, she has probably either met, or lost, or found. Therefore, however uncomplimentary this may sound to those charming and devoted creatures, which of course they always are in ladies' – young ladies' – society, a lady past her youth may be well content to let them go before they depart of their own accord. I fear the waning coquette, the ancient beauty, as well as the ordinary woman, who has had her fair share of both love and liking, must learn and show by her demeanour she has learned that the only way to preserve the unfeigned respect of the opposite sex, is by letting them see that she can do without either their attention or their admiration.

Another source of contentment, which in youth's fierce self-dependence it would be vain to look for – is the recognition of one's own comparative unimportance and helplessness in the scale of fate. We begin by thinking we can do everything, and that everything rests with us to do; the merest trifle frets and disturbs us; the restless heart wearies itself with anxieties over its own future, the tender one over the futures of those dear to it. Many a young face do I see wearing the indescribable *Martha*-look – 'troubled about many things'[105] – whom I would fain remind of the anecdote of the ambassador in China. To him, tossing sleepless on his bed, his old servant said:

'Sir, may I put to you, and will you answer, three questions? First, did not the Almighty govern this world very well before you came into it?'

'Of course.'

'And will He not also do the same when you are gone out of it?'

'I know that.'

'Then, do you not think, sir, that He is able to govern it while you are in it?'

The ambassador smiled assent, turned round, and slept calmly.

Alas! it is the slowest and most painful lesson that Faith has to learn – Faith, not Indifference – to do steadfastly and patiently all that lies to her hand; and there leave it, believing that the Almighty is able to govern His own world.

It is said that we suffer less as we grow older; that pain, like joy, becomes dulled by repetition, or by the callousness that comes with years. In one sense this is true. If there is no joy like the joy of youth, the rapture of a first love, the thrill of a first ambition, God's great mercy has also granted that there is no anguish like youth's pain; so total, so hopeless, blotting out earth and heaven, falling down upon the whole being like a stone. This never comes in after-life, because the sufferer, if he or she have lived to any

purpose at all, has learned that God never meant any human being
to be crushed under any calamity like a blindworm under a stone.

For lesser evils, the fact that our interests gradually take a
wider range, allows more scope for the healing power of compensation. Also our strongest idiosyncrasies, our loves, hates, sympathies, and prejudices, having assumed a more rational and
softened shape, we do not present so many angles for the rough
attrition of the world. Likewise, with the eye of that Faith already
referred to, we have come to view life in its entirety, instead of
agonisingly puzzling over its disjointed parts, which are not, and
were never meant to be, made wholly clear to mortal eye. And
that calm twilight, which by nature's kindly law so soon begins to
creep over the past, throws over all things a softened colouring
which altogether transcends and forbids regret. I suppose there is
hardly any woman with a good heart and a clear conscience, who
does not feel, on the whole, the infinite truth of the verses at the
head of this paper, and of the other two verses which I here add
– partly because a pleasant rhyme is a wholesome thing to cling
about the memory, and partly in the hope that some one may own
or claim this anonymous song:–

> '"Do ye think of the hopes that are gone, Jeanie,
>   As ye sit by your fire at night?
> Do ye gather them up as they faded fast
>   Like buds with an early blight?"
> "I think of the hopes that are gone, Robin,
>   And I mourn not their stay was fleet;
> For they fell as the leaves of the red rose fall,
>   And were even in falling, sweet."
>
> "Do ye think of the friends that are gone, Jeanie,
>   As ye sit by your fire at night?
> Do ye wish they were round you again once more
>   By the hearth that they made so bright?"
> "I think of the friends that are gone, Robin,
>   They are dear to my heart as then:
> But the best and the dearest among them all
>   I have never wished back again!"'

Added to all these reasons, contentment, faith, cheerfulness, and the natural calming down of both passions and emotions, which give a woman greater capacity for usefulness in middle life than in any previous portion of her existence, is another – her greater independence. By the time she has arrived at the half of those three-score-years-and-ten which form the largest available limit of active life, she will generally have become, in the best sense of the term, her own mistress. I do not mean as regards exemption from family ties and restrictions, for this sort of liberty is sadder than bondage, but she will be mistress over herself – she will have learned to understand herself, mentally and bodily. Nor is this last a small advantage, for it often takes years to comprehend, and act upon when comprehended, the physical peculiarities of one's own constitution. Much valetudinarianism among women arises from ignorance or neglect of the commonest sanitary laws; and indifference to that grand preservative of a healthy body, a well-controlled, healthy mind. Both of these are more attainable in middle age than youth; and, therefore, the sort of happiness they bring – a solid, useful, available happiness – is more in her power then, than at any earlier period.

And why? Because she has ceased to think principally of herself and her own pleasures; because, as I tried to show in a former chapter, happiness itself has become to her an accidental thing, which the good God may give or withhold as He sees most fit for her – most adapted to the work for which He means to use her in her generation. This conviction of being at once an active and a passive agent – self-working, worked through, and worked upon – is surely consecration enough to form the peace, nay, the happiness, of any good woman's life: enough, be it ever so solitary, to sustain it until the end.

In what manner such a conviction should be carried out, no one individual can venture to advise. Women's work is, in this age, if undefined, almost unlimited, when the woman herself so chooses. She alone can be a law unto herself; deciding, acting according to the circumstances in which her lot is placed.

And have we not many who do so act? Women of property, whose name is a proverb for generous and wise charities –

whose riches, carefully guided, flow into unnumerable channels, freshening the whole land. Women of rank and influence, who use both, or lay aside both, in the simplest humility, for labours of love which level, or rather raise, all classes to one common sphere of womanhood. And many others, of whom the world knows nothing, who have taken the wisest course that any unmarried woman can take, and made for themselves a home and a position: some, as the ladies Bountiful of a country neighbourhood; some, as elder sisters, on whom has fallen the bringing up of whole families, and to whom has tacitly been accorded the headship of the same, by the love and respect of more than one generation thereof; and some as writers, painters, and professional women generally, who make the most of the special gift apparently allotted to them, believing that, be it great or small, it is not theirs either to lose or to waste, but that they must one day render up to the Master His own, with usury.

Would that, instead of educating our young girls with the notion that they are to be wives, or nothing – matrons, with an acknowledged position and duties, or with no position and duties at all – we could instil into them the principle that, above and before all, they are to be *women* – women, whose character is of their own making, and whose lot lies in their own hands. Not through any foolish independence of mankind, or adventurous misogamy: let people prate as they will, the woman was never born yet who would not cheerfully and proudly give herself and her whole destiny into a worthy hand, at the right time, and under fitting circumstances – that is, when her whole heart and conscience accompanied and sanctified the gift. But marriage ought always to be a question not of necessity, but choice. Every girl ought to be taught that a hasty, loveless union, stamps upon her as foul dishonour as one of those connexions which omit the legal ceremony altogether; and that, however pale, dreary, and toilsome a single life may be, unhappy married life must be tenfold worse – an ever-haunting temptation, an incurable regret, a torment from which there is no escape but death. There is many a bridal-chamber over which ought to be

placed no other inscription than that well-known one over the
gate of Dante's hell:

'Lasciate ogni speranza, voi chi entrate.'[106]

God forbid that any woman, in whose heart is any sense of real
marriage, with all its sanctity, beauty, and glory, should ever be
driven to enter such an accursed door!

But after the season of growing old, there comes, to a few,
the time of old age; the withered face, the failing strength, the
bodily powers gradually sinking into incapacity for both usefulness and enjoyment. I will not say but that this season has its sad
aspect to a woman who has never married; and who, as her own
generation dies out, probably has long since died out, retains no
longer, nor can expect to retain, any flesh-and-blood claim upon
a single human being. When all the downward ties which give
to the decline of life a rightful comfort, and the interest in the
new generation which brightens it with a perpetual hope, are to
her either unknown, or indulged in chiefly on one side. Of
course there are exceptions; where an aunt has been almost like
a mother, and a loving and lovable great-aunt is as important a
personage as any grandmother. But I speak of things in general.
It is a condition to which a single woman must make up her
mind, that the close of her days will be more or less solitary.

Yet there is a solitude which old age feels to be as natural and
satisfying as that rest which seems such an irksomeness to
youth, but which gradually grows into the best blessing of our
lives; and there is another solitude, so full of peace and hope,
that it is like Jacob's sleep in the wilderness, at the foot of the
ladder of angels.

'All things are less dreadful than they seem.'[107]

And it may be that the extreme loneliness which, viewed afar
off, appears to an unmarried woman as one of the saddest of the
inevitable results of her lot, shall by that time have lost all its
pain, and be regarded but as the quiet, dreamy hour 'between
the lights;' when the day's work is done, and we lean back,
closing our eyes, to think it all over before we finally go to rest,

or to look forward, in faith and hope, unto the Coming Morning.

A finished life – a life which has made the best of all the materials granted to it, and through which, be its web dark or bright, its pattern clear or clouded, can now be traced plainly the hand of the Great Designer; surely this is worth living for? And though at its end it may be somewhat lonely; though a servant's and not a daughter's arm may guide the failing step; though most likely it will be strangers only who come about the dying bed, close the eyes that no husband ever kissed, and draw the shroud kindly over the poor withered breast where no child's head has ever lain; still, such a life is not to be pitied, for it is a completed life. It has fulfilled its appointed course, and returns to the Giver of all breath, pure as He gave it. Nor will He forget it when He counteth up His jewels.

On earth, too, for as much and as long as the happy dead, to whom all things have long been made equal, need remembering, such a life will not have been lived in vain:

> 'Only the memory of the just
> Smells sweet, and blossoms in the dust.'[108]

NOTES

[1] Date of composition unknown. The sonnet was given the title 'Endurance' by William Michael Rossetti in the 1904 edition of Rossetti's poems.

[2] Any game, but especially card games, in which each of a number of persons plays on his or her own account.

[3] See Introduction p.viii.

[4] The following three examples of 'bouts rimés' appear in the 1896 and 1904 editions of Rossetti's poems as Xa, Xb, and Xc or 'Vanity Fair'. Date of composition unknown. In his notes on the poems in the 1904 edition, William Rossetti comments: 'The sonnet a (it will at once be observed) is not a true sonnet at all, having lines of unequal length. This was, of course, intentional on Christina's part, to mark the ineptitude of the young lady who is supposed to have indited a. None the less I give the three sonnets together as showing how readily Christina could utilize the same rhymes for three entirely distinct lines of thought or subject.' (*The Poetical Works of Christina Georgina Rossetti*, Macmillan: London, 1904, p. 490.)

[5] Song of Solomon 2:1.

[6] See Maude's sonnet p.10 line 8.

[7] Composed November 26th, 1848 and entitled 'Song' in the 1862 edition of *Goblin Market and Other Poems* (Macmillan: London).

[8] Composed March 12th, 1849. The 1896 and 1904 editions give it the title 'For Advent'.

[9] William Rossetti notes in the 1904 edition: 'Written during a period of illness . . . in the MS notebook . . . in our mother's handwriting' (p.467 *The Poetical Works*). Dated June 2nd, 1849 and entitled 'One Certainty' in the 1862 edition of *Goblin Market and Other Poems*.

[10] Composed June 1st, 1848.

[11] To receive the bread or the Blessed Sacrament in the Communion service.

[12] An eighteenth-century word to describe a band of singers and musicians who sing and play for gratuities at Christmas.

[13] Composed March 7th, 1849 with the title 'A Christmas Carol'.

[14] A song or poem composed for a bride and groom on the occasion of their wedding.

[15] According to William Rossetti, the epigraphs or mottoes to the three poems mean the following:
'This heart sighs, and I know not wherefore. It may be sighing for love, but

to me it says not so. Answer me, my heart, wherefore sighest thou? It answers: I want God – I sigh for Jesus.' (p.460 *The Poetical Works*.)

[16] The second of the three poems was composed on February 12th, 1849 with the title 'A Nun'. Parts one and three were written on May 10th, 1850. Another ambivalent treatment of the conventual life is found in Rossetti's 'The Convent Threshold' of 1858.

[17] Composed January 7th, 1849 and entitled 'Symbols' in the 1862 edition.

[18] William Rossetti writes: 'The tone of this lyric suggests that it was written in expectation of seemingly imminent death; in the MS notebook it stands in my mother's handwriting (quite contrary to wont), and so does another poem dated in the same month ('One Certainty')'. This poem was composed on June 8th, 1849 and was given the title 'Looking Forward' in the 1896 and 1904 editions. (p.478 *The Poetical Works*.)

[19] Date of composition unknown. William Rossetti entitled it 'Withering' in the 1904 edition.

[20] According to William Rossetti, Christina wrote a later version of this sonnet, originally written on March 2nd, 1850. The second version has a slightly modified octave while the sestet is radically altered:

> What is it Jesus saith unto the soul?
>   Take up the Cross, and come and follow me.
>   One word he saith to all men; none may be
> Without a cross yet hope to touch the goal.
> Then heave it bravely up, and brace thy whole
>   Body to bear; it will not weigh on thee
>   Past strength; or if it crush thee to thy knee
> Take heart of grace, for grace shall be thy dole.
> Give thanks today,and let tomorrow take
>   Heed to itself; today imports thee more.
>   Tomorrow may not dawn like yesterday:
>   Until that unknown morrow go thy way,
> Suffer and work and strive for Jesus' sake:)
> Who tells thee what to-morrow keeps in store?

ON SISTERHOODS

[1] The Church of England in the nineteenth century consisted of a number of groups which differed according to the amount of authority they gave to the church or the individual conscience. They ranged from the High Church (and the highest called themselves Anglo-Catholics) to the Broad Church or Latitudinarians to the Low Church, those closest to Non-Conformist or Dissenting sects such as the Presbyterians and the Methodists. Inevitably, such wide-ranging beliefs led to controversy.

[2] John Henry Newman (1801–90) was a leading figure in the Oxford Movement of the 1830s. He was then a member of the High Church wing of the Church of England but he converted to Catholicism in 1845 and was created Cardinal in 1879.

[3] The anti-Ritualists would be members of the Low Church wing of the Church of England who opposed High Church ritual because of its similarity to the Roman Catholic form.

[4] See Introduction p.xxii.

[5] Dorothy Wyndlow Pattison or Sister Dora of Walsall (1832–78). She joined the sisterhood of the Good Samaritan at Coatham, near Redcar, in 1864. In December 1865, the mother superior would not allow her to attend her father's deathbed. See *Sister Dora: A Biography* by Margaret Lonsdale (C. Kegan Paul: London 1880).

[8] *Hamlet* Act 3, Sc. 1, l. 144: 'Get thee to a nunnery, go; farewell.'

A WOMAN'S THOUGHTS ABOUT WOMEN

[1] This theme is taken up by Florence Nightingale in *Cassandra* (1860).

[2] Food or nutriment.

[3] See Introduction p. xxii regarding Craik's views on female suffrage.

[4] From the Prologue (l. 141) of Tennyson's *The Princess* (1847).

[5] Genesis 3:16, 19.

[6] Samuel Johnson *Rasselas* (1759) vol. 1 chap. xxv.

[7] See *Cassandra* pp. 213–14, edited by Mary Poovey (Pickering & Chatto, 1991).

[8] *Macbeth* Act 5, Sc. 3, l. 40: 'Therein the patient/Must minister to himself'.

[9] Ecclesiastes 9:10.

[10] Reference to Christ's parable of the Wise and Foolish Virgins in Matthew 25.

[11] Reference to the parable of the Talents in Matthew 25.

[12] Mark 14:8 referring to the woman who anointed Christ's feet with ointment.

[13] The principles of the American Amelia Jenks Bloomer (1818–94). She advocated dress reform for women which included the use of long, loose trousers gathered at the ankles: these bloomers were first worn in America in 1851. Craik's is one of the earliest references to bloomerism in England.

[14] Confirmation, marriage and death.

[15] Two of the worst slum areas in London in the nineteenth century.

[16] London slum areas in close proximity to the Thames which was badly polluted in the mid-nineteenth century.

[17] A reference to the traditional belief that the Amazons cut off their right breasts in order to use their bows effectively.

[18] A character from Book 1 of Spenser's *Faerie Queen*, who typifies the true religion.

[19] Samuel Butler *Hudibras* (1633–78).

[20] From 1859, the Society for Promoting the Employment of Women did open up new opportunities for female employment.

[21] This appears to be a reference to a Roman youth, Curtius (usually cited as Marcus rather than Quintus), who is said to have jumped into a chasm in the Roman forum which then closed.

[22] Even though the Royal Academy Schools did allow some women to study ancient statuary and plaster casts in the 1860s, academic study of the live nude model was impossible for aspiring women artists until 1893 when the Academy Schools finally allowed female students to draw from life. For further discussion of women and art in the nineteenth century, see Pamela Gerrish Nunn, *Victorian Women Artists* (The Women's Press, 1987).

[23] Written by Elizabeth Barrett Browning and published in 1857. Craik had great admiration for Barrett Browning. In the preface to her novel *The Head of the Family* (1851), Craik wrote: 'I dedicate this book to no personal friend, but to one who has for years been the good influence of my life. Nothing she knows, or ever may know of me. Yet it pleases me to offer this novel to a woman, the mere naming of whom includes and transcends all praise – Elizabeth Barrett Browning.'

[24] These arguments are reminiscent of those used by George Eliot in her essay 'Silly Novels by Lady Novelists' in the *Westminster Review* (p.442–61, vol. X, July–Oct. 1856).

[25] Alexander Pope *An Essay on Criticism* (1711) l. 625.

[26] Georges de Buffon (1707–88) French naturalist and author of *Histoire Naturelle*.

[27] Book 2, ll. 513–20.

[28] The term 'bluestocking' was first applied to a group of intellectual women who met at Montagu House in London from 1750. There they replaced the usual card-playing evening activities with literary conversation, and were renowned for their emphasis on scholarly, rather than domestic, concerns. The group included such women as Mrs Montagu, Mrs Chapone and Mrs Vesey.

[29] Sarah Siddons (1755–1831), great tragic actress; Rachel or Elisa Félix (1821–58), French actress; Jenny Lind (1820–87), singer, known as 'the Swedish Nightingale'.

[30] In classical legend, the Pythoness was a prophetess, a mouthpiece for the gods. Here she receives the inspiration or knowledge (afflatus) from the divine source.

[31] *Song of the Shirt* by Thomas Hood (1843); *Lettice Arnold* by Anne Marsh (1850); *Susan Hopley* by Catherine Crowe (1841); *Ruth* by Elizabeth Gaskell (1853).

[32] The Ten-Hours'-Bill Committees were those engaged in drafting legislation limiting the working day to ten hours. The Ten Hours' Bill became reality in the Acts of 1850 and 1853.

[33] Quotation not traceable.

[34] Craik's argument is prefigured in the visual arts by a painting entitled 'The Seamstress' by Anna Blunden, exhibited at the Society of British Artists in 1854 along with a quotation from Hood's *Song of the Shirt*. Its image is of an overworked needlewoman working in dim light to produce delicate hand-sewn clothes for middle-class customers.

[35] Benjamin Franklin (1706–90), American writer and public figure.

[36] *Macbeth* Act 2, Sc. 3, l. 56.

[37] Milton *Comus* (1634) ll. 1022–3.

[38] Craik also wrote a novel on this subject: *Mistress and Maid* (1863).

[39] A conflation of Matthew 23:11 and Luke 22:26.

[40] A reference to John Bunyan's *Pilgrim's Progress* (1684) where Vanity-fair is the centre of corruption and frivolity.

[41] Sixth – 'Thou shalt honour thy father and thy mother'; seventh – 'Thou shalt not kill'; eighth – 'Thou shalt not commit adultery'; ninth – 'Thou shalt not steal'. (Exodus 20:1–17).

[42] Christ.

[43] Colossians 3:22–4.

[44] A battle fought during the Crimean War on November 5th, 1854.

[45] Hannah Glasse (1708–70), author of *The Art of Cookery Made Plain and Easy* (1747) and other texts on housekeeping.

[46] A Metropolitan police constable.

[47] Indispensable or essential (element).

[48] *David Copperfield* by Charles Dickens published 1849–50.

[49] Proverbs 31. Selections from verses 10 to 31.

[50] The first three pairs of names are close male friends from classical legend; David and Jonathan's friendship is mentioned in 1 Samuel 18.

[51] From 1778, Eleanor Butler and Sarah Ponsonby lived together in close friendship for nearly half a century at 'Plas Newydd' in Llangollen.

[52] Johann Wolfgang von Goethe (1749–1832), German poet and dramatist.

[53] *Rasselas* vol. 1, chap. xi.

[54] Characters from Benjamin Disraeli's novels *Coningsby* (1844) and *Sybil* (1845). Craik's character 'Tape' is actually Taper in the original.

[55] The greater mystery is the relationship between Christ and the church. See Ephesians 5:32.

[56] Polonius to Laertes in *Hamlet* Act 1, Sc. 3, ll. 62, 63.

[57] Sir Arthur Helps (1813)1875), author and politician.

[58] Exempli gratia: e.g. or for example.

[59] Shelley *Prometheus Unbound* Act 3, Sc. 4, l. 200.

[60] Description of the tongue in James 3:6.

[61] Helps *Companions in Solitude*.

[62] Dissenters or Nonconformists were Protestants who did not belong to the Church of England. Independents and Unitarians were two specific Dissenting sects. (See p.153 2nd paragraph).

[63] Anna Letitia Barbauld (1743–1825), poet and essayist; Hannah More (1745–1833), writer and founder of the Religious Tract Society. The writings of both women were regarded as rather out-dated and conservative by the mid-Victorian audience.

[64] Rag-pickers or collectors of scraps.

[65] Loyal, faithful.

[66] A religious system developed in the third century AD that held Satan as co-equal in power with God.

[67] Craik refers here to the popular Victorian ideology of 'separate spheres' where man's proper area of power and responsibility was seen to be the public world and woman's, the private or domestic world. See John Ruskin's lecture, 'Lilies: of Queen's Gardens' from *Sesame and Lilies* (1865) for further development of the concept that 'woman's proper place is home'.

[68] *Othello* Act 2, Sc. 1, l. 160.

[69] On the look-out.

[70] A symbol of conventional propriety from Thomas Merton's play *Speed the Plough* (1798).

[71] Rules of behaviour or decorum.

[72] A wool or wool and cotton material.

[73] A light, open muslin material often used for ballgowns.

[74] A rare freak of nature.

[75] Possibly a reference to *Madame Bovary* by Gustave Flaubert published in 1857.

[76] 'The descent to hell is easy' from Virgil's *Aeneid* Book 6.

[77] Originally referring to the worship of Demeter (Greek goddess of the earth and agriculture). Here referring to the worship of any false god.

[78] Matthew Green *The Spleen* ll. 357–8.

[79] Its image or double.

[80] *Henry V* Act 5, Sc. 2, l. 291.

[81] *Othello* Act 1, Sc. 3, ll. 126–7: 'Men whose heads/Do grow beneath their shoulders'.

[82] Thomas Hood *The Bridge of Sighs*.

[83] Matthew 13:30.

[84] The Honourable Mrs Skewton is a character from Dickens' *Dombey and Son* (1847–8); the Countess of Kew or Lady Kew is from Thackeray's *The Newcomes* (1853–5).

[85] Anna Letitia Barbauld (1743–1825). See note 63.

[86] The chief or highest good.

[87] In medieval legend, the Sangreal or the Holy Grail was the platter used by Christ at the Last Supper and held by Joseph of Arimathea to receive Christ's blood at the cross. Sir Galahad was the only knight pure enough to achieve its quest.

[88] Wordsworth *The Force of Prayer* Stanza 1.

[89] Pope *Essay on Man* (1733–4) Epistle 4, l. 49.

[90] Hebrews 2:10.

[91] Genesis 1:3.

[92] Meaning abominably filthy. In Greek legend, Hercules had to purify the stables of Augeas, King of Elis. They held 3000 oxen and had not been cleaned for thirty years.

[93] The wife of the Roman Emperor Claudius, renowned for her promiscuity.

[94] 'Let us not speak of them; but look, and pass.' Dante *Inferno* Canto 3, l. 51.

[95] In 1842, *An Inquiry into the Sanitary Conditions of the Labouring Population of Great Britain* by Edwin Chadwick began a series of such inquiries.

[96] Jane Austen (1775–1817), novelist; Maria Edgeworth (1768–1849), novelist; *Loves of the Angels* (1823) by novelist Thomas Moore (1779–1852).

[97] Nell (Eleanor) Gwyn (1650–87), actress and mistress of Charles 11; Peg (Margaret) Woffington (1714?–60), actress and some-time lover of David Garrick, actor. A novel entitled *Peg Woffington* was written by Charles Reade and published in 1853.

[98] Possibly a reference to *Ruth* by Elizabeth Gaskell, a novel which deals sympathetically with the plight of the seduced woman. (Published 1832.)

[99] Free schools for children of the poor staffed by voluntary teachers. The Ragged School Union was founded in 1844. See a letter in *The Morning Chronicle* of March 19th, 1850 for an opinion that they often acted as training schools in crime.

[100] Mark 2:17; John 8:11 (to the woman taken in adultery); Luke 7:47 (to the woman who anointed Jesus' feet).

[101] Institutions for the reforming of prostitutes.

[102] Pope *Essay on Man* Epistle 4, l. 209.

[103] William Lennie (1779–1852) published *Principles of English Grammar* in 1816; Lindley Murray (1745–1826) published *An English Grammar* in 1795 and became known as the 'father of English Grammar'.

[104] i.e. Heaven. (1 Corinthians 13:12.)

[105] Martha, sister of Mary and Lazarus. See Luke 10:38–41.

[106] 'Abandon all hope, ye who enter.' Dante, *Inferno* Canto 3, l. 9.

[107] Wordsworth *Ecclesiastical Sonnets* Pt. i, No. 7.

[108] James Shirley *Contention of Ajax and Ulysses* (1659) Sc. 3, l. 23. 'Only the actions of the just/Smell sweet, and blossom in their dust.'